The Con Queen of Hollywood

The Con Queen of
HOLLYWOOD

The Hunt for an Evil Genius

Scott C. Johnson

HARPER

An Imprint of HarperCollinsPublishers

Portions of this work were originally published in different form in the *Hollywood Reporter*.

THE CON QUEEN OF HOLLYWOOD. Copyright © 2023 by Scott C. Johnson. All rights reserved. Printed in the United States of America. No part of this book may be used or reproduced in any manner whatsoever without written permission except in the case of brief quotations embodied in critical articles and reviews. For information, address HarperCollins Publishers, 195 Broadway, New York, NY 10007.

HarperCollins books may be purchased for educational, business, or sales promotional use. For information, please email the Special Markets Department at SPsales@ harpercollins.com.

FIRST EDITION

Designed by Nancy Singer

Library of Congress Cataloging-in-Publication Data has been applied for.

ISBN 978-0-06-303693-2

23 24 25 26 27 LBC 5 4 3 2 1

For my mother, Lee

Contents

Author's Note

In the spring of 2018, I received a tip about a case of identity theft in Hollywood: an imposter was running amok around town, co-opting the identities of prominent female executives. A corporate security firm in New York, K2 Intelligence, was looking into it. At first, I didn't think the tip would amount to much; Hollywood was rife with petty scams, and I didn't expect this one to be much different.

Then I began speaking to people who had been swept up in the scam, and a very different picture started to take shape. People who had encountered the imposter described an operation that was far more elaborate and sinister than I could have imagined. In the story that resulted from that initial burst of reporting, "Hunting the Con Queen of Hollywood," I recounted the hunt for an elusive criminal gang and the disturbing female impersonation at its center, operating from within a matrix of online obscurity, stealing identities from the rich and famous to bilk money from the dreamers of the world. The story included two short recordings of the Con Queen in action. I was inundated with messages, tips, and leads. One of those set me on the journey of discovery that led to this book.

Over the following three years, I interviewed dozens of people who had come into contact with the Con Queen, from family members and childhood acquaintances to victims, private investigators, federal law enforcement officials, and lawyers. Eventually I met the mysterious figure behind the mask. I traveled across the United States, to Europe and eventually to Southeast Asia, tracking the Con Queen's movements and tracing the development of a fascinating and troubled criminal mind.

IN MOST CASES, THE DIALOGUE that appears in this book is taken directly from recordings, videos, emails, journals, and photographs from people who had direct access to the Con Queen, or from recordings of the Con Queen provided to me by victims or investigators. In a few rare instances I have re-created dialogue based on extensive interviews with victims who were recalling events they experienced. Wherever possible, I use the real names of people I interviewed. I have offered a few individuals the mask of anonymity, providing them with an alias and noting the cover as such in the text. I also obtained several hundred pages of court records and police investigations from California, Illinois, and Nevada as well as the United Kingdom and Indonesia. Finally, I relied heavily on the many hours I spent talking to the Con Queen, both in person and by telephone.

The research and writing of this book led me in unexpected and sometimes troubling directions as a journalist and a human being, becoming in the process an inquiry into the nature of deception.

PART I

The Quarry

Nibble, nibble, where's the mouse?
Who's that nibbling at my house?

—The Brothers Grimm,
"Hansel and Gretel"

Chapter 1

The Drone Operator

On the afternoon it all began, on a fall day in 2017, Will Strathmann stood in a field in eastern Nebraska, south of Omaha. The sky was overcast; it was one of those dreary, midwestern fall days that threatened heavy rain but delivered only drizzle, when clouds trembled with gray-white fissures that wouldn't break open until they hit the Great Divide, far off to the west. Will stood underneath the canopy of a large oak tree whose leaves were beginning to turn gold and orange, and like a hunter he watched his quarry, a stone-walled building in a muddy construction pit that was to be the seat of some foundation or other. He had set up a slider to which he'd affixed two tripods with cameras for a twenty-minute reveal time lapse. His boss on this commercial shoot, Deren Abram, who ran a production company from Denver, was tending to engineers elsewhere, and Will had some time to himself. The wind was gentle on his face, and while the apertures gawped and the autumn light flowed in, he reached into his pocket to check his email. Someone named Amy Pascal had written to him. The name sounded vaguely familiar, so he googled it. Ah, he chuckled, *that* Amy

Pascal, the Hollywood producer of *The Post*, *Spiderman: Homecoming*, and scores of other movies. Pascal was perhaps most famous as the primary victim of the 2014 Sony hack, in which her private email correspondence was leaked.

Could she call him?

His phone chirped. After introducing herself, Amy Pascal got to the point. She told Will she had sought *him* out because she was looking for a "dark horse DP," a director of photography. Will was eager, of course, to hear more, but he was on a shoot at the moment, and short on time. Could they speak that night? Sure, sure, Pascal told him.

"Do you know Amy Pascal?" he asked Deren later when they were seated in the SUV they'd rented, rolling north toward their hotel.

"Yeah," Deren said. He had worked in Hollywood for years. He'd even met Pascal once, at a party.

"I just got off the phone with her," Will said.

"No, you didn't," his boss said.

That night, Pascal told Will that she was developing an idea for a television show for Netflix. Pascal's vision was dreamy and compelling, and it appealed to what Will found most exciting about photography: culture wasn't locked inside storied monuments or cherished tourist sites. Truth was best extracted from unobserved corners. They bonded over the idea that it was in these overlooked places that gems of understanding might slip into view, like quiet but welcome intruders. As a framework for the show, she had in mind a children's book, JonArno Lawson's *Sidewalk Flowers*. Published in 2015, and illustrated with poignant drawings, it told the story of a young girl who finds and distributes flowers—to a dead bird, a homeless person—and in so doing reanimates a drab world with color and meaning. Pascal wanted to highlight a female perspective; the story's young female protagonist would be a proxy for the viewer. She wanted a partner who was talented and hungry, someone who loved exploring the world and appreciated the challenge of working in a strange and perhaps even unsettling foreign land, a land like Indonesia, a rich and fascinating culture unfamiliar to most Americans where she wanted to set the travel show she had in mind. She had studied Will's portfolio, and thought they would make a great team.

During college, Will had studied Buddhist philosophy in Dharamshala, India, for a year. One day he found himself in Varanasi, India's holiest city, sitting near the statues of the cremation gods watching as pilgrimaging families carted their dead to the sacred ovens, their ashes destined for the currents of the holy Ganges River, which flowed nearby. When he returned to the United States, he abandoned a notion he'd nurtured for a while of becoming a clinical psychologist, and devoted himself instead to photography.

Will couldn't help but feel that this opportunity had been tailor-made for him.

Amy Pascal had a blunt and disconcerting way about her, Will thought, and she hinted at things he didn't fully grasp. The tone wasn't sexual, exactly, but it veered awfully close. She asked how he felt about working with powerful women. He fumbled, and then felt bad about fumbling, not entirely sure why. She sensed his hesitation, almost before he sensed it himself. She called him "darling" and "honey." By the end of the first phone call, they were on a first-name basis. "The business Amy is very different from the personal Amy," she murmured.

"How's it going with Amy?" Deren asked the next day.

"Good," said Will. "Weird."

He told Deren about the job, the odd questions and the tone—he wasn't sure if it was suggestive, necessarily—in which Amy had posed them. Harvey Weinstein, the lecherous Hollywood producer accused of raping women, was all over the newspapers. Who was to say Amy wasn't the same breed of cat?

"Just don't go into a locked room with her," Deren joked.

Then Will showed his boss the emails Amy had sent from what appeared to be her work account: amyp@pascalfilms.com. Deren shrugged. It was a *little* unusual, he said, but the documentation seemed legit.

"It would be hard to turn down this kind of opportunity," he said. Will agreed. It would be hard to turn down. Too hard. "Whatever you do," Deren added, "don't go out of pocket."

Amy had what seemed to Will a rich and deeply nuanced appreciation of Indonesian culture and history, which Amy felt would be the ideal setting for an adventure travel show. She described the sacred Buddhist temples of Borobudur, in the ancient city of Yogyakarta, and spoke about the Dutch colonial expansion, kings and concubines, trade routes and the Dutch East India Company. She also shared stories of other deals she had worked on, or those still under way, a project about Cleopatra with the director David Fincher that had fallen apart. Everybody knew about that, she added, almost as an aside. "So many fascinating stories there for you to look at a little bit more," she said. Will was entranced. Together they began to explore the idea in more depth. She tasked Will with devising a storyboard for a pilot episode, and they agreed that Will would travel to Indonesia to scout locations and develop potential story lines.

The trip was already organized; she had taken care of that herself. A concierge car service run by her friend "Soli," short for Solihin Kalla, the son of Indonesia's vice president, Jusuf Kalla, would be put at his disposal. Will would have to pay for $2,740 in up-front expenses, she said, before warning him that Indonesia, like Mexico, another country with which she seemed to be familiar, was rife with fraud. He should only extract cash from ATMs in full view of CCTV cameras. "Please don't think of me as racist," she pleaded. She went over minutiae, describing the drivers ("not very talkative"), the payment methods ("no credit cards; cash only"), tipping ("don't"), even meals ("I don't know how much of a foodie you are . . ."). Having flooded Will with this torrent of logistics, she tidily summed it up. "So, uh, that's the entire setup—the premise. I just need your phone to be on," because she wanted to be in touch with him every day. "You've traveled a lot," she told him. "This should be a breeze."

Will had traveled some already, it was true, to other cities in India and Asia. Pascal seemed to have picked up on a subtler ambition: Will was looking for meaning, something to eclipse transitory epiphanies. Pascal was giving him that opportunity. She sent him more documentation to firm up the practical side of their partnership, itineraries, and an elaborate nondisclosure agreement. "Are you good?" she asked. "I just want to make sure you understand conceptually because I've devoted so much of my time to this."

Pascal was a fan of Anthony Bourdain's *Parts Unknown*, and she likened Will's upcoming journey to a cultural version of Bourdain's popular travel show, updated for the millennial generation. In the days leading up to his departure, he compiled articles about Buddhist temples, Hindu religious sites, and cultural landmarks, but Pascal gently discouraged this. "Stop doing research," she said. "Just show up, and discover."

Will landed in Jakarta around midnight on October 15 and was met by a Mr. Rusdi. The gentleman, in his sixties, a chain smoker of cigarettes who spoke very little English, seemed generous, and the two managed to communicate well enough. The night air was thick and warm, and from around the base of lampposts that lined the highway luminous blooms erupted. "An explosion of bright purple flowers," Will wrote in his journal. "Even in the dark of the night."

On his first full day in Indonesia, Will stood atop the National Monument, a towering 433-foot-tall obelisk, and studied the unruly metropolis of Jakarta. From far below wafted the pungent, halfway pleasant odor of burning trash and the muffled din of traffic. Will's thoughts drifted. While waiting to buy his ticket, he had spotted a young couple with two children, including a girl who looked to be about eight years old and was stealing cautious glances at him from behind the safety of her mother's legs. Atop the tower, the girl ventured to the white metal protection bars at the edge and peered through a set of stationary binoculars. What if *he* were a young girl lost in a big city, he wondered. Where would he go to get his bearings? This perch seemed like a logical starting point. The day was crushingly hot and Will worked steadily, shooting more than seven hundred frames. That evening, jet lag and exhaustion washed over him, and as he lay in bed, thrill bled into fatigue and anxiety. If he failed, Amy had warned him, there were plenty of other talented DPs eager to take his place.

After a week of steady work, Will returned home, but a few days later, at Amy's request, he was back in Indonesia. The second trip didn't go as well as the first. Will was exhausted. His back hurt. He was concerned about his expenses. Between flights, cars, and hotels, he had spent close to $15,000, none of which Amy had reimbursed. He hoped an upcoming trip to Yogyakarta, the last remaining monarchical city in Indonesia, home to the sultanate, would improve his mood. But after two days spent touring the Kraton palace and the Green Temple, and an afternoon walking blindfolded through a grove of banyan trees as part of a tourist attraction, a sense of fatalism crept into his observations. "My soul is fucked," he wrote.

This time when Will left Indonesia, he flew straight to Los Angeles to meet Amy and two Netflix showrunners. No sooner did he land than Amy called. The Harvey Weinstein scandal had become a conflagration. The Netflix showrunners were suddenly unavailable and Amy's own staff recommended she not meet with anyone alone. Anyway, an additional complication had arisen. She needed Will to return to Indonesia, specifically Bali, to photograph a new location, or else one of the showrunners would pull the project. Just four days after arriving in LA, and a one-day layover in Taipei, Will returned to Indonesia for the third time. The promised reimbursements still hadn't arrived. His own savings were gone and Will was now asking his parents for help. The Strathmann family was in for close to $30,000.

On November 12, he made his way to an ATM in Jakarta to gather the final funds for Bali. His flight was scheduled to leave in two hours. But when he put his card into the machine that morning, his account was frozen. He tried calling his bank's customer service line but couldn't get through. Mr. Rusdi and the bagman said they couldn't drive him to the airport until they had been paid, but eventually relented and drove Will for free, with the condition that Will tell his boss he had taken a taxi—should word get back to her, they would both be in serious trouble. Amy found out anyway, when Mr. Rusdi failed to turn over the usual driving fees. She was livid. With his thoughtless dismissal of protocol, Will had jeopardized her long-standing relationships and imperiled their project. She ordered him to cancel his flight and withdraw enough cash to "make this right." Later, she called again to say the Bali trip wasn't going to happen after all. Now more conciliatory, she urged him to return home and assured him that he had proven himself worthy.

Will hadn't slept properly for weeks, he wasn't eating, and all the melatonin he'd been taking had left him constipated and bloated. He cried himself to sleep that night. The next morning, he left Indonesia. Shortly after landing in Seoul, South Korea, Will was changing planes when Amy called: Bali was on. Could he return to Indonesia?

Having invested so much time and effort in a project whose contours he no longer understood, he decided it made little sense to abort. He stumbled from counter to counter trying to rearrange his itinerary, and after much haggling, and more money, he was once again in the air. That night, for the fourth time in less than a month, he passed through Jakarta Customs.

Will was sleeping when his phone began buzzing around 2 a.m. He figured it was Amy. She had called him only a couple of hours earlier, just after midnight, to go over his trip to Bali the next day. Mr. Rusdi was scheduled to arrive in just under four hours. Bracing himself for another "crazy Amy call," he picked up his phone and instead saw a slew of text and voice messages from his father that he had somehow missed. Fred's voice was firm, but he sounded on edge. "This is an emergency," he said. "Call me ASAP. Do not go anywhere or get in any cars with anybody."

The Screenwriter

Gregory Mandarano had moved frequently as a kid. Born in Connecticut, he had spent some time in Howard Beach, Queens, and then a few years in the Florida Keys, where his father, a surgeon, oversaw an

ER. The family had relocated to Long Island when he was in middle school and Mandarano had been there, on and off, ever since. He was thirty-seven.

He dreamed of being a screenwriter and had drafted a couple dozen feature film scripts, but unfortunately none sold. He often sent his projects to www.scriptshadow.net, a website and online community that offered screenwriting resources, feedback, and, sometimes, encouragement to aspiring writers. Winners of the site's featured monthly competition occasionally received calls from Hollywood executives. A few people had gotten agents and even deals based off projects they had submitted. While Greg was a frequent visitor, he often rankled other members with unsolicited and unwelcome critiques. He had earned what he admitted was "a bad reputation." To make matters worse, he remained unrepresented and his screenplays unproduced.

While the constant rejection had been frustrating, he and his writing partner, Jay Shapiro (a pseudonym), were hopeful that fortune would soon break in their direction. One day that summer while surfing the web, Greg came across what appeared to be a website affiliated with the China Film Group, www.thechinafilmgroup.com, which was soliciting ideas for screenplays. It was an encouraging development. CFG was a major player in China's burgeoning film industry, considered the go-to destination for American studios in search of mainland partners on big-budget productions. Greg quickly sent off an email pitch for a movie titled "Shadows Below." The quick summary, or logline, read, in part: "After terrorists attack China on the 4th of July, a submarine commanded by the President's Daughter and a team of Navy SEALS are all that stand between a rogue Chinese doomsday sub and Nuclear Armageddon." Before long, he received a message back from a CFG executive named Jing Huilang. Interesting pitch and synopsis! she wrote. Over the course of numerous emails, Greg outlined his vision of the movie, providing Huilang with detailed notes about the script's tone, feel, and themes.

In a subsequent phone call, Huilang said she was looking for someone to write a blockbuster American script, set in China, for an international audience. CFG was a mainland Chinese outfit, but Huilang sounded more like she hailed from Hong Kong. Her English was strong and fluid, with the British inflection common to wealthy Hong Kongers, a legacy of the long historical connection to the United Kingdom. She laid out how competitive this opportunity would be and stressed that, if Gregory and Jay were chosen, their work would be subject to strict oversight by China's censors. The Chinese market was growing fast; big American studios and streaming networks like Netflix and Hulu were racing to get a foothold. More traditional American studios were teaming up with Chinese outfits on projects that had appeal in both places. This was the break Greg had been looking for. It wasn't Warner Bros., exactly, but the world was changing; a big hit in China might be even better. He and Jay responded right away: Yes, they were interested. What did Huilang need?

In the days following Huilang's last email, Greg and Jay complied with a series of elaborate requests. They wrote essays about their movie idea, which Greg had already pitched as a big-budget sci-fi extravaganza set in Asia, involving sea monsters and ninja warriors. At Huilang's request, they created a forty-page "mood board," a blueprint of sorts for the movie. They answered long questionnaires providing personal details about themselves and their work habits. And then they waited, hoping their "application" to have their screenplay selected by the China Film Group would be approved.

It was.

Over emails and phone calls Huilang explained the next steps and connected Greg with other CFG staff. She needed them to travel to Indonesia, where CFG maintained offices and oversaw production on its many projects. She explained that CFG operated differently than most Hollywood studios. China's all-powerful censorship board played a big role in developing scripts, down to the smallest level of detail. It was partly for this reason that the company wanted writers to spend time in Indonesia, where they could visit key locations that the studio would likely want to have featured in the movie. Greg consulted with his entertainment attorney. The lawyer was skeptical and told Greg that he should be, too, but Greg insisted on moving ahead. The lawyer warned him to proceed with caution. "Look," he said, "you're going to a foreign country. You're dealing with China. For all you know, your rooms are going to be bugged."

They arrived in July 2015 and settled into their rooms at the Hotel Santika Premiere, a four-star resort in downtown Jakarta. Huilang had told them that they would be meeting with one of her colleagues, a senior development executive from CFG. After a night of poor sleep and anxious half-dreams, Greg and Jay woke to a humid morning and took a cab to a high-rise in the business district.

Eventually a man emerged through the glass doors on the street level and greeted them. He was of medium height, with a dark complexion and a buoyant demeanor, accentuated by a smile that stretched across his face. His eyes seemed unusually large, and Greg wondered whether he was purposely widening them for effect. He had dyed parts of his dark hair bright green and the contrast with his skin was striking. Greg thought he looked a little like Max Landis, the Hollywood screenwriter; he exuded a similar buzzy energy and powerful charisma. He introduced himself as Anand Sippy and explained that his father had been a well-known director and producer in Bollywood. He handed over a business card that identified him as "Vice President of Creative and Development—Film Division, China Film Group." Although his nationality was left unaddressed, he spoke nearly flawless, American-accented English. Greg immediately warmed to what he described as Sippy's "LA attitude." They chatted during the elevator ride. Greg had written more than twenty scripts and Sippy indicated that he had read some of them. He complimented Greg on his style.

Sippy led them to a glassed-in conference room on an upper floor. Greg and Jay had come prepared to give a PowerPoint presentation, and Sippy went about setting up the TV console in the corner. At one point, Sippy pressed a button on the TV and an image of the two

Americans sitting at the other end of the room suddenly appeared on-screen. Greg wondered if they were being secretly recorded through the television monitor. He remembered what the lawyer had said. Doing business with Communist China, even if you were in Indonesia, was different than doing business in the United States; one should expect a certain amount of light surveillance. The two Americans presented their ideas for "Shadows Below." For more than an hour, Sippy listened and provided detailed feedback on the scope and direction of the film, commenting on plot points, locations, and thematic ideas. Greg and Jay left the meeting confident that they had finally found their footing as screenwriters. That night, Greg sent Sippy a new treatment for a "fantasy variant" of "Shadows Below," which took place in an alternate universe.

When Greg informed the scriptshadow community that a project of his had been green-lit by a major Chinese film studio, former detractors clamored to pitch their own projects. A single mother from Kansas told Greg she had recently been in touch with the people from CFG. She would have to borrow money to make the trip and first wanted to ensure it was legitimate. "Go for it," he reassured her.

The rest of Greg's family viewed the trip with a mixture of exhilaration and alarm. Within days of the initial contact, Huilang began communicating directly with Greg's mother, Lisa. Huilang called from China almost every day and kept Lisa on the phone for hours. In time they would all be dragged into the project; over the course of the next several months, Greg's parents would provide them upwards of $100,000 in funding. Greg brought in his sister Melanie, an artist, as a "creative consultant." They traveled to Indonesia and Hong Kong together and she produced more than a hundred ink sketches and watercolors for a "journal" to be featured in the movie. When the international financing that CFG had insisted upon became too overwhelming, Greg asked another sister, a senior vice president at a major New York City investment firm, to help. The family's entertainment attorney charged them tens of thousands more to manage the legal thicket. The project was all the family could think about. Huilang referred to the Mandarano clan as "the dream team."

The Photographer

The bedsheets had begun to feel sticky. Caleb Kotner, who asked that I use a pseudonym when referring to him, wasn't sleeping anyway, so he threw them aside and rolled off the bed onto the tiled floor. He glanced briefly out the hotel window at the buzzing, spitting lights of Jakarta. For the past few weeks, Caleb had been documenting his travels across Indonesia with a Canon and a Leica. He, too, was working for Amy Pascal, who had sought him out for a film project she was developing. He'd muted the alarm on his phone but a bedside clock shone bright red: 3:30 a.m. Amy would be calling soon.

Earlier that fall of 2017, the producer had sent him an email, asking if they could speak. Caleb had been puzzled but intrigued. At twenty-seven, he was building a career as a freelancer. He had worked for the *New York Times*, the *Wall Street Journal*, and the *New Yorker* and was developing a portfolio that, in addition to media outlets, included several corporate clients. A personal phone call from someone of Amy Pascal's professional stature, while welcome, was unusual, to say the least. But when they did finally speak, Pascal was engaging and friendly. She name-dropped, which was to be expected, mentioning Martha Stewart and *New Yorker* editor David Remnick, and demonstrated a casual familiarity with several of Caleb's corporate clients. Pascal explained that she was looking for an enterprising photographer to help with two short documentary films about world-class athletes, shot in Indonesia, projects she hoped to turn into a big-budget multipart series with Netflix. He warmed to her right away.

Within days of their first call Caleb had signed on, and he soon boarded a flight bound for Jakarta. His assignment in Indonesia involved touring the country extensively, documenting iconic landmarks such as the ancient stone ruins of Borobudur, in Yogyakarta, on the island of Java. He worked steadily from early morning to late at night. When they spoke by phone, sometimes after midnight, Pascal updated him on the project, always peppering her conversation with the names of powerful people.

When it came to travel logistics, Pascal was very specific about the smallest details. She insisted that Caleb use a taxi company owned by a man she affectionately referred to as Soli. Caleb pointed out that there were probably less expensive options, but Pascal said that working with this company would help them access certain Hindu religious sites where filming was generally prohibited.

Caleb worked hard; seemingly, so did Pascal. They exchanged reams of paperwork and dozens of emails. She drafted complex contracts outlining the expectations of the job, the travel budgets, the locations where he was to shoot along with expected timelines, and strict NDAs to maintain the secrecy of the project. Pascal promised Caleb that he would be reimbursed for all his expenses once the project was complete. The travel across the sprawling archipelago was demanding, but also rewarding, and before long he had built up a substantial portfolio of images.

But in other ways, the job was less satisfying. Pascal was an exacting, and sometimes impulsive, boss. She called all the time. Caleb began to wonder if she was a little unhinged. At the very least, she was unusual, and at times disarmingly forthcoming. She had explained that she wanted to work with an up-and-coming photographer like him because more established artists were difficult, less flexible. She also confided that the Sony hack had been devastating. Since leaving Sony, she had been trying, in fits and starts, to rebuild her career and reputation but it had been a struggle. Part of her own reinvention, she said, involved finding younger talent that she could mold and shape. This was why the phone calls were so important—it was this process of working together, building something from the ground up, that would tell her if Caleb was going to be worth her time, and her money, if he was going to be a good investment.

In anticipation of her volatility, and her penchant for calling at all hours, he began setting his alarm for the middle of the night, energizing himself by doing push-ups or taking a cold shower. Amy called so often, and the calls became so stressful, that the standard Apple ringtone he used began to haunt him. About halfway through the trip he changed it to a happier, chirpier tone. If the phone sounded more excited, perhaps he would feel it, too.

So it was that morning when he'd rolled out of bed at 3:30 a.m. When his phone lit up, he answered before it could ring.

"Good morning," he said, trying to sound bright.

"Are you okay?" Pascal asked.

"Everything's fine."

"It doesn't sound fine," she said.

"I just woke up."

"Caleb," she snapped, "in Hollywood we don't get tired. We're driven."

Caleb felt the familiar knot in his stomach tighten. He wanted so badly to please her. And now he wondered, not for the first time, what his employer would do next.

"I can find someone else for this job," she said. "If you're going to be too tired to do this, you can go home now."

He blamed it on jet lag. "I'm great, I'm good to go," he said, trying to wrap it up. "Excited for the day."

Lately, conversations like this had become the norm with Pascal, who berated him for seemingly minor infractions, even as she suggested they build their personal relationship. She knew Caleb's parents lived on the East Coast, and she told him she would be his "mommy in Los Angeles."

Yet the work moved forward. On two occasions Caleb traveled by plane several hundred miles southeast from Jakarta to Yogyakarta, where he stayed for a few days and photographed ancient ruins. After he traveled to the Hindu temple of Prambanan, she pressed for details, as if she knew the place intimately. During one trip to Yogyakarta,

Caleb broke with protocol and accepted an invitation from his local fixer to dine with his family. Amy called during the dinner and when she learned where Caleb was, she grew furious and ordered him to leave immediately. She explained that she never wanted him to do anything that she hadn't explicitly organized. She told him she worried for his safety, but to Caleb it felt like she just wanted to be in control.

Whether on the road or back in his hotel in Jakarta, Caleb logged hours on the phone with Pascal coordinating details, discussing story ideas, and poring over contractual details—but something nagged at him. He had never actually seen Pascal, even via Skype, her preferred method of communication. She never activated her camera, explaining that to do so would pose a security risk.

Over a month into the project, he was growing nervous. It was standard practice within the industry for freelancers to pay for their own travel, accommodation, and logistics with the expectation that those expenses would be reimbursed once the work had been turned in. Caleb had successfully completed dozens of assignments this way without much trouble at all. Yet the expenses involved in this new job were in a different realm: within the space of a few weeks on the road he had somehow—he wasn't quite sure how—racked up close to $50,000 in credit card charges and ATM withdrawals in Indonesia. Thus far he had been able to rationalize this obvious problem: for working freelancers like him, it was a lot of money. On the other hand, Pascal was worth tens of millions. Perhaps she had simply lost financial perspective?

Caleb's entreaties to meet Pascal in person, even via a Skype video chat, went nowhere. Even though the project hadn't been completed, she assured him the money had been sent, but he hadn't received anything. Whenever he began to suspect he was being played, his thoughts inevitably returned to the same question: To what end? Pascal had obviously poured hours of her own time into the project. It *had* to be real. She had even offered Caleb's father, who also worked as a film editor, a job in LA. While his father didn't have time to pursue the opportunity, the offer spoke volumes—didn't it?

Still the doubts niggled at him. After several weeks in Indonesia, Caleb had returned to the U.S. but now Pascal told him she needed him to go back one final time. She explained that a prominent Hollywood producer—she let a major A-list name slip—was interested in their project, but he wanted that "extra something."

In the first days of January 2018, he finally screwed up his courage and sent her an email. He told her he was excited for Bali, his bags were packed, but before he departed for this final trip he wanted to clear up one thing. "I just need to confirm that I am truly dealing with you," he wrote. And then he waited for her to respond.

Chapter 2

Nicole Kotsianas was a Garden State girl, born and bred. "Jersey through and through," she told anyone who asked, as if it wasn't already abundantly clear. In high school, she drove a dirty white 1990 Buick Century her grandfather had given her, with cowskin interiors and the fuzzy dice—the "Buey Beast." Her hairstyle, complete with bangs, harked back to her days as a teenager holding a lighter aloft for Bruce Springsteen, who had attended her same school. When, as an adult, she finally made it out to Los Angeles, she wandered down to the Venice boardwalk and strolled past head shops and haunted houses and didgeridoo-playing Rastafarians. It reminded her of the Jersey shore, only with more weed.

Nicole's employer, a corporate security and investigations outfit called K2 Intelligence, didn't discriminate much when deciding which clients to take on. They'd help an unsavory regime with as much gusto as they mustered for a widow who'd been bilked of her savings. For a time, they'd even asked some pointed questions on behalf of Harvey Weinstein, in the months before he was arrested, which earned them a few cycles of bad press. Around the firm's offices in Manhattan, K2 investigators sometimes referred to the company as "the CIA for the corporate world," which could be interpreted as a compliment or a slight, depending on one's perspective.

Nicole worked on the Investigations and Disputes Team, where there were more women than men. Jules Kroll, K2's founder, liked it that way; he believed that women were better listeners. Most of Nicole's work was tied up with the kind of meat-and-potatoes research that comprised the bulk of her team's caseload: due diligence for companies, asset searches, and investigations for high-net-worth individuals, a specific kind of deep-pocketed client.

Hollywood, and this half-formed slip of a case that had landed on her lap in October 2017, felt so foreign. It had come to her from a lawyer in LA whose client, a well-known Hollywood movie producer, was being impersonated. But when Nicole looked into it in those first few days the whole thing struck her as a bit off and, as far as cases went, even a little bit weak. The lawyer's client was Amy Pascal, who had produced *Molly's Game* and the *Ghostbusters* reboot. Pascal was a big deal, but the extent of the impersonation didn't seem to add up to a whole lot.

Someone pretending to be Pascal was making calls around town—Hollywood was a "town," Nicole now learned, a small and tidy place with its own etiquette and language. In some of the conversations, the fake Pascal flirted with the men on the other end of the line. But the caller was also tentative, like someone toying with an idea whose true shape she hadn't quite grasped. Nicole thought it sounded a little like the Harvey Weinstein scandal, which had erupted in the press that very month, with the gender dynamic powerfully inverted: an exceptionally influential woman was taking advantage of her position to lure unsuspecting—and, most importantly, unknown and powerless—men into awkward compromises. Yet, compared with the firestorm erupting around Weinstein, this was penny-ante stuff. Probably just a weird lady somewhere pulling a prank, she thought; a few phone calls here and there, none of them were very long, and they didn't seem to lead anywhere. Now and again, the fake Pascal was said to have probed about people's availability to work on nonexistent projects. Bizarre, Nicole thought, but no one had been robbed of any money—not even Pascal, a multimillionaire and the obvious financial mark.

The real Amy Pascal had been targeted before. Pascal had built an illustrious career in Hollywood. Beginning as a secretary at a production company, she had risen to become the vice president for production at 20th Century Fox and ultimately the chair of Sony Pictures Entertainment. Along the way she had earned a reputation as a hitmaker, involved in some of the most successful movie rollouts of all time, including the 2012 *Skyfall*, the first James Bond movie to gross over $1 billion at the box office. After a decade at Sony, her reign came to an abrupt and humiliating end in 2014, when a previously unknown group from North Korea, calling itself the "Guardians of Peace," hacked into Sony's computers. The group released a trove of private data, including scores of embarrassing emails between Pascal and famous actors, like Angelina Jolie and Meryl Streep. In an instant, Pascal, whom *Forbes* had once ranked as the twenty-eighth most powerful woman in the world, was brought down hard, and she had been trying to rebuild her reputation since. Now she was in the crosshairs again, and needed to nip it in the bud quickly.

NICOLE HAD A PERFORMATIVE STREAK. Once she got going, she was not inclined to stop. Her high school classmates voted her "most dramatic," and she was a runner-up for "Class Chatterbox." Maybe it was the years of theater—six years in *Annie* in an off-Broadway production, nine shows a week, when for a while it seemed like she might make a career of it. Then there was the Model United Nations. And in college Speech and Debate, the art and science of linguistic persuasion. She spoke quickly, ideas flowing, connections hopscotching. She could build an argument or hurl an insult with equal measure. She was also practical, a doer with a mind for details and numbers, graphs and flowcharts, and cold logic that binds them.

She had always planned on studying communications at Emerson

College after high school, but when the dot-com bubble burst and gutted her father's investments she settled for Rutgers, the New Jersey state school, where she studied economics. In hindsight, she came to view it as the best decision she'd ever been forced to make. She immersed herself in the bustle of the *Daily Targum*, the country's second-oldest collegiate newspaper, whose student journalists had produced award-winning coverage. She became the paper's opinion editor and sat on the editorial board. An imaginary future spooled out before her in which she might one day become a war correspondent. In the end, the lure of home was too strong—and it seemed like newspapers were dying by the dozens. After graduating, she got a job in Manhattan probing securitizations and derivatives for a subsidiary of the *Financial Times* that offered a premium service for paying customers, and later for a bond-rating agency doing qualitative research. She fell in love with finance. But as much as she felt the lure of the city, she also knew that one day she would return to the suburbs of New Jersey, and settle there in her very own "oasis."

Over drinks at the annual Christmas party one year, she started chatting with the K2 investigators, whose firm shared a bathroom on the same floor. This "journalism" job wasn't really journalism and she was growing tired of it. K2 wasn't journalism, either, but she was intrigued by what they were doing, and whether it might be an opportunity to put her investigative talents to good use for better pay. K2 hired her in 2015. Most of her work was focused on white-collar crime. Fraud. Identity theft. Even impersonation. By 2017, she and her husband, Anthony, a Manhattan litigator, had one small child and another was on the way. At thirty-three, she was providing for her family. This was her perfect life.

ONE OF THE MOST INFLUENTIAL women in Hollywood, Amy Pascal existed on the other end of the socioeconomic spectrum, yet here she was entrusting the fate of her public persona, and perhaps her private one as well, to an unknown investigator on the other side of the country. Maybe that was by design; the "town" *was* small. As she began her investigation, Nicole heard variations on the same basic story: "Amy Pascal" was calling industry professionals inquiring about their availability for work. The conversations had turned awkward and, in some cases, oddly flirtatious. She got her hands on a few short voice mail recordings but they added very little. Nicole needed something more to go on.

And then, one day in October 2017, Nicole's office phone rang. A distraught father was on the other end. He told the investigator about his twenty-six-year-old son, Will, who was right now stranded in Jakarta, caught up in something gone horribly wrong involving Amy Pascal. "He thinks he's working on this project," the father, Fred Strathmann, said. "Something doesn't seem right."

WHILE WILL STRATHMANN HAD BEEN running around on his Indonesian goose chase, Fred and Francy Strathmann had made their own inquiries. Fred took a closer look at the websites and emails of his son's supposed benefactor, Amy Pascal. He had found a number for Pascal's office in LA and placed a call. He explained to an assistant that Will was working with Ms. Pascal on a project in Indonesia for which he hadn't yet been paid. Almost immediately he was patched through to one of Pascal's assistants, who delivered a series of revelations: Amy Pascal was not involved in any projects in Indonesia. And Fred Strathmann wasn't the first person to call—though he was the first to identify the connection to Indonesia. Pascal's identity had been compromised by some unknown criminal enterprise and the Los Angeles County district attorney had already opened a preliminary investigation. Pascal had hired a private investigator in New York. The assistant was sympathetic and said she would put Fred in touch with all of them.

It was 2 p.m. in Pennsylvania, where Will had grown up and where his parents still lived, when Fred began frantically calling and texting his son.

Will's initial reaction to the revelation that he had been conned was denial: he accused his father of inventing a story of fraud and deception, in order to lure him home for some as-yet-unknown purpose. It simply made no sense, he pointed out. What on earth would compel someone to invent such a complex and elaborate scheme? The hours and hours of telephone conversations? The hotels in Indonesia that, in some cases, had been prepaid for him? The pages and pages of nondisclosure agreements, logistics packets, itineraries, and emails outlining every aspect of his three trips, down to the dour temperament of a shabbily clad Indonesian driver with horrible English. There was simply no way it could *not* be real. Suspended between fear and rage, alternating in those first few minutes from shock to incomprehension, he tried to explain these complexities to his father, who was unmoved. But as dawn approached, the strength of his father's love and concern proved overpowering, and a crack appeared in the artifice. And as it did, fear settled in.

Will's phone rang just minutes after he hung up with his father. The LA district attorney told him he needed to make his way to the U.S. embassy. Moments later his phone rang a third time. The woman on the other end of the line said her name was Nicole Kotsianas and she was an investigator from K2 Intelligence, a corporate security firm in New York City.

ON THE OTHER SIDE OF the world, Will sat alone on the hotel bed, his phone to his ear, wondering if he was being watched. He turned his ire on this supposed investigator, Nicole. He asked her: How could he be sure that she, in fact, wasn't part of . . . whatever this was? Then his anger gave way to a wave of cascading fears. He wondered whether he would even be able to make it out of Jakarta safely. Nicole urged him to skip the visit to the U.S. embassy and get to the airport as quickly as he could. He took an Uber, leaving his hotel room just after two in the morning, and used his phone to buy a ticket home. He spoke to Nicole again as the now-familiar scenery passed by, and she tried to reassure him again that she was on his side.

At the airport he waited for three hours in a large outdoor amphitheater, hemmed in by wire fencing and guards, watching the milling crowd until, at 6:30 a.m., half an hour after he had been scheduled to meet Mr. Rusdi at the hotel, he finally boarded an Ariana Afghan Airlines flight. Fake Amy had already called him three times, and sent several messages and a voice mail. "WHERE THE HELL ARE YOU? YOU'RE SUPPOSED TO BE HERE." More messages poured in as he listened to the airline attendants run through routine security protocols. The reminder to fasten his seat belt felt oddly comforting. He spent the flight to Japan staring out the window, running through worst-case scenarios; even after landing he worried that *she*, *his* Amy, would find a way to cancel the final leg of his journey home. If Amy was capable of creating a completely fabricated world for him in Jakarta, he wondered, what wasn't she capable of?

Will didn't sleep for four days after arriving home. He had never felt so vulnerable in his life. The criminals knew virtually everything about him: his parents' names, his address and bank account information, his work history and his contacts. And those long hours of conversations with "Amy" had at times veered into deeply personal, revealing territory.

On the fifth day, his phone rang. It was Amy. He stared at the screen and let it ring. She didn't leave a message.

INVESTIGATIONS PROCEED IN FITS AND starts. Like kaleidoscopes, their shapes change constantly as new light flows in; a sudden break on the heels of a long period of inactivity can feel like the curtains being ripped open to reveal a blazing sun. Nicole's conversation with Will had changed everything.

Until Fred Strathmann's call, Nicole had no inkling that the grift was in any way connected to Indonesia. She later described her reaction to that revelation as "whiplash." A few hours later, when she spoke to his son, she registered the fear that gripped the young man; even separated by twelve time zones, she could sense Will trembling as he shared his story. When he revealed the elaborate setup that had preceded his trip, and the huge amount of money he had lost since, the two-dimensional prism through which Nicole had been viewing the strange phone calls from Pascal shattered. The picture she was looking at now was shadowy and dark, and unmistakably malevolent. In time, Nicole would speak to hundreds of people who expressed the same pain and confusion about their run-ins with the Con Queen. But she would never forget the fear she heard in Will's voice, and the twisted story he unfurled.

Finally, she had an angle into the case. The impersonation of Pascal was just a gateway, an opening that led almost certainly to a criminal enterprise, with a female impersonator at its center. Luring and potentially kidnapping people, perhaps for their organs, across East Asia. Stealing large amounts of money in the process, in Will Strathmann's case more than $50,000.

Eventually, Will would provide Nicole with recordings that gave her direct insight into how the scam worked. Will had recorded one conversation before leaving the United States on his second trip to Indonesia. She turned the volume up on her computer. To Nicole, the voice Will had understood to be "Amy Pascal" sounded nothing like the real person, but then Will had no way of knowing that. And the impersonator was smooth, convincing, and highly knowledgeable. She spoke with a distinct air of authority that didn't leave much room for disagreement or doubt, and her repertoire of persuasive skills was especially impressive.

The conversation began breezily enough, as they discussed Will's upcoming return trip to Indonesia. But eventually, when Will tried to steer the conversation around to the several thousand dollars he was owed by that point, the fake Amy Pascal expertly threw him off the scent.

"I just want to make sure . . . I saw the other stuff about the funds getting through," Will began. "Um, how—"

"Can you, just a sec, can you hold on just a second?" Amy interrupted him.

"Yeah . . ."

Now Amy, in a slightly muffled but still audible voice, was talking on another line, to someone else.

"Marsha," she said softly, "the whole idea of getting the team to finish the editing . . ." Sounding slightly exasperated, Amy gently instructed Marsha that she would "follow up with Donna" as soon as she was finished with this call. But before she hung up, she added, "I'll be fine, thanks for asking. I'll call you back." She paused.

"Hello?" she said brightly, returning to Will.

"I just wanted to check in on the money and finances of it all," he resumed. "Because I'm a bit strapped for cash right now."

"No, I know, I *know*," she said, her tone turning impatient, frazzled. "This is what I'm trying to say." She explained that she didn't want to "overspend" and complained about delays and postponements that had plagued her in the past. He wasn't the only one worried about money. To ensure that it all went smoothly, she promised to secure him a business-class flight for his next trip. "I'm figuring it out," she insisted.

A lengthy explanation ensued, as she dove enthusiastically into the particulars of her accounting methodology for a full two minutes. At one point she referred to the payments required as a "one-time cost," while later she spoke of her "European offshore account." She explained that when she "put out large sums of money I usually do it through the company," but since Will didn't have a business account the payments would have to go through a separate channel, one that had to be delicately negotiated with her attorneys, an accountant, and a "relationship manager."

"I understand you're strapped," she concluded. "But I'll make sure you get the reimbursements by next week so when you're on that trip, you'll have it, so don't worry about it." She then implored him to "focus on the flights, that's all I ask, the rest, let me take care of this."

Will asked if he was going to have to bring cash with him on this next trip, and she said that yes, he would, as part of the one-time deal she had described.

When he admitted to being a "little surprised" that he had to return to Indonesia at all, especially so soon for another trip, she jumped on him.

"Why are you surprised?" she asked, sounding genuinely taken aback. She explained how all of these trips were simply part of a production schedule. "I don't know how it is in your world of photography," she said, "but this is part of production, there's nothing to worry about."

Will quickly backtracked, clearly nervous about ruffling her feathers. "I wasn't surprised in, like, a negative way," he said.

"I'm just crossing my fingers, making sure that you get this job," Amy said, sympathetically. "Because it's a lot of money out, it's not a lot of money out for me, it's not a big deal, but it's also money out, so I just want to ensure that you did the right thing, that *we* did the right thing and, you know, have that faith that you'll deliver accordingly—which I do."

She told him to have a "positive outlook," to focus on the work, and assured him that after this next trip, they would meet in LA. Perhaps sensing a growing skepticism within Will, she tried to keep the mood light, and tossed in what sounded like a sexual innuendo. "There won't be any merchant fees cuz I'll strap myself there with a seat belt when you're around," she said playfully, emitting a breathy giggle.

"Just book the tickets," she added. "Okay?"

"Thanks, Amy," Will said.

Within forty-eight hours, he had returned to Jakarta.

NICOLE URGED K2's HEAD OF research to engage the FBI, thinking that the agency would take the case and run with it—a naïve expectation, it turned out. As word of Nicole's case spread throughout K2, her colleagues began making calls to their police contacts in New York and Los Angeles, trying to generate interest in the case. As Nicole would soon discover, the FBI had a track record on this particular scam, and it wasn't a good one. Back at her desk, she created an Excel spreadsheet, with tabs: victims, money, method of contact, and the identity the impersonator assumed. She called it "Victim Tracker," and placed Will's name at the top. Alongside that she kept a running memo with notes. That night she curled up next to Anthony. "They're getting people to go to Indonesia," she said. They had to get up early but stayed up talking as their children slept in the next room. Together they gently began to peel back the first thin layers of the case that would consume Nicole for the next three years.

In almost every case Nicole had ever worked, grift fell into a relatively predictable pattern. The chief motivation was financial, and the people running it fulfilled their obligations with little or no enthusiasm for the role-playing. Greed caused people to fumble, exposing cracks through which a clever investigator could slip. Nicole imagined bored thieves clocking in and out of work in the back of an abandoned warehouse. Those cons were commonplace affairs, less interesting but also easier to detangle than the one sitting on her desk now.

Nicole had never worked on a case quite like this, nor had anyone else at her firm. Not even, remarkably, Jules Kroll, who founded J. Kroll Associates as a private detective agency in 1972. Nearly fifty years later, Kroll Inc. had offices in sixty countries and three thousand employees. In 2009 Jules and his son Jeremy founded K2 Intelligence. Jules wanted his investigators to learn how to build cases the FBI wouldn't be able to refuse. Kroll had been guided by this ethos for years. "The FBI," Jules liked to say, "is busy."

After learning about the Indonesia connection from Will, Nicole encouraged her client to spread the word: anyone who had traveled to Indonesia should get in touch. Several more victims had since emerged and now Nicole was receiving emails and calls every day. One fact stood out: time and again, people had boarded airplanes to Indonesia for Hollywood-related projects, even though the country had little infrastructure for the entertainment industry, and even less history as a venue for locations.

As she spoke to more victims, she began to discern a pattern. Will was, in some sense, representative of a certain breed of professional traveler. As a general rule they were creative and adventurous, with a strong interest in other cultures and countries. Most were well-educated, middle-class white people with means. The scamming outfit lured people to Indonesia and then convinced them to fork over hundreds or thousands of dollars, in cash and up front, for inflated travel costs involving drivers or translators, pocketing the difference. By the time the marks grew suspicious it was too late. Their money would never be reimbursed.

In those first days, Nicole cast a wide net and quickly discovered that other private investigators in Hollywood had also been making calls. Former policemen and military types by and large, they tended to see it as another romance scam of the sort detectives the world over are forever swatting away from their prestigious clientele. In 2018 the Federal Trade Commission received reports of more than 21,000 such scams, costing victims some $143 million, nearly quadruple the amount reported lost just three years before. Some of the cons stretched credulity. A California man named Jeffrey Lash convinced several women that he was a secret government agent who conducted interplanetary travel and hunted hostile space aliens. Over the course of two decades his marks forked over roughly $600,000, which he used to buy some 250 firearms and war paraphernalia. The scam only fell apart when Lash died in 2015, and his decomposing body was discovered in an SUV on a desolate road in Malibu.

The other investigators who had heard about the suspicious calls tended to view each one as a singular event and weren't receptive to the idea that they could be connected—or, if they were, they didn't believe that much could be done about them. Nicole, by contrast, approached the scam without any preconceived notions, and quickly determined something the other investigators had overlooked. Whoever was impersonating these producers wasn't just doing it for the money; the sums in question were generally small, usually in the $2,000 to $5,000 range. The only other group of criminals who had displayed such intense persistence were counterfeiters, and perhaps this wasn't all that surprising; the counterfeiting of money, or of a person's identity, ultimately spoke to a penchant for deception.

October turned into November and Nicole divided her time between the case and errands to the grocery store and evenings spent preparing stuffing. As the Thanksgiving holiday approached, she took stock of what she had, which included the preliminary emails the imposters had sent to an earlier group of victims and, from Will, a website domain: www.pascalfilms.com. But this data alone yielded only limited information. The scammers were using a virtual private network (VPN), a kind of roving, hidden server that bounces and cycles off other servers scattered around the world, continually masking the location and identity of its user.

Unless they are encrypted, emails contain metadata, with details about various pathways an email takes before it lands on a given computer. Metadata scraped from large email providers like Gmail or Yahoo isn't always helpful because the traffic gets routed through servers that cover huge geographic areas. But individual, vanity domains, such as pascalfilms.com, can provide more specific information. And in this case, the domains had been linked to Microsoft 365, a simple email platform with relatively weak security. Nicole could see that the metadata in the scammer's emails originated from within a single IP address, suggesting that it was always coming from the same router, located somewhere in the United Kingdom. The emails from the earlier set of victims shared the same IP addresses as those used in the Pascal Hollywood scam. It was reasonable to conclude that the same people were probably responsible. Nicole had uncovered her first digital fingerprint.

It came into even clearer focus when she began scrutinizing the PDF files of contracts, NDAs, and itineraries that the fake Amy Pascal had sent to her victims. These documents also contained valuable metadata, including time stamps. They appeared to have been created in London, by the scammers, and then opened later, in Indonesia, by the victims. The scope of potential financial beneficiaries, which ranged from hotels to airlines to drivers and guides, was vast. The logistics involved were mind-boggling.

DURING THOSE EARLY, CONFUSING WEEKS, K2 continued trying to enlist the help of the FBI by reaching out through back channels, but kept running into the same hurdles. Whatever financial arrangements existed between the victims and the scammers could be interpreted as business deals that had soured. The money had changed hands in a foreign jurisdiction, where U.S. federal agencies had no authority. The United States shared no extradition treaty with Indonesia. The identity theft of the Hollywood figures was more straightforward, but none of those victims suffered any direct financial loss. And even if they had, the FBI only took on cases in which damages exceeded a million dollars. One day, Nicole ran into a colleague who had gone to work for the FBI. "The FBI will never do this," he told her. The agency limited its involvement to terrorism, drug trafficking, murder, and the occasional white-collar crime involving tens of millions of dollars. None of that was evident here.

As Nicole considered this obstacle, she decided the scammers had thought this through and adjusted accordingly. In other words, the imposters were cleverly gaming the international judicial system. It was ingenious. It felt in some ways like a swindle from long ago, the kind advertised in fading primary colors on the side of a carnival traveling wagon, an elaborate card trick performed by a top-hatted gentleman wearing the stylized Guy Fawkes mask favored by members of the hacktivist group Anonymous. When Nicole really thought about it, it felt . . . crazy.

She needed to find more victims. As it turned out, there were plenty. For every person who had traveled to Indonesia, there were several who had not. Now she realized why: the group doing the impersonating had established a kind of screening process. At least one reason for the initial calls was to identify people who might be lured to

Indonesia. If the scammer couldn't convince her marks that she knew of and appreciated their artistic achievements, no one was going to get on a plane bound for Jakarta. But nor were they likely to travel if their lives were constrained in other ways—by wives, husbands, kids, obligations. The initial raft of phone calls allowed her to filter out unlikely candidates, zeroing in on those who would be likely to hop on a plane at a moment's notice. Once the scammer had homed in on a real target, she could, as Nicole put it, begin to "groom" them for the next stage of the scam.

While some victims were talented photographers, by and large their true dominion was social media. They had mastered the art of self-promotion, and were comfortable posting—advertising—the details of their lives. Masters of the selfie, they crossed back and forth between journalism and the more nebulous but profitable world of branding. Nevertheless, some, like Will, had a strong sense of social justice, and were eager for projects that aligned with their ethics. By cross-checking the victims' stories with the details they had posted about themselves online, Nicole began to discern patterns. The impersonator's seemingly deep knowledge base could have easily been scraped off the internet, an open vault where ambition and oversharing collided. Once in possession of a mark's professional trajectory, along with the names of past collaborators or clients, the impersonator could weave a tale to suit each one.

Technology was the scam's great enabler. It allowed the imposter to be multiple people at any given moment, anywhere in the world, often all at once. It exponentially increased her ability to adapt to the needs and insecurities of victims in real time. A blank Skype screen—in which the victim, but not the imposter, was visible—reinforced the power imbalance at the heart of the relationship. And the speed and frequency of communication—whether by email, text message, Instagram, WhatsApp, Skype, or even a straightforward, old-fashioned cell phone call—provided her with a constant opportunity to keep at bay, for ever-longer periods of time, the one thing that would kill any scam: doubt.

Each new victim provided Nicole with "a different little piece" of the puzzle: another phone number, domain, or email, a new IP address. One victim had told her a story about how he had confronted the driver while still in Indonesia. The driver had obligingly called his "boss" in the United Kingdom, whereupon a man, speaking flawless English, said, "Hi, this is Rio Wirya." She added the name to the Victim Tracker. She found a victim in South Africa who referred her to a Navy SEAL and ten of his buddies who had all gone to Indonesia. Soon her Excel spreadsheet had half a dozen tabs going, and the list was growing. She thought of this process as "collecting victims."

The more she dug, the further back in time the scam seemed to stretch. A group of makeup artists in London who had been scammed in 2016 gave her domain names for a Chinese firm called Huaxia, a film distribution company. Another cohort believed they had been hired by the China Film Group, a mainland company that was helping to develop China's film industry. The metadata was helpful for obtaining location data, but useless when trying to determine who was behind the fake domains. Whoever had set them up was hiding behind a privacy wall. Unlike the Guardians of Peace hack, which had targeted Sony, the group responsible for this impersonation was training its sights on specific individuals. The imposter and her minions were intimately familiar with the horse-whispering language of Hollywood; good enough, Nicole discovered, that in addition to Pascal, they had passed themselves off as several other powerful women as well: Lucasfilm's Kathleen Kennedy, 20th Century Fox CEO Stacey Snider, and former Paramount chief Sherry Lansing.

Around this time, Nicole also began to develop a rudimentary picture of what the scam looked like from the Indonesian side. She learned the names of the driver and a series of moped-riding bagmen who collected money from the victims and carted it off to an as-yet-undetermined location. The travel arrangements had been made through booking.com. In many cases only the first night's stay would have been paid for, which left the victims to pick up the rest of the bill. She collected pictures of all these local helpers and enablers that victims had taken and then later posted about on Facebook. She learned that they had stayed at virtually every three- and four-star hotel in Jakarta, from the Santika to the Shangri-La. There were different directives, depending on a victim's role in the "production": makeup artists were told to visit local food and craft markets in Jakarta to seek design inspiration; cinematographers visited historic sites to get ideas for scenes; screenwriters were immersed in the culture and mythology of Indonesia through trips across the archipelago.

An early victim connected Nicole with a translator who told her he had been recruited by a cousin who worked for "a guy who does travel projects for Americans and Europeans, visiting museums," so Nicole found the cousin and then the cousin's brother. They told her they worked as money collectors and explained that they were employed by a man named Rio Wirya—the same name she had heard just days earlier. Exactly how this tangle of people was caught up in the scam remained obscured for the time being. But there existed, somewhere, a mastermind: an English-speaking puppeteer going by the name Rio Wirya, presumably working from the United Kingdom, who controlled at least some of the strings being manipulated seven thousand miles away in Indonesia.

NICOLE WORKED FROM HER HOME in New Jersey three days a week and traveled into Manhattan by bus on the other two, but even with that flexibility, between soccer practice, dance lessons, and karate, most days were rushed and overfilled. She felt guilty checking her phone while sitting on the floor during Saturday Mommy & Me classes, singing along to songs from India and Brazil while her toddler gazed at her in expectation.

One night she received a call just as her kids were exiting the bath. She needed to take notes but didn't have one of her leatherette journals handy, so she seated her kids at the kitchen table, filled her son's bowl with a distracting mound of Cheerios, and grabbed a glittery, mermaid-themed notebook with a tiny lock on the cover that belonged to her daughter. Before too long the notebook had become the reposi-tory for all things related to the imposter, the tiny lock protecting the case details from prying eyes. It remained on her bedroom office desk until she reached the last page.

By late 2017, however, Nicole had hit a wall. She was no closer to identifying who had set up the domains, or how to stop them. At her suggestion, Pascal's lawyers in LA filed a lawsuit that they hoped would give them subpoena power to go after the telephone and domain hosting companies that were being used by the criminals. The idea had come to her during a conversation with Pascal's attorneys in which she learned that they had developed a juridical innovation a few years earlier, while helping Microsoft defend itself against a massive hack by an army of bots.

In order to dismantle the bots, they had to destroy the hubs con-necting them. But without a named defendant, they had no one to target and they had to obtain subpoenas against *somebody*. So, in a novel legal maneuver, they *invented* a defendant. This was unusual. In legal strategy, Jane Does were typically added as plaintiffs to existing lawsuits. In this case, however, the primary *defendant* was to be Jane Doe. It worked and Microsoft prevailed over the bots. Nicole wondered if something similar could be done with her Indonesia case. The suit, submitted on behalf of Pascal against the imposter, now known as Jane Doe, was filed a few days before Halloween.

In spite of her frustration, Nicole's boss seemed pleased; she was building a reputation as a curious and persistent young investigator. She had what one supervisor described as "a healthy dose of paranoia" that allowed her to navigate her way through theories and conspiracies. And her "collecting" approach was yielding results. Her memo on the scam had expanded to fill five single-spaced pages detailing notes, numbers, emails, and observations. Nicole had discovered two more Hollywood notables who had been impersonated: the producer and billionaire philanthropist Gigi Pritzker and *Homeland* director Lesli Linka Glatter. There were at least fifteen names on Victim Tracker, going back two years. She had drawn a dotted line between Huaxia and the China Film Group to the impersonations of Hollywood notables. She also had email addresses and telephone numbers, as well as metadata from NDAs and itineraries, which placed some part of the scam in the United Kingdom. Finally, she had a name: Rio Wirya.

With the successful filing of the lawsuit, the attorneys sent out dozens of subpoenas—to the phone companies, the internet domain hosting giant GoDaddy, and a host of smaller phone forwarding companies based in Europe and the United States. Then, they all waited.

NICOLE OFTEN FOUND HERSELF THINKING about the toll the scam took on its victims. There was a sadistic undercurrent to the interactions, in the casualness of the manipulation, the construction and subsequent dismantling of worlds; there was a cruelty in the godlike annihilation of dreams. Whereas the victims began their journeys believing themselves talented and worthy of discovery, they ended them mired in self-loathing and doubt.

The scammer had figured out how to target each of them as individuals. The differences between the scams were subtle, and carefully considered. Vulnerabilities were like fingerprints; afterward, each blistered pad looked different.

Sometimes she continued speaking to some people for weeks even when it was clear they would never go to Indonesia. Whoever was doing the impersonations had another goal in mind. This was how Nicole stumbled into a new category of victims: the connectors. These people functioned like an army of personal headhunters, introducing the scammers to a wider network of potential travelers. The person at the center of the web promised these connectors rewards if they got her what she wanted, including finder's fees or future jobs.

NICOLE DECIDED IT WAS TIME to brief Kerry Sulkowicz. A professor of clinical psychiatry at New York University's Grossman School of Medicine, Sulkowicz helped K2's investigators build psychological profiles for the agency's clientele in his capacity as the founder of Boswell Group consultants. Based on what Nicole had told him, Sulkowicz speculated that whoever was behind the voices likely had an ambivalent and troubled relationship with female authority figures, along with a profound identification with them. Seen from this perspective, the impersonations could be thought of as a grand and cruel psychodrama in which unresolved childhood trauma was playing itself out; Sulkowicz said he wouldn't be surprised if the imposter had experienced intense neglect at the hands of a cruel mother, or perhaps abandonment. For such a person, the feeling of power that came from manipulating people could be intoxicating, compensation, perhaps, for a corresponding lack of power in childhood. After listening to Nicole, the psychiatrist said he believed the con might be the work of a psychopathic mind.

Chapter 3

The water on the lake near Nicole's home froze in winter. The birdsong quieted. In the first week of February 2018, the results of the subpoenas began flooding in. A pattern quickly emerged: the phone numbers used to reach out to victims were all Voice over Internet Protocol, or VoIP, numbers with British, New York, and Los Angeles area codes. Long before internet-based telephone services like WhatsApp and Skype made calling internationally essentially free, VoIP was an inexpensive and reliable workaround. From anywhere in the world, users could buy a forwarding number that appeared deceptively on the receiver's end as local. More recently, with the advent of internet calling services, VoIP had come to be seen by people in Nicole's line of work as an obscuring tool, almost always a sign of fraudulent, "scammy" activity. But VoIP was undeniably effective; sometimes K2 investigators themselves used it if they wanted to anonymously contact someone. The numbers the impersonators had used to call victims had been registered with small, mom-and-pop outfits based in Europe that gobbled up discarded phone lines and recycled them in the VoIP ecosystem. Nicole cross-checked the subpoena results with the numbers she had recorded in Victim Tracker. One of the British numbers identified in the subpoenas as a forwarding destination—one of the deceptive local numbers—was the same number that an early victim had tied to Rio Wirya.

Another name she had never seen before popped out: Cabin Yim. He was listed as the purchaser of one of the phone numbers associated with the fake Gigi Pritzker. Nicole looked up Yim's Instagram account. He was a Bangkok-based gamer and entrepreneur. As far as she could tell, Yim had no criminal record. His account was a blur of stock market and forex trading graphs, nutritional advice, and a few snapshots of outdoor scenes. It was all very ordinary. But she did find one tantalizing thread. For months, a London-based Instagram account called Purebytes had been tagging Yim almost every single day. The site's host, a middle-aged man who looked to be of South Asian background, often referred to Yim as his "best friend." The adoring tone of the posts reminded Nicole of the way children, especially young girls like her own daughter, spoke about their closest friends.

To safely study Purebytes more closely, she created a fake Instagram account and curated it to look like that of an electronic dance music fan. The pictures, and a few videos, of elaborately prepared soufflés and tarts, kebabs, and rotis that populated the Purebytes posts seemed professionally produced, but had limited engagement from its 52,000 followers. The host, on the other hand, remained largely off-screen. "Purebytes," the site's bio read, "Every Meal Has a Story." As she scrolled back in the timeline, she saw that he often included Indonesia and Jakarta in hashtags.

Just days earlier, in early February, Purebytes had linked to a popular Bahrainian restaurant in London whose chef he praised. The chef responded with a note of her own: "Thank you Gavin Lal @purebytes for your visit . . . hope to see this and more shows [*sic*] Netflix!" *Gavin Lal.*

Yim's name was tied to other numbers linked to the scam as well. If Yim was the registered administrator of the phones, Nicole reasoned, perhaps he was also responsible for setting up the fake domains. Pascal's attorneys sent Yim a "cease-and-desist" letter titled "Your Unlawful

Impersonation Scam" and demanded that Yim cease all his fraudulent activities and identify anyone else involved in the scam. Cabin responded immediately and within an hour he was speaking to Nicole. After introducing herself as a private investigator, she asked him if he had set up the Amy Pascal domain. Yes, he had helped set up www .pascalfilms.com, he acknowledged, but only at the bequest of his friend Gavin, the creator and host of Purebytes, who worked in Hollywood. Some of the victims had described speaking to someone named Gavin, but with a different last name: Ambani.

"Gavin Lal is Purebytes," Nicole said, matter-of-factly.

"Gavin, yes," he told her. He sounded scared. "I don't know his last name. He's not very technically savvy." Nicole thought he was holding back, but pocketed her doubt for the time being.

"I need to talk to Gavin," she said. Yim told her he felt sorry that people were getting scammed, and promised he would tell Gavin to take care of it.

"What can we do to make this right?" he asked Nicole.

It was Presidents' Day weekend and Nicole and Anthony needed a night out alone. They left their kids with Nicole's mother and headed for Jersey City, where they hit the Golden Cicada, a karaoke bar popular with hipsters and whose Japanese owner "assigned" songs to patrons. Sizing up Nicole, he gave her "The Impossible Dream," from the Broadway hit *Man of La Mancha*, and later Aretha Franklin's "(You Make Me Feel Like) A Natural Woman." Around 1 a.m., they stumbled back to the apartment of Nicole's brother-in-law, who was out of town. The next morning, Nicole was nursing a hangover, a Bloody Mary, and a plate of huevos rancheros at a hole-in-the-wall Mexican brunch spot, skimming through the pages of the Sunday *New York Times*, when her cell phone rang. The call showed up as "Anonymous" and she didn't answer. It rang again. And then again.

Suddenly, remembering Cabin's promise to call Gavin, she picked up.

"Oh, Hi, Nicole? Oh, no, no, no," said a man with an American accent and a frenetic manner. "I really need to talk to you. I really need to clear my *name*. My family is very disturbed that I've been dragged into this whole thing."

He told her his name was Gavin. He said that he knew she was investigating some scam, but that it was all a big misunderstanding. He wasn't involved.

"This is it," she whispered to Anthony.

Gavin told her he would call her back soon with more information and quickly hung up.

NICOLE AND ANTHONY HAD PLANNED to visit a museum that day in Jersey City. But now Gavin was on the hook.

"We have to go back," she said. They cut the meal short and returned home. That night, she listened again to the few recordings she possessed of the female impersonator. In her notes, she jotted down her first impressions of Gavin. "Accent sounds like the woman on the phone. I think he's more involved than he says."

Gavin called Nicole several times over the following week, always from a restricted number so that it showed up as "Anonymous" on her screen, as it had the first time he had called. Once she woke at 7 a.m. to find thirteen missed calls from Anonymous. He called during her daily commute into Manhattan, sometimes as early as 5 a.m. She had a couple of conversations with him while standing in the Port Authority terminal, waiting for a subway train heading uptown. Every call seemed harried and frantic, as if she had caught him in the middle of an important meeting, and while he was energetic and polite, he provided little of value. When she asked him if he knew anything about the fraud, he encouraged her to pursue it. Gavin told her that he was involved in the movie industry in Asia, primarily India, employed by a woman named Maggie Ling, who was working to secure distribution deals with female producers like Amy Pascal and the actor Angelina Jolie. Gavin told her that Ling had contacted him two years earlier and asked him to take a scoping trip to Jakarta—just the kind of trip that many of the victims had taken. Gavin conceded that he had, with Cabin's help, set up the Amy Pascal domains, but that he had done it at Ling's direction. He suggested that Ling owed him money and said he thought she was responsible for the calls to victims. He lamented that he had gotten involved with her at all.

"Oh my gosh," he gushed. "Oh, no, no, no. I've been swept up in this, too. Like, I didn't actually do anything wrong. This woman has fooled me. I want to help you."

Nicole wasn't sure what it was, exactly, but there was something *off* about Gavin. She asked if he had any connection to Indonesia. No, he said; he was an American citizen.

He spoke quickly, with rapid-fire interruptions and a kind of breathy urgency. "Listen, I want to help you however I can. She is *hurting* people." He promised to provide her with the names of people who could help in her investigation.

The subpoenas had yielded a list of domains for several Hollywood notables and high-net-worth individuals, including a site she had never heard of: ambanihouse.com, another suggestion that the mysterious "Gavin Ambani" was in some way connected to the scam. The surname "Ambani" originated in Gujarat, India; Mukesh Ambani was one of India's wealthiest people. Nicole also discovered a fake domain purporting to be a website for Christine Hearst Schwarzman, an intellectual property lawyer and the wife of billionaire Republican heavyweight Stephen Schwarzman, CEO of the hedge fund the Blackstone Group and, for a brief time, the head of President Donald Trump's Strategic and Policy Forum. As far as Nicole knew, Schwarzman hadn't been impersonated. But the presence of her name in this web of numbers and domains was puzzling. Then she realized that she wasn't necessarily viewing evidence of crimes that had been committed, but rather, clues for crimes yet to come. Schwarzman was a potential *future* victim. The road map for the scam was expanding in two directions at once, into the past and now the future.

Cabin had already revealed that he had purchased several global forwarding numbers used to impersonate Gigi Pritzker and Amy Pascal. The links tying emails to domains to phone numbers suggested that the same criminal enterprise was responsible for scams spanning more than two years. The originating internet provider information on the metadata scraped from emails and documents throughout that time, and from all the victims, also matched. But what was the end-game? And what was the connection with Indonesia?

"What's the deal with those other women?" Nicole asked the next time Gavin called.

Gavin grew exasperated. "Maggie really took me for a ride," he said bitterly. "She claimed she had a relationship with Amy Pascal and all these other women." When Nicole posed more pointed questions he began to slip, sometimes into incoherence, which fed her skepticism. Gavin, in turn, seemed to intuit something was wrong because one day, while Nicole was probing, he grew wary.

"You don't know my legal name," he said. "You don't know who I am."

"I know your name is Gavin," she replied. "Unless you're lying."

"I respect you," he said, by way of a response. "I know you're just doing your job. I get why you have to ask these questions. I *understand*, we have to get to the bottom of this, but I'm not *involved*. You've got the wrong guy. I need to clear my name." She didn't know yet whether Gavin was his real name, but she was confident that over time it would all come out; he was a *big* talker. He told her that he had attended Bradley University, in Peoria, Illinois, and the Wharton School of the University of Pennsylvania; that his parents, now dead, had been heavily involved in Bollywood, and that he had lived in Los Angeles when he was younger. Unsure what was true and what was fantasy, she clocked those details away.

"I don't know who you are. But you should probably tell me because I'm taking this to the police." She could "go away" and never talk to him again, she explained, if he would just shut down the Pascal domain.

Gavin switched tacks. On their next call, he threatened to sue

Nicole and K2 if she didn't stop coming after him. He let slip details about her personal life, only some of which were correct, in what felt like a deliberate move to scare her. As an *American citizen* he would be caught—unfairly, he added—in the crosshairs of a justice system gone horribly awry. He insisted that his "team of lawyers" was reviewing the matter carefully, sorting through what they could and could not disclose to Nicole. He began calling her from blocked numbers at all hours of the day and night. One morning, he called half a dozen times while she was scrambling to get the kids out the door. When she finally answered he said he was consulting his lawyer about pursuing legal action. He said he had just spoken to Angelina Jolie, and that she informed him that Nicole's client, Amy Pascal, was a "bad person."

K2 offered Nicole protection, but she declined. Nicole had confronted stalkers and harassers, the criminal and the mentally ill alike, extorters and grifters, even impersonators. And when she tracked down these adversaries, came face-to-face with them, they usually listened. Confrontation in this form typically worked, however uncomfortably. Except on the rare occasion, such as now, when it didn't. Nicole felt a knot in her stomach, a sense that she had encountered a human being who lacked a fundamentally human lever: fear. Gavin never delivered the names of the lawyers, as he had promised, or any further information about the scam. He did, however, take down the Pascal domains. "This is a horrible thing," he told her in their last conversation. "Why would anybody do this?"

Then Gavin went dark, never to call again. Perhaps Maggie Ling was the female voice, Nicole thought to herself; for a brief time, this became her operating thesis. Something along those lines had been the working supposition all along, in fact: a criminal enterprise led by a female impersonator, all working in concert within the hive of online obscurity. But the email she sent to Ling at the address Gavin had provided bounced back, and she realized he hadn't intended to help her at all. She didn't bother to ask him about the email that had bounced.

Nicole reached out to Schwarzman, the wife of the billionaire hedge fund manager. She described her investigation and explained that there was a fake domain in Schwarzman's name. She suggested they might want to take preventative measures. K2 would be happy to help. The response from Schwarzman was tepid: thanks, but no thanks.

Chapter 4

An inchoate kind of comprehension begins two and three layers, and possibly more, beneath the level of words. In scientific jargon, this is called prosody, the physics of language: pitch and modulation, emphasis and timing. *Prosody* refers to the emotional power inherent in language, when words are stripped of their meaning, and sound alone does the heavy lifting. Think of a song whose lyrics you have garbled to the point of absurdity, but whose emotional resonance remains powerful simply because of the way the words *sound*.

Linguists sometimes talk about "prosodic features." These are fragments of language that are typically longer than a vowel or a consonant, but sometimes as short as a single, gasping syllable: "*Oh!*" Rather wonderfully, they call these fragments "suprasegmentals." Charles Darwin hypothesized that the music of language predates language itself. Then there are those fastidious and untamed students who devote themselves to the mechanical mastery of monologues, poetry, and dialogues so as to learn a language's secret rhythms—but now we're getting ahead of ourselves.

LANGUAGE OFFERS CLUES TO A person's background, and sometimes even to their psyche. In some societies, specific words can function as gender markers. The word *okay* is such a linguistic tic in some Asian cultures, typically signifying a male speaker. In Japan, where gender roles are starkly drawn, many words have a "male" and "female" form, depending on the speaker. In the romance languages, nouns themselves are gendered. In the Atayal language, spoken by several thousand people in the mountains of Northern Taiwan, men and women use different registers and vocabularies, a tradition thought by some to have its origins in a "secret" form of communication used exclusively by men. Across the world, in fact, gendered differences crop up in languages in a variety of ways small and large. But culture isn't the only factor that influences how people speak. So, too, does biology, especially when personality disorders are present. Psychopaths use language differently than most people. They tend to display more disfluencies, *um*'s and *ah*'s, than non-psychopaths.

Nicole wasn't aware of the linguistic complexities inherent to the scam yet, but in her own manner she began siphoning off the subtle linguistic markers that were shared by the impersonator and the impersonated. Nicole carved out time after her children were asleep to play and replay recordings side by side, one from Purebytes, another from a victim. Beside her, Anthony offered questions and observations. He was invested in the case as well at this point. They were both now professionals in white-collar New York, and they had each other's back. And Anthony was a good lawyer, skilled at finding the smoking gun during long and tedious depositions.

Verbal tics began to jump out at Nicole, starting with the phrase "You know . . . ?" She listened repeatedly to recordings in which a Gigi Pritzker or a Kathleen Kennedy trailed off as their intonations rose when saying these two words, just as Gavin, she now remembered, had done when they had spoken. *You know?* Nicole had also noticed other words and phrases that seemed unique to Gavin. "Just a real heads-up," he had said, and "No, no, no, no, no." Meanwhile, on the recordings the victims shared there was a wide range of accents—Chinese, American, British, Indian, Persian—and there were women in their sixties and men in their twenties.

The real Kathleen Kennedy was American, but in one recording Nicole listened as the fake Kennedy tossed off a series of Briticisms—"monies" instead of money, "solicitors" instead of lawyers. Whoever was doing this Kathleen Kennedy was, at least in the banalities of her day-to-day routine, soaking more in British, not American, waters. Nicole considered herself to be pretty good at accents, thanks to years of high school debate and drama, and she began to think the American voice in the recordings sounded put-on, as if someone were faking a midwestern accent while also, simultaneously, trying to sound "Californian." No, she thought, almost with a tinge of disappointment, that's not how you do it, that's not it at all.

Nicole had grown up more attuned than most to the vagaries and nuances of language. Her grandfather had arrived in the United States by steamer from the tiny village of Kalesmeno, near Karpenissi, situated in "the Alps of Greece," one of the country's poorest and remotest regions. He waited fifteen years before he was able to bring the rest of his family over, including Nicole's father, Dimitrios. Her mother was a second-generation immigrant from Italy. Her parents named her Nicoletta, meaning "People of Victory." Dimitrios, known to his friends as "Jimmy," liked to tell his daughter that he learned English by listening to *All Things Considered* on NPR, and half a century on he still spoke English with a Greek accent. Jimmy worked as a janitor at the warehouses of AT&T and later at a series of diners and dry cleaners. But he liked being a father more and so he passed up opportunities for promotions to coach his daughter's soccer team. Nicole's mother presided over their home in much the same way she ran the middle school where she was a principal: like an affectionate drill sergeant.

In the weeks following Nicole's conversations with Gavin, she noticed a change in the patterns of the calls. Victims began hearing from male "producers" who worked with the female executives. Within a matter of weeks, she received a new set of recordings that sent the investigation in a new direction. She downloaded a recording of Gavin speaking as the host of Purebytes and played it several times for a South

African makeup artist who had traveled to Indonesia in 2016. Then she asked if the man in that recording could possibly be the same person as the Chinese female executive the stylist had known as "Leslie." The victim was unequivocal: no. Nicole repeated the experiment with other victims and always got the same result. Not a single victim believed that the voices of the men—whether Gavin on Purebytes or an unnamed male producer—could conceivably also belong to any of the impersonated women. She had asked victims if their conversational partners spoke over one another, the way people tend to do in the course of normal conversation. In some cases, they insisted they had, which had suggested there had been multiple people on the same call; in other instances the victims only ever spoke to a single individual, one Amy Pascal or one Gigi Pritzker. Recently Nicole had spoken to an actor, a contestant on the Australian edition of the reality show *The Bachelor*, who traveled to Indonesia thinking he was working for Wendi Murdoch; he told her he had spoken on the phone with three different people—two women and a man—at the same time.

Wendi Deng Murdoch was arguably even more high-profile than Amy Pascal. Born in China to two engineers, Deng studied economics in California and ultimately obtained an MBA from Yale. Launching her career with an internship at Star TV in Hong Kong, she had soon become a vice president of the network's music feed, Channel V. In 1997, Deng met and married Fox NewsCorp chairman Rupert Murdoch. They had two children together before divorcing in 2013 after reports surfaced that Deng had carried on an affair with former British prime minister Tony Blair. By the time the scammer began impersonating her, people once close to the real Wendi Murdoch, including then–first daughter Ivanka Trump and Deng's former husband Rupert, were publicly accusing her of being a "Chinese spy."

The actor who had spoken to the fake Murdoch now told Nicole about a single, lengthy phone conversation that included Murdoch, her male assistant, Aaron, and Apple cofounder Steve Jobs's widow, Laurene Powell Jobs. Murdoch spoke in her clipped British accent,

Aaron in a New York twang, and Laurene in a "typical, middle-aged American woman" accent. Three voices at the same time, but how many people had actually been on the call? The idea that three people would participate in such a ruse was almost as fanciful as the notion of a single person performing three voices at the same time.

There was one exception. An early victim had told Nicole he thought the person on the other end of the line might possibly be a man pretending to be a woman. A few stragglers with similar suspicions surfaced occasionally, but none had traveled to Indonesia, and none had spoken to their impersonators for very long. Among the victims who had developed relationships with their imaginary benefactors, none had hinted at any uncertainty about the gender of the person on the other end of the line. Some laughed when Nicole raised the possibility that they might be confused. The people who had spent the most time, hours and hours in some cases, carrying on long conversations with their imaginary totems, their Amys, Kathleens, or Gigis, were the most certain of all.

As a result, Nicole had stopped entertaining the idea herself. But with every new Instagram video from Purebytes, each new "story" from the dandy gallivanting around London, Nicole began to wonder less about what wasn't, and more about what exactly she *was* hearing, which increasingly felt to her like Gavin's voice in some of the voices. The lens was narrowing; the idea that a sprawling criminal enterprise was behind the scam seemed less and less plausible. It was more likely a smaller operation, perhaps just two or three people. Gavin was almost certainly the male "producer," working with the elusive Maggie Ling, whom he had described as "the one hurting people."

The consensus had also begun to shift inside K2. One of Nicole's colleagues was certain the culprit was, to use his term, a "drag queen." His had been a dissenting voice until then, but now more people began to come around to his view. Nicole began to place other observations she had made into this new matrix. When the person being impersonated was a man, Nicole often heard background noise, as if the calls were being made in public. But the female voices only ever emerged in the quiet. In her mind's eye, Nicole saw herself passing a counter in a coffee shop and noticing a figure talking animatedly on an iPhone, seemingly oblivious to the surrounding chatter. In that setting, she thought, a man pretending to be a woman might turn some heads.

FROM A LINGUISTIC STANDPOINT, THERE are several tangible differences between average female and male voices. Female voices generally fall within 196–293 hertz, the standard unit used to measure frequency. The male range dips down to 110 Hz. The "gender ambiguous" range is somewhere in the middle. Certain letters, such as *M*, *N*, *Y*, *L*, and *R*, called resonant consonants, have an even higher-than-usual frequency in females than males. Females also generally have a wider pitch range, called prosodic variation, than men. They speak faster, and with more breath. Men speak with more "creak," a quality often referred to as "vocal fry."

A computerized measurement of the voice of Elizabeth Holmes, the deep-voiced CEO of Silicon Valley unicorn start-up Theranos who bilked investors out of hundreds of millions of dollars, was found to sit comfortably within the range typically associated with males. Studies have shown that deeper, male voices tend to elicit more trust and credence. Holmes's real voice sat naturally higher, at a more typical female register, but she deployed the lower tone in all her public appearances and only infrequently slipped out of character.

JOSIE ZANFORDINO IS A TRANSGENDER woman, now in her sixties. A licensed speech pathologist, she directs the Voice and Communication Modification Program for People in the Transgender Community, at Ithaca College. "Your Voice of Choice Awaits You" proclaims her website, where interested people learn that vocal transformation is a nonmedical option that requires "diligence, experiments, and adventure." Zanfordino trains people how to modify their voice to become, in effect, other people, specifically how men can become women and vice versa. Zanfordino believes there is nothing more central to that process than one's voice, particularly its prosody: a voice conveys the essence of a person, enabling connection, communication, and expression. People may hide, protect, or otherwise ignore their genitalia; they may wear makeup to change their faces. But they must, as a matter of survival, use their voices every day, all the time. Successful vocal transition requires an immense psychological shift. One must, like an actor, become another, even to oneself.

On one level, it's a technical exercise. Zanfordino takes measurements of her clients' voices using pitch voice monitors. Effective vocal transition requires subtle shifts. In the case of a male transitioning to a female, it encompasses several nuanced stages: a lighter contact in the throat, less friction between the vocal cords, a loosening of the two muscle groups that control the vocal tract and the thyroid region, an awareness that what is now occurring in the throat should be moved forward into the facial "mask." She teaches clients how to modify the pitch of their voice to match the tone of the gender they are seeking to inhabit. She stresses inflection, helping to lighten a voice, making it breathier, more "legato." Students learn that sounds can be thought of as having color values. A consonant like *P* has a lighter shade, but is darker than *V.*

The deeper work, which proceeds "very, very slowly," is psychological. Zanfordino's patients must persuade themselves, in a sense, of the authenticity of their own identities. Zanfordino describes it as "peeling off the layers of ourselves that have kept us from our true sense of where our heart beats." Transitioning from one voice to another can take anywhere from three to six months. She puts her clients through deep-breathing and relaxation exercises designed to reorient their perspective on their own bodies. She helps people to identify what she calls the feminine and masculine "aspects" of language, the nuances in sentence structure. Some seemed simple, even reductive: women prefer to use an upward inflection when finishing a sentence, or posing a question, whereas men prefer to get to the bottom line very quickly and speak in a more staccato tone. She adored Gregory Peck and thought his rendition of Captain Ahab in the 1956 film adaptation of *Moby-Dick* was exemplary of an ideal male voice. "Rise now ye white whale," Ahab utters, in that deeply sonorous bass, moments before he is yanked from his dinghy and towed into oblivion. "Show us your crooked jaw, show us your wrinkled brow. Rise!"

The great white whale of Zanfordino's world was, unquestionably, talking on the telephone. No other everyday act presents a greater challenge to somebody in the throes of a vocal transition. Among the twelve modules Zanfordino teaches, which include "Body language" and "How to laugh like a man or a lady," the most difficult segment is "How to succeed on the telephone." Research has shown that it is both easier for a listener to detect deception over the telephone than it is in-person, and also much harder to pull off for the person doing the deceiving. Untethered to a wig or makeup or any other physical crutch, this aspect of a transformation leaves little room for error. There is a long history of trans people being maligned unfairly as deviant impersonators, and Zanfordino wouldn't describe the process she teaches as deception, of course. Nevertheless, she does have a specific protocol to help her clients be more convincing when speaking on the phone: be light and confident, choose your first sentence in advance, and then coach yourself about how the conversation might unfold before you ever dial a number. When the other person answers, spell your name out loud; the methodical enunciation of each letter of, say, a "Christina" or an "Amy" reinforces the narrative. One tiny slip, and your story could be blown.

The imposter had seemingly perfected the art of vocal transformation, all without ever setting foot in Zanfordino's offices, at least as far as the speech pathologist knew.

Nicole had never given much thought to accents; now she found herself obsessing about them. She had started to think of the imposter's different vocal constructions—the aggressive New Yorker; the East Asian sophisticate; the hard-charging Middle American—almost as distinct people in their own right. The trick was to find the common denominators in their speech, the verbal tics. It was painstaking work, but slowly she came to isolate at least one clue. Gavin and the impersonated women seemed to punctuate their enthusiasm for a conversation's meandering journey with a similar exclamation. Gavin said it in a nasal, slightly pleading upswing—*Okay?* So did the impersonated women. *Okay?*

NOWADAYS, OF COURSE, PEOPLE TEXT. The phone feels anachronistic. Maybe it's the intimacy, a voice literally whispering in your ear. There's no filter available to dull its effect. No gloss. You can hear a voice's crackle and hiccups, its fry and swallows and half breaths as if it's inside your head.

That missing tic, for instance, that Nicole picked up on every time she listened to a recording of the fake Amy Pascal, whose somewhat nasal, midwestern drawl was otherwise pretty good. What made the real Amy Pascal's voice so unique was the scratch in the marbled Madonna, its singular flaw, her distinctive lisp. But only if you were really paying attention. When it came to Pascal, at least, the mental picture victims shared was of a female, roughly in her middle-age years, possessed of a nonregional but distinctly American accent—precisely, in other words, what they had been led to expect.

Zanfordino often saw psychological changes in her patients once they began to get more comfortable in their adoptive voices. Most of them had suffered from deep gender dysphoria going into the process; they hated their bodies and their voices. Those who underwent successful vocal transitions found a sense of calm, and were more able to enjoy the "vibration of their voice inside their body," which also eased their minds. But did a vocal transition ever cause a person to splinter into several people? Did one voice ever become many?

Zanfordino knew of no such cases—but Nicole did. The more time she spent with the voices, the more complicated they became. Inhabiting several voices at once, the imposter played people against each other by maneuvering them into baroque theatrics. At the imposter's instruction, victims found themselves yelling, chastising, and scolding one of the two people on the other end of the call. It was as if a couple they had only just met had invited them to help broker an intense and very intimate disagreement. These sorts of three-way conversations weren't sexual in substance, but in the forced aggression there was a kind of eroticized menace, an intimation of comforts that lay just beyond the horizon. Nicole kept asking: How do you know there were two people on the call? The answer, invariably, was simple: they had spoken over each other. The contradiction puzzled her.

The mechanics weren't always perfect. Occasionally the imposter made grammatical mistakes. And more than once the scammer tried a voice on a victim who had actually spoken to the real Amy Pascal or the real Kathleen Kennedy, and the gig was up before it even began. But for the most part, the recordings Nicole heard wouldn't have given the casual listener pause.

At this point Nicole wasn't a casual listener. It was no longer just a matter of the voices' tone and pitch and timbre; it was what the imposter discussed, and the way she discussed it, that began to fascinate her. For a powerful conversationalist, most people are playthings; their wit is outmatched, their pace is quickly overtaken. In real life, these influential women were exceptionally persuasive; so, too, were the imposter's representations of them. *She* seemed able to talk about anything, at any time: the eight- or twelve-hour day meant nothing; she was always available. Conversant on an astonishingly wide array of topics, she could speak about Jamaican bobsledding to a member of that country's national team as easily as she could connect with alpine mountain climbers, Filipino chefs, or mercenaries from the heartland who'd lost friends beyond the wire in Iraq or Afghanistan. She seemed to know the ins and outs of every deal in Hollywood, and who was really behind them. It was this facility not just with voices, and not even just with knowledge itself, but rather with the intangible frequencies, the thrum of her marks' ambitions, that elevated her game. Having laid such a strong foundation at the core of the con, she was able to easily vanquish any momentary doubts her marks might entertain.

Consider what happened when, after sending her an email demanding clarity, photographer Caleb Kotner next spoke to his Amy. He had told her he needed confirmation that she was who she claimed to be. Insulted by his skepticism, she threatened to end their collaboration. A vein of menace began to pulse in her voice as she grew angrier. He was violating their contract and she would take him to court over the breach.

Caleb was shaken. His voice trembled.

"It's *doubting me*," she said. "Where did that come from? I'm giving you money. You have to tell me: Where did that come from?"

She told him she was "a woman of my word."

Caleb fumbled for a bit and then he unwittingly laid out a hypothetical scenario that mirrored perfectly the one in which he was currently enmeshed. "If, God forbid, someone wanted to impersonate Amy Pascal, everything that we've talked about has been, you know, somewhat public knowledge because, you haven't wanted to, rightfully so, tell about—"

"Why are we talking about impersonating?" she interrupted. "If you think I am impersonating someone else, I would be in trouble."

In that moment, in which she had both recognized and denied reality, the conversation took on a new flavor of sadism. It was as if Amy was almost taunting Caleb with the possibility that he might, in fact, be right, and at the same time scolding him like a child for entertaining the idea. If this *was* an impersonation scam, Amy posited, what was she getting out of it? Nothing.

"Why would I want to put myself through hell? Everything can be traced back through paperwork and everything. That would be a stupid thing to do. For what?"

"Let's just say you're someone completely different—"

"Who?"

"You're someone completely different, who studied Amy Pascal and learned everything there is to know about Amy Pascal, who her friends are, who her family is—"

He wanted to know that he wasn't "living some crazy dream."

"You're not living some crazy dream, and it's real," she said. "I am who I am. I'm never going to change for everybody. Unfortunately, that's me."

"You're very intuitive," he told her. "You always know."

"You can't impersonate intuitiveness," she agreed. She instructed him to travel on Friday. His money was on the way. She wanted him to know he wasn't a nobody, that he could accomplish his dreams, that he could work with anyone, including Clint Eastwood. He was *that* good.

Now it was Caleb who was on the back foot.

"If I didn't fuck it up, my bags are still packed," he said. The call had lasted close to an hour. Caleb did take that one final trip to Indonesia. He spent one night in Bali and then he returned, still unpaid, to the U.S. Eventually he found the office of the real Amy Pascal, where one of Pascal's assistants revealed the truth: the whole thing was fake. Then she delivered another slap in the face: he was one of dozens of people who had gone to Indonesia at Fake Amy's behest.

In other words, he now learned, he was nobody special.

Soon Caleb, too, was talking to Nicole.

Chapter 5

Grey's kids were screaming in the background. "You have a family?" Christine Hearst Schwarzman was curious. She was putting together a movie project that would involve security work in Thailand, Laos, and Cambodia. She and her billionaire husband were financing it. In security circles, these types of clients were referred to as "high-net-worth individuals," and of all the clientele, they were the most coveted. Three kids, Grey told her, and a wife. Grey was David Grey: former U.S. Marine. Texas native. From the hardscrabble part. With tumbleweeds. After a stint as a private security contractor in Afghanistan, he returned to the U.S., taught firearms and tactics for a while, and then departed again, landing in Thailand. America just wasn't adventurous enough. Schwarzman asked Grey to give her a list of qualified candidates.

Of the twelve soldiers Grey passed along, Schwarzman chose six husky U.S. Marines with blond hair and blue eyes, six feet tall and over. One of them was Jared. After fighting his way to Baghdad during the Iraq invasion, Jared had left the Corps in 2003, but stayed abroad. As a combat veteran, he was highly qualified to provide security and close protection, and he had landed several jobs in the private sector, catering to the superwealthy. Jared was interested in the opportunity, and Schwarzman was interested in Jared. When the two finally spoke on the phone, Schwarzman was joined by her executive assistant, Jason.

Schwarzman intended to begin a second career as a director and producer in the film industry, she told Jared. Her first project was to be in Indonesia, but to get it off the ground she hoped to create an "advance team" to scout and secure film locations, find lodging, and map safe routes for travel around Jakarta in case of emergencies. Before hiring Jared, Schwarzman needed to be sure that he had the requisite decisiveness and leadership qualities to be a suitable addition as a TL, or team leader. She wanted to engage in some light role-playing: Jared was to "order" her assistant Jason off the call in a prompt and efficient manner. "Just be aggressive," she told him. "Let me see you can be mean to somebody. Yell at him. Tell him that you're in charge now."

Jared thought it was a little strange, but he acquiesced. He had been taking orders for so long, from so many demanding, unrelenting people in such a wide array of impossible scenarios, that the request didn't set off any alarm bells. There was something else: Schwarzman was offering obscene amounts of money. If this project went through, Jared stood to make up to $500,000.

And so it began.

"Jason, if Christine tells you to do something, you do it," Jared barked. "If I tell you to do something, you do it. I want you off this call. Now." Jason obliged and Jared was alone on Skype with Schwarzman. Schwarzman let out a breath. That's when the sex play began. Really, it was more of a domination fantasy. She asked him to activate his video so she could see him, but she kept hers off, explaining that for security reasons she couldn't expose herself to potential hackers.

"Now," she demanded. "Give me kisses."

"What?" Jared wasn't sure what was being asked of him.

Schwarzman made some kissing sounds.

"Kisses," she said. "Give me kisses."

Jared was immediately put off, and said so. But Schwarzman

laughed and turned it into a joke. She explained that she wanted to form a "team" but that it should also feel "like a family."

Again, reluctantly, Jared obliged. But on the other end of the line he could hear her moaning.

She asked him to take off his shirt.

"I've got a lot of tattoos," he said.

"Let me see your tats," she said. He took his shirt off.

"Oh, I like that," she cooed.

JARED GOT THE JOB. EVENTUALLY he would recruit more than a dozen of his close friends and colleagues for Schwarzman. "She's going to go all Harvey Weinstein on you," he briefed them. But the promise of real money was so enticing that the soldiers went along with it. Schwarzman told the men she liked the idea of having a close-knit unit, similar to what they had in the military. "Like a family," she assured them all, and indeed among themselves the men began to refer to her as a "big sister" and felt in some way that she *was* protective of them, perhaps in ways that their government, their generals, and even in some cases their own families had not been. "Guys were masturbating on cam for her," Jared said. "One guy who was getting engaged left his house, rented a hotel room to do this thing, because he thought he was going to get this high-paying job."

The impersonator had clearly thought through the power dynamics at play in this particular con. The men receiving the phone calls were incentivized to believe they were speaking not just to a woman, but to a powerful woman; it strengthened their view of themselves as chosen ones, the selected or the strong. And because they were heterosexual, gender-conforming types by and large, to think otherwise would have meant a wholesale abandonment of their well-established identities.

Jared took one two-week trip for Schwarzman in March 2018. One night, Jared was riding in the back of a car in Jakarta that Schwarzman had organized when, for reasons he didn't understand, his driver began ignoring his directions. When Jared asked him to stop, the driver refused, and Jared lost patience. "If you don't stop the fucking car," he yelled, "I'm going to beat the shit out of you."

The driver, in turn, was screaming into his cell phone to a third party. Jared didn't understand a word.

Then his own cell phone rang.

It was Christine. He described the situation in which he found himself.

"Can you just get away?" Christine pleaded in her nasal New York twang.

"I told you to fucking stop," Jared yelled at the driver. Then to Christine: "You're paying these guys $117 a day to drive me around . . ."

"You can't talk to them like that—"

"I feel like I'm being kidnapped," Jared snapped, starting to panic. He'd fought his share of Iraqi insurgents blowing up Humvees via roadside bombs, or themselves with suicide vests. This was not how he had survived. He hung up on Christine, then went full bore on the driver.

"Stop the fucking car!"

The sedan lurched to a halt and he jumped out. The driver careened off.

Christine called back immediately.

"Are you away? Where are you?"

He spotted an Indomart. Like a 7-Eleven back home in Ohio. Only smaller. Brighter. Somehow scarier.

Eventually he made it back to his hotel and left the country. The calls tapered off but Schwarzman wasn't done with him yet. The promised funds, a few thousand by now, still hadn't arrived in his account. One day she called again. She needed more résumés. This time she wanted a Latino man, so Jared connected her to another buddy who fit the profile. But when that contact turned out not to be available for the times she wanted, Schwarzman called him, screaming, "This fucking Mexican, I'll have him deported." Jared tried to calm her down but she hung up on him. Extremely unprofessional, she texted. I'm not interested.

Absolutely disgusting behavior from your friend. Jared was contrite and confused. He wrote back, I tried to find you a Hispanic like you asked for ma'am. I'm sorry for his behavior. It's not me who did that. I'm available for you 24/7 like I have been. Jared continued sending her one candidate after another. When she declined to work with a former Scout Sniper and mixed martial arts fighter whom Jared had put forward, he wrote, Ma'am I'm running out of white English no accent Americans that can protect you. I'm calling people that are not looking for a job. You have the best guys in the world of security at your fingertips. These guys will not embarrass you and they will fight and die for you. But Schwarzman seemed unmoved.

Soon after, Jared began avoiding her calls. Without Schwarzman's voice in his ear, he began to listen instead to the suspicious thoughts he had been tamping down. One day he reached out to a friend who worked as a financial adviser at JPMorgan Chase and explained the story. A day later, the friend called him. Schwarzman didn't have an assistant named Jason, the friend told him; the wire instruction numbers she had provided to Jared weren't real. Including the jobs he had forfeited in order to be available for Schwarzman, Jared was out more than $12,000. Jared reached out to Blackstone, the firm run by Schwarzman's husband. Blackstone's in-house security team wanted to see the contracts, but when Jared complied with their request the firm went dark.

For a period after the scam, Jared signed on for jobs that were intentionally high risk and morally ambiguous. He spent time infiltrating the student protests in Hong Kong. Another mission had him working to uncover a cigarette-smuggling operation in Thailand worth billions of dollars. But the weeks he spent inside the toxic world of the fake heiress haunted him. The voice he got to know so intimately remained embedded somewhere in his psyche. He wished he didn't have to hear it anymore, but he did, and it angered him. She owed him for how she had corrupted him. First, he'd sold himself. Then, to help his friends, he'd helped them sell themselves. She'd screwed them over, too.

NICOLE FOUND HERSELF THINKING ABOUT Norman Bates more than she would have liked. More than once, the imposter had expressed a desire to become a "mommy" to the men who believed themselves in her employ. So many of these men, strong and battle-hardened, perhaps weakened by the desire for a magic escape hatch, were fooled. One of them "straight up thought he was in a relationship," Nicole said. "For months. And his friends were like, 'You're not though.' And he was like 'Yeah, she's gonna fly me here, she's gonna fly me there, she's going to give me money every month. Like, I'm going to be a kept man.'" The imposter professed affection and even love, but often under the guise of some kind of brokenness: her marriage just wasn't working out, it was a sham; or she was going through a divorce.

For Nicole, this was a new theater of operations. Most of the victims were U.S. military veterans. The prospect of money was a constant in the scam, but the powerful undercurrent to the conversations was the promise of intimacy. This is how we're going to end the call, the imposter would tell her marks: give me kisses and tell me you love me. Nicole felt uncomfortable discussing it with the soldiers' wives, who, if they talked about it at all, were more concerned with the longer-term safety implications. Were they going to be hacked? Did they need to change their credit cards? Nicole didn't have the heart to tell them that the imposter might have, at least in some cases, videotaped their husbands in compromising positions. One night, Nicole called a number associated with a Navy SEAL who had been lured to Indonesia. A woman answered.

"This is going to sound absurd," Nicole began. "But is your boyfriend in Indonesia right now? I tried to reach him but his phone isn't working."

The woman on the other end hesitated.

"Yes," she said, "but who the fuck are you?"

Nicole grew emotional telling this story. "The number of wives I've talked to who are like, 'Why are you texting my husband?'" she said. They had no clue what their spouses were going through.

"All these Navy SEALs who are just, you know, a lot of them are really damaged. They've had hard, shitty lives. They've been in deployments. They come back. A lot of them are divorced and they think this is going to be their meal ticket. And they're going to turn it all around. They're going to be a bodyguard for a billionaire."

Nicole now thought back to the earliest calls she had heard about more than six months ago. They, too, had been flirtatious and awkward, but nothing on this scale. They had evolved; the imposter was improvising as she went along, changing and adopting the scam to fit her whims. The voices were multiplying, taking new shapes as they spread. Now, with these sexual games that seemed to border on abuse, she was also taking more risks, taunting her trackers to follow her into darker corners.

Of all the victims Nicole had so far encountered, the military veterans struck her as the most vulnerable of all, and their pain lingered with her the longest. She knew that even before the scam, they were more susceptible than nonveterans to divorce, self-harm, and substance abuse. If they survived the wars in Afghanistan and Iraq, many set up shop in Asia as security contractors for hire. But freelance work was sporadic and unsatisfying, and some of the men had drifted into unemployment and even episodic criminality. So, when a Christine Hearst Schwarzman—or, during one intense flurry of calls that targeted a network of Canadian soldiers in 2018, a Melinda Gates—came calling, they jumped at the opportunity. But in spite of their external toughness and years of military experience, they weren't prepared for the enemy they encountered. They were sitting ducks.

In May 2021, police in Thailand arrested Jared, the former U.S. Marine, and charged him with attempted kidnapping, extortion, and attempted murder after he and several accomplices allegedly abducted a Taiwanese businessman and briefly held him hostage. He was later released on bail. People who knew Jared well wondered whether this criminal turn of events could be traced back to the scam. "As soon as I heard about his arrest, I thought of his experience with Christine

Hearst Schwarzman. I think that experience set him on a downward spiral," said one of his acquaintances, who was also a victim. "He was so raw, you could see the PTSD in his eyes, and then the scammer took advantage of that." The scammer had ravaged his savings, damaged his self-confidence, and set him on a path of desperation.

Some of them, perhaps to save face, insisted that they had been caught in an Indonesian "intelligence" operation and offered to travel to Indonesia and sort it out for Nicole. As politely as she could, she declined, but of course she empathized with their deflection; it helped them avoid the pain of having been conned. Only when she thought about it later did she realize they weren't entirely wrong. It *was* an intelligence operation of a sort; an enemy had gotten inside their heads and brought them to their knees. They worried that if they had been taped, the videos might be used by a terror group as a kind of blackmail that could pose security risks to future U.S. operations abroad. This might have seemed like a fanciful abstraction, even paranoid, to an outsider. But it was a real threat for the soldiers, many of whom broke down in tears while recounting their stories to her. For Grey, the emotional fallout lasted for months. *He* was supposed to be the hero who caught bad guys and investigated evildoers. But Christine had slipped through his defenses.

THERE SEEMED TO BE NO depth to which the impersonator wouldn't sink. Nicole couldn't shake the story of the seventy-two-year-old veteran photographer. One day he received a call from a woman, a prominent figure in the media landscape, with whom he had a casual acquaintance. She said her daughter, who was sixteen years old at the time, was getting interested in photography and wanted his advice about what kind of camera she should purchase. Moments later the sixteen-year-old "daughter," now on the line, initiated explicit, graphic phone sex with the older man. He immediately realized the call was fake, and not only that: a single person was performing both voices, mother and daughter. He hung up and reported the call to the authorities. Nicole had given a lot of thought to what, from a legal and financial stand-point, might transpire if the imposter was eventually caught. Would the victims be able to recoup their losses? What sorts of penalties would follow? But when she listened to the cracking, distraught voice of this abused septuagenarian, the dollars and cents of it all felt irrelevant. "What is that even about?" she wondered. "What *is* that?"

One day, Blackstone's in-house security team called Nicole. They wanted to know if she would consider taking Schwarzman on as a client. Nicole chuckled. She had tried to warn Blackstone about the scam months earlier, when it was just a speck on the horizon, and they had declined. Now, as she had predicted, they had been hit, and the details the ex-Marine Jared had provided were depressing in their fa-miliarity. Anthony joked that she was like Carl Hanratty, the dogged FBI agent who spent years tracking the legendary con artist Frank Abagnale Jr.—a true story of cops and conner chronicled in the 2002 film *Catch Me If You Can*. Abagnale's fabulist exploits turned him into a doctor, a lawyer, and a copilot for a major American airline, though he was neither trained nor qualified for any of them. The movie, which starred Leonardo DiCaprio as Abagnale and Tom Hanks as Hanratty (based on real-life agent Joseph Shea), revealed a disturbingly symbiotic relationship between the two men. Nicole didn't yet know who she was chasing, only that whoever it was remained just out of reach. At home, Anthony had started to quote famous lines from the movie back to Nicole when they were lying in bed, or driving to the mall. "You walk out of that door," he teased her, echoing Hanratty, "they are going to kill you!"

BACK IN THE 1980s AND '90s, phone sex lines were automated. You could see them advertised on billboards at ninety-nine cents a minute: 1-800-976-SEXY, and so forth. They were ubiquitous and soon became a cultural staple, spoofed in music videos, movies, and late-night com-edy shows. As a widely available technological interface that simulated intimacy, nothing beat the phone in those years, and the popularity of

976 numbers foretold the explosion of internet porn. From the ether came a voice with an erotic tale replete with moaning and exhortations. Real intimacy through sex is a terrifying enough narcotic. But this kind of numbing exchange could also be addictive. In years to come, for an additional charge, flesh-and-blood people materialized on the other end of the line, and then you were in serious trouble, a state of real extremis: anonymous intimacy. The very idea of an actual person sitting in some location, unknowable and unknown, who followed your orders or ordered you around? Intoxicating.

Nicole thought back to that phone call with the Australian contestant on *The Bachelor*—his name was Damien Rider—who had spoken with three people at the same time: Wendi Murdoch and her assistant, Aaron, along with Laurene Powell Jobs. As it turned out, there was more to his story.

Eventually Laurene had asked Murdoch and Aaron to get off the call; she wished to speak to Rider alone. At that point, Laurene turned the conversation in another direction. Would Rider like to visit her in Malibu? Would he accompany her to an event as her date? Did he find her attractive? Rider was baffled and felt it necessary to state the obvious: they had never even met. Yes, Laurene agreed but, surely, he'd seen a picture of her? Did he find her attractive? Would he want to kiss her? "Say my name," Laurene commanded. Rider complied, but Laurene wanted him to say it again and again. As he did, Laurene moaned and carried on moaning until, as far as Rider could tell, she climaxed.

Many other actors had similar experiences, and all of them bore similar features: the same vocal signatures, the same lurid patterns. In one episode that would eventually become part of a lawsuit, an impersonator pretending to be the producer Donna Langley lured an actor into a phone sex call that turned explicit. After some preliminary "kissing," she began moaning and breathing heavily, and asked if the actor was "getting hard." She wanted to "hear it," she said, and asked him to place the phone near his crotch. He pretended to masturbate by slapping his leg. She told him to "stroke it faster, faster, faster" until she came loudly while repeating his name over and over.

Another actor, who believed he was being groomed for a part in a movie with Tom Cruise, to be financed by Elon Musk and filmed in outer space, wound up in a similar setup, having erotic conversations with two different women, one of whom was the same fake Donna Langley. One night, he found himself standing shirtless and staring at a camera at 2 a.m. for an audition. "Do you feel aroused?" his Donna Langley asked. "Are you touching yourself?" He lost it. "What the fuck is wrong with you!" he shouted. His computer screen stared back impassively. By that point, "Donna's" work was done. The humiliation was complete. To top it off, over the preceding weeks she had also unburdened him of more than $6,000, which he had sent via Western Union to an account in the Philippines.

Chapter 6

Each New Jersey morning, before rolling out of bed, before her morning coffee, before anything, Nicole checked Purebytes on Instagram. While she had been playing therapist to the growing number of soldiers whose names had been added to the Victim Tracker, she had continued to keep an eye on Gavin. There he sat day after day, alone at a Michelin-starred restaurant, resting his jacketed elbows on white linen, fiddling with his iPhone, making it appear as though he had friendships with solicitous bartenders and waiters, managers, or an ever-tolerant concierge, when she knew that the reality was likely very different. With the Pascal and Schwarzman domains dismantled, her obligation to these clients was largely satisfied. But by then Nicole understood that the scam wasn't going to end until the perpetrators were arrested. She convinced her bosses at K2 to stay on top of the case. She couldn't shake her hunch that Gavin was somehow involved in the scams. As the days turned into weeks and the lake near her house grew warm, she kept watching and waiting. The skies above her house filled with birds. The strange world of Purebytes grew even stranger.

THAT SUMMER OF 2018, SHE returned to Greece to visit her Yaya, her ninety-seven-year-old grandmother, who still lived alone in a stone house reachable via a long drive along treacherous, winding roads in the shadow of the mighty summit of Tymfristos, and then along the banks of the Megdovas River, which flowed under the ancient stone bridge at Viniani and emptied into the Ionian Sea. There she was once again a child at play, safe among nonagenarians who had spent their lives largely, and happily, cut off from the rest of the world.

BUT THE WORLD INTRUDED. A few weeks earlier, I had received a tip about the scam from a colleague of mine at the *Hollywood Reporter*, a glossy industry publication where I worked writing features and investigations. For most of my career, I had worked as a foreign correspondent in the Middle East, Africa, and Latin America, covering wars and politics and other assorted conflicts. Hollywood was still relatively new to me at that time but, as I was to discover, target-rich in its own special way. On the day Nicole arrived in Greece, the magazine published a cover story I had written about the scam, and Nicole's role as lead investigator, "Hunting the Con Queen of Hollywood."

Kathleen Kennedy, the coproducer of *E.T. the Extra-Terrestrial* and many other iconic films, had reportedly hired K2 Intelligence to help stave off the predations of an unknown identity thief. At the time I didn't think that the tip would amount to much. Hollywood, perhaps like Indonesia, was a land rife with scams and grifters. But when I began to report on the story, it immediately felt different. One of the very first people I spoke to was the photographer Caleb Kotner. His account was raw, and his pain was clear. What kind of person would implement such a sadistic scheme? And to what end? Embedded in the article were two short voice recordings I had obtained in which the Con Queen could be heard castigating different victims in two separate incidents. One of the voices was American, the other British. Both were women and both, I thought, were very convincing.

The story struck a chord. A few national outlets picked it up. Almost immediately, my inbox was flooded with more tips. Many people were certain they knew who it was, and offered up tantalizing avenues for me to explore—an American grifter with ties to the Indonesian mob, now living in France; an albino man who ran an Indonesian restaurant in Manhattan; a convicted felon from Texas who had swindled his way to the highest echelons of the Democratic establishment in Washington, D.C. The list of possible culprits began to grow.

Nicole didn't have great internet access at Yaya's place, and had to wait a few days to digest the article, which described her central role in chasing the imposter, and to peruse the hundreds of emails that flooded her inbox from people who claimed to have information. Instead she sat on her grandmother's ancient stone patio and gazed out across pine forests to the jagged cliffs of the Pindus mountain range, the Spine of Greece. The name of the highest peak was Velouchi, which meant "arrow"—homage to the ancient Aetolian archers who fended off successive waves of invading Celts and Persians.

Almost a year into her work on the case, the list of names on the Victim Tracker had grown by between ten and twenty per month and she now had well over a hundred victims. She also had a name: Gavin. While almost certainly fake, it was still something. She had Gavin's Instagram account, Purebytes, in which he touted his long-standing connections to Indonesia. She had pictures and videos of him. She knew he was in the United Kingdom, which the metadata had indicated was one of the scammer's locations. She had even spoken to him, and concluded that he had impersonated at least some of the male producers. At this point, Nicole still had no hard evidence for who was responsible for the leading impersonation, the ubiquitous female voice. By this point, she had exhausted nearly all of her leads.

There was, however, one person who she had long believed might yield something valuable—if only he would talk.

IN FEBRUARY 2018, WHEN THE subpoenas had first arrived, Nicole had been surprised to find that Cabin Yim wasn't the only person in the

United Kingdom assisting Gavin. Buried in the list of phone numbers that had been used to set up websites on Gavin's behalf was a second name: Matt Crane.

A high-end personal trainer, Crane worked at an Equinox gym in Kensington, an upscale neighborhood in central London. The subpoenas revealed that it was Crane who had set up the fake Christine Hearst Schwarzman domain, along with a few others, including a fake site for Dee Bakish, the wife of Viacom CEO Robert Marc Bakish. But when Nicole had first reached out to him, Crane claimed he knew nothing and abruptly ended the call. Thinking Gavin might be tempted into further disclosure, she dropped Crane's name in their next conversation, but Gavin just exploded with rage, and accused Crane of "harassing" him. Nicole had noted Crane as a potential suspect and decided to return to him later, when she had more information. Over the course of the following months, Nicole had reached out to Crane several more times, but he ignored her.

Now she tried him again, and to her great surprise he picked up the call. She immediately detected a familiar emotion. Matt Crane was scared. A brawny former rugby player, Crane had taken Gavin on as a fitness client during the spring of 2017, he told Nicole. At first Gavin seemed like a quiet, pleasant type, if a bit eccentric and prone to name-dropping. He boasted of a friendship with the American actress Jessica Chastain; yeah, yeah, thought Matt, who knew people, too. From time to time, Gavin asked Matt to make purchases on his behalf, usually clothes, and Matt wondered why Gavin couldn't do it himself. But when he asked, Gavin had a plausible explanation: his wealthy family watched his credit card charges and kept him on a tight leash. It was no skin off Matt's back; Gavin always paid him back right away, in cash. But then Gavin had asked Matt for another kind of favor: to help him register a website for his personal friend, Dee Bakish. Matt was hardly a technical guru, but this task would require very little expertise, just a few emails and a credit card payment. He told Gavin he would get to it sometime in the next few days. Gavin broke down in tears, pleading that it was for a "client" and that if Matt didn't set the domain up immediately Gavin stood to lose his entire business. Matt paid the seventy pounds and bought the domain. Not long after, Gavin grew even more demanding and Crane, increasingly fed up, cut him off entirely.

Cautiously, Crane began to open up to Nicole. Another group of investigators from Viacom had recently told Crane he was being investigated as part of a federal criminal probe. The FBI was sniffing around. His details were "all over" the fraudulent account.

Crane told Nicole the reason he hadn't spoken to her before was that he was convinced that she was somehow in league with Gavin. He went on to explain that he had also been making payments via Western Union on Gavin's behalf to a website designer who lived in Athens, Greece, and he showed Nicole the emails to back it up. Not only did this new information tie Gavin firmly to Matt; it suggested Gavin was possibly benefiting financially from the whole arrangement. This email chain in particular was the clearest evidence Nicole had yet seen that Gavin's role in the scam was more central than she had previously imagined. Crane informed the police his identity had been stolen.

From an investigative standpoint, the emails were a "slam dunk." When Nicole had originally spoken to Gavin there had been some deniability; the elusive Maggie Ling was the real mastermind. Now that deniability was evaporating quickly. Gavin was clearly involved at every level of planning but the question of who was behind the female voices remained unanswered. Nicole reached out to the Greek web designer.

"I've been waiting for someone like you to call me," were the man's first words to Nicole. The designer explained that for years, dating back to at least 2012, he had designed websites for a woman he had known as Eileen Lehman. Eileen always made sure he got paid via Western Union, from a man named Armando Rio Wirya. The Greek believed that he was designing sites for legitimate, Asian subsidiaries of real companies like HBO and Annapurna Pictures—including one where screenwriters could submit screenplays directly online—but he'd stopped working after he received several legal threats, including one from the real China Film Group. Nicole then played for the Greek a recording of the fake Gigi Pritzker, one of the Hollywood producers who had been impersonated.

"That's her," the Greek said. "That's Eileen Lehman."

A gear clicked forward in Nicole's mind as all of the voices began to merge into an undifferentiated stream. She had entertained the possibility that the imposter was a man, but the idea had never fully gained traction, in part because the majority of victims had unanimously opposed that view. She thought back to the victims who had been convinced they'd been speaking to two people. They had insisted that they had heard two people talking over each other, but they were wrong. Their minds had played a trick on them. They had been told they were talking to two people and they believed it, filling in the logical gaps with their own imagination; armed with one half of a story, they completed it on their own.

The only common denominator between Eileen Lehman and Gigi Pritzker was Gavin. If Gavin was, as Nicole now believed, both Eileen and Gigi, based on phone numbers that tied him to both of them, it stood to reason that he was also every other woman who had been impersonated, including her very first client, Amy Pascal. She sprang up from her desk, careful not to upset the tiny bottle of ouzo, a keepsake of her grandfather's journey by boat from Greece, and ran out into the hall at K2.

"It's a man!" she shouted. "It's a man!"

NICOLE WAS STILL MISSING A key piece of the puzzle: Gavin's real name. During their conversations, Gavin had talked about living in Los Angeles, and attending the Wharton School in Pennsylvania. She hadn't been able to find a record of him in either place. Private investigators have access to Credit Header databases that are largely unavailable to most people. One of them is called Accurint. Another is PLO. Anyone who has ever signed up for a credit card in the United States winds up on one or both of them. From the beginning of her investigation, anytime Nicole received a tip on a possible name, she had run it through Accurint or PLO, hoping for a hit.

Now she brought up the databases again and began trying new combinations of names and fragments of names she had picked up. She reasoned that since Gavin had used an Indian name as an alias, he might have an Indian background; Indians had begun migrating to Indonesia in waves since the early twentieth century. She had played around with various prefixes and suffixes, combining names she already had—Gobind Tahil, Gavin Ambani—with combinations she thought might yield something: Gavin Tahil, Gobind Lal. Nothing. Then she worked her way through the alphabet, using single letters as stand-ins for possible first names: A. Tahil . . . B. Tahil . . . C. Tahil . . . It was a stab in the dark, but certainly more useful than looking in the United Kingdom, which didn't even maintain such databases. Nothing.

Stumped, she returned to Instagram, which had been such a useful repository of information in the past. Victims of the scam and acquaintances of Gavin like Cabin Yim and Matt Crane had heard him use various names, including Gavin Lal, Hargo, Gavin Tahil, and Gobind Tahil. She began scrolling through the list of people Gavin followed, focusing on those who might actually know him, and be Indonesians of Indian extraction. Soon she had compiled a list of nearly fifteen people, all of whose last names ended with the suffix *amani*. Unbeknownst to her at the time, Nicole had stumbled onto a quirk of the Sindhi language, one of several languages in the Dravidian group that are influenced by Hindi, Urdu, Persian, and even ancient Sanskrit. The *ani* that ended many Sindhi names could be traced back to *ansh*, a Sanskrit root denoting descendance from a common male ancestor. Turning back to the databases, she typed in "Gobind Taheel Amani," thinking that perhaps Taheel might be a middle name. The computer calculated for a second and then spat back a name: Mar Gobin Taheel Ramani.

Mar Gobin?

She tried it again and got the same response. But when she took a closer look, she noticed a glitch. The system wasn't autocorrecting, exactly, but appeared to be returning a mistaken variation of a different name, as if whoever had input the name in the system the first time had misspelled it, and now the system was conducting a "looks like, sounds like" algorithm to find an answer. By the computer's logic, Mar Gobin "sounded like" something closer to the actual name. And then she saw it. Twenty years earlier, in 1999, there was a student address record tied to Bradley University for someone with a differently spelled, but almost identical-sounding name to Mar Gobin Taheel Ramani:

Hargobind Tahilramani.

Just to be sure, the first time she typed a name in the Google search bar she used the first name she had found: Mar Gobin Taheel Ramani. A spotty English translation of a headline in a local Indonesian news outlet came up: "Hargobind Punjabi Tahilramani, Proposed Terrorists Can Remission Christmas." It was dated December 27, 2010. A rough interpretation provided by Google Translate described Tahilramani as "a terrorist prisoner who had shocked the United States Embassy office in Jakarta in 2008." He had been living in a cell in Cipinang Penitentiary, a Class I prison that normally held political dissidents, terrorists, and murderers. The author of the piece had interviewed him and learned that in 2008, from inside the prison walls, Tahilramani had gotten hold of a cell phone and called the U.S. embassy. Using an alias, "Michel," and speaking in different accents, Iranian and Russian among them, he told the duty officer that a bomb would explode at the embassy within seventy-two hours. He called back twenty minutes later and threatened the Pentagon and the FBI headquarters in Quantico, Virginia. He had giggled his way through the interview he had given to the Indonesian journalist who had written the story, flippantly discussing the bomb threats alongside his skills with accents.

Within days, an Indonesian antiterror squad had tracked the cell phone to the prison and found Tahilramani, who promptly confessed.

A judge sentenced him to three years and four months behind bars, on top of a preexisting charge of embezzlement for an unrelated crime about which no details were given. In 2011, Tahilramani and ninety-nine other "Christian" inmates had been offered early release for good behavior, in time for the Christmas holiday.

Nicole had often wondered about the discrepancy between the work that went into the scam and the relatively modest payoff. Here, finally, was an answer: Hargobind was bragging and giggling about the psychological terror he had caused.

For Nicole, the most exciting development was the picture that accompanied the article. It showed a large crowd of people in whose midst was a figure of unmistakable distinction. He was a little heavier and, absent the trappings of fashionable clothes or the health benefits that a membership at an expensive gym in Kensington would confer, a little less elegant, but the face clearly belonged to Gavin Ambani, aka the host of Purebytes.

And also, Nicole now wondered, a terrorist? What was more logical, two or more people working together, coordinating schedules and voices, passing calls off to one another in some warehouse basement? Or, simply, that there was just one person? *This* person—a convicted felon who was adept with voices, currently living in London? It was as if Keyser Soze, the iconic criminal mastermind of *The Usual Suspects*, had appeared and then walked out of the building. She stared at the screen.

Of course, it was him all along.

Nicole immediately called her contact at the FBI.

"I think I found him," she said, barely able to contain her excitement.

Nicole sent along her running memo, which had grown to twenty-five single-spaced pages of detailed information.

"Maybe there's a case here," the FBI contact told her.

WHEN NICOLE BEGAN HER INVESTIGATION, the scam had seemed like little more than a series of naughty phone calls. A year and several dozen victims later, she was staring at a photograph of a man convicted on terrorism-related charges. She wasn't quite sure who was staring back at her. That night she and Anthony celebrated with a cocktail, but in truth, Nicole was also a little afraid. "He spent time in jail already," she told Anthony. "Should I be concerned?"

PART II

The Outlaw

I would be sitting pretty,
but for my curiosity.

—Vizier, *The Arabian Nights*

Chapter 7

In the years before World War II the province of Sindh lay on India's far northwest flank, bordered on the west by the tan hills of Balochistan, and the mountainous Punjab region to the north. Raised there in the 1930s, Lal Tahilramani went on to serve as an engineer in the Indian Marines during the war, dispatched to East Asia. When the war ended, he returned home, only to face additional upheaval. The Partition of 1947 cleaved the country in half and gave birth to a homeland for India's Muslim minority, the Islamic Republic of Pakistan, to which the region of Sindh now belonged. However, not all of Sindh's denizens were Muslim, and Lal, a Hindu, soon joined other Sindhis in search of a new beginning beyond the borders of the subcontinent.

In those tumultuous postwar years, tens of thousands of Sindhis settled across the Indonesian archipelago, including on the islands of Aceh and Sumatra and in the capital, Jakarta. For more than fifteen centuries India had exerted a powerful influence on Indonesia as successive religious and economic tides swept eastward carrying new ideas and possibilities. In the nineteenth century, Dutch colonists brought Indians from the subcontinent to work Indonesia's plantations in the first wave of what became the modern Indian diaspora. Sindhis who remained in India after partition helped build the country's entertainment and media industries, while those who fled to Indonesia became successful traders, entrepreneurs, and textile merchants. The community was small but tightly knit, with deep family and business ties that fueled a thriving middle class, marked by an insular and conservative streak.

Lal traveled frequently, including to nearby Hong Kong. On one of those trips he met a young woman named Kavita Rukhana. They fell in love, eloped, and returned to Jakarta, exiles in an adopted land. Kavita's childhood hadn't been easy. Also born in what was to become Pakistan, her parents had moved to Hong Kong before Partition, when she was still a young girl. Raised in a conservative Islamic home, she broke away from her family and religion to marry Lal, a scandalous decision for a young Muslim girl in the 1960s. Severe depression and a history of suicide ran in Kavita's family, alongside a rare cancer gene that killed several of them, including Kavita's own mother. Her father was abusive and drank himself to death. Despite this grim inheritance and a propensity toward anxiety, she developed a keen interest in history, a love of conservation, and a fascination with Indonesia's indigenous cultures. Both she and Lal valued giving back to their communities, and whenever they landed in a new place, she made friends and connections by volunteering in orphanages and impoverished hospitals.

Throughout the 1970s, Lal moved his family frequently for work. The Tahilramanis never stayed in one place for long, and as Lal hopscotched from engineering project to project, the family adapted. By the middle of that decade, he and Kavita had two young daughters, Amisha and Yara, and were eager for a son. The long-awaited child finally arrived on the night of October 31, 1979. They called him Hargobind, a name with Sikh and Punjabi origins meaning "a part of God." Over the next several years they lived for brief periods in Nigeria, Italy, Japan, and Singapore before finally returning to Indonesia in the mid-1980s.

THE BRIEF HISTORY ABOVE, AS well as the story that follows here, only began to take shape late one evening in the summer of 2020 when I received an email from Amisha, the younger of Hargobind's two older sisters. It had taken months to convince her to correspond with me, but once the door had been cracked, she offered many insights, and was open and vulnerable in ways a journalist rarely encounters. She poured her heart into her messages, and I responded in kind. She seemed damaged, and that had its own centrifugal force. But I also wanted her to keep writing to me; I told her I hoped she felt safe—and I did. At first, she wanted our conversations to be off the record. Later, when I asked for her permission to use the details she had provided, she consented, with the caveat that I use an alias.

When I said "safe," I had meant safe in sharing the details of her life with me. No one, at that time, was particularly safe from the other scourge: Covid. Throughout the spring and summer of 2020 my wife and I, like everybody else, had been shut-ins. At least one and sometimes both of our two children, one of them a toddler, were at home every day. Our days were spent juggling an impossible schedule of online classes, meetings, and outings to the few remaining places that the pandemic restrictions hadn't shut down. I struggled to get much done. In the claustrophobia imposed by the virus, Amisha's correspondence, while distressing, was nevertheless a breath of welcome air from the other side of the world.

Amisha declined to use Hargobind's actual name, or any of the abbreviations or aliases he had come to be known by over the years. Instead she referred to him as "Monster." As she explained over the course of several email messages, Hargobind's childhood had been marked by troubling behavior. He suffered frequent nightmares and often woke screaming about ghosts who lived in the ceiling, and children who crawled out of walls. He dreamed of drowning in the ocean, dragged to the depths by an unknown figure. He had an aversion to animals and human babies. Lal and Kavita told the girls that their brother had trouble comprehending language, that he could "read but couldn't learn." He didn't start forming words until the age of five or so; once he did, he talked constantly, including to himself, and on occasion it seemed as if he were conversing with another person.

Amisha enjoyed the memory of a happy, safe home, where she felt secure and loved. As she began to open up, she revealed brief but intense flashes of compassion and empathy, a mourning for a lost time and even, on occasion, for her brother. She described her earliest memories of him as an indecipherable "weirdness." She did not detect any obvious malevolence or "devilish" behavior.

The children's mother saw Harvey (as Hargobind was known in the family) as her sensitive, brilliant son. He was gifted with math and puzzles. Kavita dismissed his outbursts as the fruits of a raw and keen imagination. Absorbed by science and languages, he enjoyed conversations with an imaginary friend but shunned extracurricular activities and, unlike his sisters, struggled to bond with other children. He wasn't rewarded for bad behavior, but nor was he overly punished. Frightened of most things, he tagged after his mother whenever possible. Friends and family urged tough love but Kavita only retreated deeper into their special relationship. Lal urged her not to coddle the boy but the more special and different he became, the more inclined she was to do just that. Harvey was her treasure, and she was his. He gorged himself on junk food and spent hours playing video games and watching movies. But when his sisters cried during emotional scenes in *The Lion King* or *Bambi*, he showed little feeling, preferring to sit by himself, reading or listening to music or, increasingly, just observing everyone else.

When Harvey was still very young, the family was living in Italy. One day, Kavita left Harvey at home with a visiting relative and went to fetch the girls from a recital. While Harvey and his caretaker slept, a fire erupted in a neighboring building and spread to their home, trapping them inside for half an hour before a rescue team arrived. Harvey spent three days in a hospital for smoke inhalation. The incident only solidified the special place Harvey already held in Kavita's heart and she prioritized him even more, especially when his nightmares evolved to include fire and burning houses. She began covering for him when he misbehaved at school or failed to turn in an assignment. When the other members of the family challenged her on her choices, she said Harvey was just born different, and required deft handling. With the girls, she was more measured, offering little sympathy in times of trouble and, when they excelled, muted praise.

Everybody knew the Tahilramani house in the upscale Jakarta neighborhood of Bungur, next to an old film studio and not far from the English-language Gandhi School. Cousins and uncles and aunties—some actually related by blood and most not—moved in constant flux through the Tahilramani household, standing guard against the unwelcome intrusions that the culture, mores, and influence of Indonesia presented. Theirs was a worldly and cosmopolitan set, with networks of extended family in several countries, including the United States. Every July Lal took two weeks and carted his family off to visit one clan or another. These trips helped nurture a dream that his daughters, at least, might one day continue their travels, helping people in tough circumstances, perhaps joining the ranks of Doctors Without Borders. Harvey, on the other hand, still seemed scared of everything: noises, the outdoors, the dark. He always slept with the lights on. He told his family their house in Bungur was haunted by ghosts. One wished him to throw his belongings into the street; another wanted him to fling himself off the balcony.

Lal stressed the importance of hard work, respect for others, and the avoidance of debt. When it came to parenting, he was efficient and rational, with a strict and even disciplinarian bent that emphasized just reward in exchange for hard work. Raw talent mattered less than effort, he told his children. Blessings were the fruit of labor and grit. When the girls weren't doing sports or other extracurricular activities, they heeded this dictum—working as dishwashers in a friend's restaurant or folding clothes in shelters for the poor. Harvey was often excused from these duties because of his, as the parents explained, "limitations."

Since Harvey had been old enough to walk, his parents had worried about his health. In quiet moments, Kavita wondered if he suffered from a personality disorder. Doctors speculated about possible physical ailments, structural problems in his brain that might account for his troubling behavior. In the 1980s, in Indonesia, mental health wasn't widely acknowledged, much less treated. Nurses often doubled as speech pathologists. Lal and Kavita were underinformed and over-whelmed. There were no guidebooks, and the internet did not yet exist. Doctors told Lal that Harvey might suffer from dementia or motor neurone disease, a rare condition that attacks the nervous system, as he aged. No one spoke about a conscience or the possibility of future crime.

Lal prioritized education above all else. The girls went to summer sports or science camps, often in other countries, and sometimes to budget camps to learn about money management, which Lal thought would help instill a sense of fiscal prudence and personal responsibil-ity. Harvey didn't attend the camps. He didn't enjoy traveling, and the sisters didn't enjoy having him along. In any event, he seemed to prefer a more self-directed education. By the time he was ten, he was immersing himself in Broadway musicals and reciting monologues and songs from memory. He performed ballads from *Victoria*, *Ragtime*, and *Chicago* in front of his family, mimicking Audra McDonald and Barbra Streisand, whom his father adored.

By high school, his childhood tantrums had subsided, but he had become withdrawn and increasingly manipulative. Harvey's intelli-gence masked his antisocial impulses. He spoke some Japanese—a result, perhaps, of having lived there, and he also understood some Spanish and Russian. When the Hollywood awards season rolled around, he stood perilously close to the television screen and shouted out the correct answers before winners were announced. He told his family an imaginary friend had given him the answers. His mim-icking skills had continued to improve, and he often wowed guests by performing full-bodied impersonations, like the kind featured on *Saturday Night Live*. If people laughed at the wrong place, or didn't know the answer to a trivia question he asked, he snapped at them in character.

When Harvey was fourteen, doctors at Mount Elizabeth Hospital in Singapore, where his mother had been sent for more specialized care, detected cancer in her breast. It soon metastasized to her liver and spinal cord and from then on, Kavita remained in the terminal stages of the illness, heavily medicated and subject to frequent, intense hallucinations. Clumps of her thick black hair fell out as the cancer spread to her bones.

According to Amisha, Kavita spent her waning years lost between hallucinations brought on by her cancer treatment and a state of near-constant worry about Harvey, "the love of her life but also the concern of her life." On one visit to the hospital, toward the end of her life, a nurse told Harvey that visiting hours were over and asked him to leave the room. He began yelling at her. "Are you completely crazy?" his mother asked. "What is wrong with you? How could you do that?" Harvey broke down and wept.

Kavita died in pain. During a moment of silence at her wake, a cabinet fell on top of Harvey. He told his family he saw his mother calling to him, and that an evil spirit had startled him.

Amisha's account of what happened in the years that followed was a story of disintegration—disintegration of family and of identity, as well as an epistemological breakdown. Part of Amisha believed that Kavita's death had "derailed" her brother's mind, that he was slipping into insanity. His identity "cracked." He lost interest in school, in grades, and in life. He stopped eating or looking after his personal hygiene and one day, in a fit of rage, destroyed his favorite toys. He began hallucinating, seeing his mother everywhere. Lal was traveling alone for long stretches, while his sisters were living elsewhere for school and work, leaving Harvey alone in the house with a widowed aunt who curled up with him at night on the floor of his mother's bedroom, surrounded by pillows. Other times she found him sleeping on the floor of the kitchen or in the living room. When he told her about speaking to angels and demons, she would rush him off to the local clinic to be sedated.

One day, Harvey skipped school and traveled two hours to the temple where his mother had been cremated. Upon witnessing another cremation taking place, he grew hysterical and had to be escorted out by a security guard who later told his family that he thought the boy had fallen into a trance. Another day he called the doctor who had first treated her in Singapore: Was his mother still there? When would she be coming home? He sought out mediums, and when his aunt stopped giving him money, he stole his mother's jewelry to pay for them himself.

GARDNER, A DISTINGUISHED DIPLOMAT AND son of an admiral, was a father of two girls. His wife, my grandmother Helen, was a classically trained opera singer who studied at the Juilliard School and then abandoned what might have been a brilliant career before it ever began, choosing instead to follow her husband around the world. For that compromise, at least, she never forgave him. As a child I would sometimes visit the home where they had retired, a sprawling house in Chevy Chase, Maryland. After the cocktail hour, dinner was served in a stately room with a view to the garden and Helen's bird feeders. We were expected to be properly dressed and groomed for the occasion. Gardner sat at the head of a table long enough to accommodate eight people with room to spare. At the other end of the room, above a wooden credenza where the china was stored, hung a painting my grandparents had picked up at a flea market.

It was, to use my mother's description, "a dark oil of a horseman riding past a tower in the night." In the foreground was a winding lane upon which the traveler approached. Off to the left, rising from a forested hillock, was a small church with a belfry whose window shone brightly in the moonlight. My grandparents entertained often, and when they did, Gardner, seated comfortably in his Windsor chair, would draw a visitor's attention to the painting.

In the manner of a master of ceremonies conducting a parlor game,

he asked, What did they see? Some saw it. Some didn't. Hiding beneath the belfry window was another image, the pale face of a man who
seemed to watch the traveler. Once you saw the face, he often pointed
out, it was impossible not to see. But people often didn't see it, just as
they certainly never saw my grandfather for who he really was.

Years later, my mother wrote a semi-autobiographical short story
called "The Tower," about a woman who, while walking along a cliff
and spotting a dilapidated house, is reminded of her sexual abuse at
her father's hands. Whereas I had always seen a man, my mother understood the pale face as belonging to a woman "locked up." She took
to avoiding the painting, pretending it wasn't there. My grandfather,
having placed himself at the head of the table, directly opposite the
painting, was content to stare at it, night after night.

PART OF AMISHA COULDN'T SHAKE the conviction that her brother was
becoming, or perhaps had always been, a manipulative sadist. He began
making phone calls to 1-800 numbers that offered phone sex, horo-
scopes, Tarot readings, and the services of psychics and mediums. He
stayed on the phone so long sometimes that he fell asleep. One night
his family caught him on the phone rehearsing lines from a play with a
complete stranger, an older woman whose identity they never learned.
Lal eventually discovered the astronomical phone bills. A maid told
Amisha that Harvey had been making the calls every day at 1 a.m. on
the dot. Lal called the phone company and asked that all international
lines to the house be cut. Harvey was outraged. How could Lal stop
him from speaking to this disembodied voice from another world, his
new "best friend"?

He threatened to kill himself and told Lal that he, and not his
mother, should have died. He brazenly violated groundings and pun-
ishments. Lal took time away from his work, devoting hours to ferrying
Harvey to swimming and tennis lessons, anything to wean him of his
phone addiction.

Harvey's actions became tormented, and so too did Amisha's

account of them, all these years later. She seemed genuinely anguished; she wanted to help other people, she told me, who might fall into the "traps" her brother had laid. She also had a more nuanced understanding of the larger family dynamics. In the years after her mother's death, she began to understand her complexities. The guilt, miscarriages, and experimental IVF pregnancy that preceded Harvey, and the rare codependency that followed, led Amisha to conclude that Harvey's toxicity was in no small part also her mother's.

These struggles diminished Lal. He sold the big house in Bungur and moved to a more modest three-bedroom bungalow. Eventually he retired but to keep himself busy he started a small textile trading firm, assigning inventory to Harvey. Lal took refuge in an imagined future, where everything might be okay, and told his daughters not to worry. As always, the large Indian community surrounded the house with love. Friends and neighbors stopped by with plates of food and stayed for hours playing cards with Lal.

When Harvey graduated from high school in 1997, he asked Lal to let him continue his studies in the United States. Before Harvey left, Lal made sure to teach him the basic skills required to live alone, how to make a bed, do laundry, and study road maps, and then accompanied him to the United States. Lal wanted him to study accounting at the University of California, Berkeley's Haas School of Business. After Lal returned to Indonesia, Harvey neglected to enroll and moved to Los Angeles instead.

HARVEY RETURNED TO JAKARTA IN the spring of 2001. The figure who walked off the plane looked depleted. And now Harvey's family learned that his four-year sojourn in the United States had not had the desired effect. He had lost the suitcases Lal had lovingly prepared for him and instead had checked his clothes for the flight home in a black plastic garbage bag. When Amisha went to LA to clean up the mess he had left behind, inside his abandoned apartment, scattered about the floor and on tables, she found piles of materials related to movies, boxes of screenplays, head shots, and tapes for auditions he had apparently done.

With Harvey living at home again, once-familiar patterns reasserted themselves. On the advice of a friend, Amisha took Harvey to see a hypnotherapist at Jakarta's Medistra Hospital. Harvey was seated in a chair, and as the therapist began to speak, he grew quiet. At first Amisha thought he was pretending, but then, from the dreamlike state into which he appeared to have fallen, he spoke like a child. But soon those gentle and careful whispers splintered into the shouting of adults, who cursed and spoke of abandonment and resentment, of self-hatred, of death. He longed to be with his mother. In shock, Amisha listened as her brother, seemingly still in a trance, switched into a language she didn't understand and carried on his tirade. Upon awakening, he didn't remember a thing. But Amisha never forgot it, and in a moment of charity she wished that her brother had been able to "step out of his body and see himself."

Instead he returned to the source of his adolescent solace: movies, 1-800 numbers, and the constant murmur of disembodied voices. The static of technology sustained him. He memorized lines spoken by the women in the computers, fell asleep listening to their hum. An old habit of calling strangers now grew into a compulsion and eventually he took on the role of the women he'd been listening to, seducing, hoping for a response. The better he got at becoming other people, the more his true self died, Amisha thought.

"Cunt," "whore," "bitch," he called his sisters, along with slurs they had never heard before. As for Lal, he was a "loser." Demoralized, Lal began avoiding the community whose company he so enjoyed, and whose doors were increasingly closed to him and his daughters. When Harvey began stealing again, Amisha asked whether he was taking drugs. He punched her in the nose and pushed her down a set of stairs, fracturing her collarbone.

Somewhat chastened by his behavior, Harvey reluctantly agreed to an inpatient stay at Doulos, a Christian-affiliated treatment facility whose stated purpose was to help drug addicts and juvenile criminals. He didn't last. Increasingly, Amisha said, Lal felt it was his responsibility to protect people from Harvey. Lal was insistent: with constant attention, they would weather this storm. Harvey could be a better man. To his daughters he confided his concerns: it was as if another *being* had inhabited his son, as if he had been "possessed."

That emergent *being* forged Lal's checks, stole money from his sisters, his aunts, and the housekeepers. One day, two debt collectors from American Express demanded to speak to Lal about an unpaid run on his credit card. Harvey told people that his family had locked him up at home and that his sisters' partners were criminals and thieves, intent on killing him. Amisha grew scared, not just for the family but for anyone who crossed his path.

By 2003, Lal had retreated from social life almost entirely. Eventually he suffered a stroke, which weakened him further. He told his daughters he was sorry for what they had gone through, that he had done his best to protect them. None of this was their fault; he urged them to continue to see the best in people. He didn't want their experience with Harvey to harden their hearts. If there was a silver lining, he told them, it was that at least they had already seen "the worst human in our midst."

As the end of his life approached, Lal took steps to prepare his daughters for a world without him, one in which they would be left alone to contend with Harvey. Lal cut his son out of his will, and urged his daughters to distance themselves from him. He explained that they would face two great challenges in life: cancer and Harvey. He died soon afterward. More than two hundred people attended the funeral. Harvey "killed my father," Amisha told me.

After Lal's death, Harvey's harassment escalated. He called Lal's friends, and their friends in turn, asking for money, for favors, for a place to stay. A few people had some advance warning and were able to steer clear. Others accommodated him. He threatened to blackmail those who refused his requests. He lied that Amisha had been involved in a car crash and asked for money on her behalf; he called neighbors and told them his sisters were abusing him; he called banks and tried to obtain confidential information. Amisha and Yara begged Harvey to stop but he was unfazed. They felt like prisoners in their own lives. "He became our invisible captor," Amisha said.

Without Lal's guidance, they had run out of options. The extended family gathered and in 2004, as a group, decided to forcibly commit Harvey to an institution called Dharma Graha. Doctors there performed an MRI scan and diagnosed him as "psychopathic with personality disorder." According to Amisha, he underwent sessions of electroconvulsive therapy. Placed on a heavy antipsychotic medication, Harvey improved. He expressed remorse and was lucid and thoughtful for long stretches. Amisha visited once a month. "He actually owned up to everything he did," she told me. She had never seen that side of him.

The peace didn't last. Harvey fled Dharma Graha and within weeks had resumed his manipulations.

IT WAS AT THIS JUNCTURE, with her brother having fled to an unknown future, that Amisha concluded her account. She had given of herself so completely in these long messages, the total length of which equaled something like a midlength novella, that I couldn't help but wonder if she had ever really unburdened herself of the story to anyone else outside her family before. I had no doubt of her sincerity, and the depth of her pain. Even so, her account felt incomplete. I asked repeatedly if she would speak to me on the phone, but perhaps fearing this would somehow open a door through which her brother could creep, she would not allow that.

Instead she went on the offensive. Amisha's appraisal of "the Monster" was pitiless. She saw him as a social predator devoid of empathy or remorse, a man without conscience who viewed other people as sources of personal gratification and gain. He was unable to love, a manipulative liar who had alienated his entire remaining family. He had no friends, no one to rely on. She described him as a "malignant tumor," and said that even employing the terms *brother* or *relative* to describe their biological kinship was itself "cruel." People who wished him harm, she said, were justified. Yet I couldn't shake an image of Amisha adrift in an ocean in a glass-bottomed boat, peering at a creature clinging to the underside of the vessel, staring back at her.

Amisha lived in self-imposed seclusion. By design, she had no social media presence. She never posted photos of herself with those she loved, for fear, she said, that if she did Harvey might attack them. She had given up trying to mend bridges. Despite these drastic measures, he still found ways to reach her. He sometimes left threatening messages on her phone, saying he wanted to stab her, or to set her and her pets and everyone around her on fire. Almost always the threats were followed by an apology, and then again by more threats. He called her ugly, fat, a whore. He was very wealthy, a Hollywood producer. He said he was transgender and undergoing transition. He said he wanted to pay back what he had stolen. He said he was sorry.

"All of these messages have gone to trash," Amisha said. She felt so traumatized that she had abandoned the idea of having children, for fear of "even one gene transfer." So, too, had Yara. Neither of them wanted anyone else, least of all their own children, to endure what they had.

Chapter 8

A generation of Americans hates talking on the phone—or so I've been told. Ali, my wife, and a millennial, counts herself among them. Phone calls "terrify" her, she says, only partly in jest. For Harvey, phone calls were a haven.

Picture picking up the phone not to text but to call a stranger. This won't be the prank call of your youth, or your parents' youth, but a true performance requiring unswerving commitment. You're a different sex and your voice will have to reflect that. You'll speak quickly and confidently, a challenge even in ordinary circumstances. If you don't, you'll be found out. You are a corporate titan: powerful, intense, unrelenting. You're no longer a citizen of your nation. Age? Ethnicity? Race? Gender? Those are different, too. You have to own your new identity, sometimes for hours on end. And you will not quit this charade until you have convinced whoever is on the other end of the line to get on a plane and travel halfway around the world to a country they have never visited. Once there, they will have to believe in you enough to shell out thousands and sometimes tens of thousands of dollars to a series of moped-riding strangers you have managed to pass off as trustworthy. Over and over again you will repeat this exercise, sometimes as the same person but often as someone entirely new.

My wife marveled at this. She has an unironic—and I think lovely—habit of slipping into hyperbole when she's excited about something. She took a sip of wine. "I mean, imagine," she said. "The nerve. The absolute nerve!" We might loathe the con artist, but we lie when we say we don't look forward, even just a little, to the next bit of spectacle.

FOR ORDINARY PEOPLE DOWNLOADING THE world onto their screens, the barriers that once separated the relative safety of "reality" from the constant intrusions of online life have been breached. This is true to the point of cliché. People are not just online; they are "hyper online." The internet has made possible a world in which anybody, by virtue of a few clicks, can taste the elixir of escape, of fame and fortune, of financial security. Likewise, they may be canceled or incur the wrath of the mob. This entire matrix of fluidity—call it the Fifth Wall—is no longer just a theoretical construct; it is a permanent feature of reality. Our favorite stars are just behind this veil on Instagram, speaking directly to us. Dreams, romance, jobs—every ambition can be made to seem possible with a few taps.

The single greatest illusion of the internet is the illusion of proximity; people who would otherwise be far removed and inaccessible are made to seem closer and more familiar. The illusion is that they are—or better yet, that they *could be*—intimates. This blurring is of great value to a con artist who works exclusively behind the Fifth Wall. As long as a con artist can maintain the illusion of intimacy and proximity, a mark will remain vulnerable.

In the fall of 2019, a writer named Natalie Beach penned a widely viewed article on the Cut about being the brains, the true voice, behind Caroline Calloway, an Instagram personality who rose to prominence in the early 2010s for her fanciful, witty insights and carefully curated pictures from her world travels. As the hidden author of Calloway's writing, and arguably the engine of her stardom, Beach's piece was a lamentation of her own relegation to obscurity, and it detailed her conflicted feelings about how much credit she deserved for Calloway's fame.

In response to the piece, Caroline Calloway, the actual person, responded with a series of dismayed Instagram posts. Tracking this performative back-and-forth was the *New York Times*, which noted, "As Caroline Calloway responded to the essay, broadcasting her reaction, her Instagram following grew as well. The essay was marketing for both women. It was writing. It was performance. What the moment made clear is that the line between the three has become blurred beyond recognition."

Around the same time, a Russian fraudster named Anna Sorokin had washed ashore in New York and was busy transforming herself into Anna Delvey, a Russian heiress worth $60 million. The daughter of a truck driver and a convenience store clerk, Delvey nevertheless proceeded to convince her marks, which included a photo editor for *Vanity Fair*, to pay for a series of lavish trips, spas, and lengthy stays in luxury hotels. Before she was caught and convicted of grand larceny and theft of services in 2019, Delvey had racked up more than a quarter of a million dollars in expenses, and her Instagram and Twitter feeds were filled with the details of her opulent lifestyle.

One could argue that there is nothing new here, and there might be some truth in that as well. Take the fraudster John Brinkley's rampage across World War I–era America. Perhaps most famously, Brinkley convinced impotent men that they needed goat testicles transplanted into their ailing bodies and later advertised the surgery to both men and women as a panacea for everything from dementia to cancer. Citing his "organized charlatanism," the Kansas medical board revoked his license after several of his "patients" died. The dynamics of Brinkley's time—the so-called "age of flimflam"—were a large factor in his success as one of America's most talented con artists. But while we look back on Brinkley's shenanigans with some amusement, future generations might not be so indulgent of our era. To be a citizen now, to try to be a human being, is to confront these forces constantly. Is it worse than in the past? Look no further than what is in your hands and the hands of virtually everybody else on the planet, that machine of addiction and pain: the phone.

The scale of online treachery is breathtaking. Scams populate the fields of our perception, each a subspecies with its own signature and its own name. There is the Shopping scam, the Nigerian scam, the Fine Print scam, a particularly insidious type that borders on corporate fraud. The commonest scam of all, conjuring a sense of a lazy and pleasant pastime but one that costs Americans millions of dollars each year, is simply called phishing, which is the practice of luring people to divulge important information through fraudulent emails; a subset of the genre is the adventurous-sounding spear-phishing, a more targeted form of the same. Should you escape the spear-phisher, let not your guard down, lest you be digitally kidnapped, held virtually hostage, and extorted for your online secrets. Different varieties of online deception abound: lotteries, surveys, charities, prizes. Opportunities! Romance scams inflict an average $21,000 hit per victim annually, the total cost doubling roughly every year. You could call tech support for help, but there's a scam for that, too, just as there's a disaster relief scam for people whose homes were detonated in tornados. In the Genus of Scams, ranging from the improbable to the inane, one species, the Imposter scam, cost Americans $1.2 billion in 2019. But of all the imposters, only one racked up such an immense array of victims from across the globe. By repeatedly transporting these curious or bored wayfarers to another material reality entirely, the Con Queen ushered a physical and mental removal so complete his victims believed they had been stolen from their very own lives.

Unfortunately, the wild proliferation of such a vast array of scams is symptomatology. Deception springs from deeper wells: it is a tunnel in which we all live; its entrance and exit are invisible.

"Every journalist who is not too stupid or too full of himself to notice what is going on knows that what he does is morally indefensible." So begins *The Journalist and the Murderer*, Janet Malcolm's seminal exploration of the fraught journalist-source relationship. Since its publication in 1990, the book has become required reading for anyone interested in the ethics of journalism. Malcolm tells the story of how author Joe McGinniss agreed to split the profits of a book he was writing with his subject, a convicted murderer. The book McGinniss eventually published was not to the killer's liking, and the two were soon embroiled in a bitter lawsuit. The way Malcolm saw it, McGinniss had betrayed his subject; she described him as "a kind of confidence man, preying on people's vanity, ignorance or loneliness, gaining their trust and betraying them without remorse."

Not all journalist-source, or journalist-subject, relationships get to the point where these questions of morality become relevant. But over the years I have been involved in a few stories where they have. I have never paid, or offered to pay, a source or a subject for their story, or for information about another person's story. But a familiar process unfolds in stages: You come to people and ask them, persuade them in many cases, to speak to you because you are interested in their story—and indeed you are. However, you also need them to speak to you so you can meet your obligations. To be clear: this is not to say that you're *not* interested. Presumably, the reason you became a journalist in the first place is that, at your core, you are interested in the experiences and stories of other people, the contours of human nature. But that is now a secondary concern. It is what brought you here, but it is not what is going to get you where you need to be. Only a conversation with your subject, perhaps a confession *from* your subject, will accomplish that. Later, when you sit down to write about what you have learned, the fealty you once felt to the subject will find itself competing with the blank page.

WHEN I WAS FOURTEEN MY father revealed that he was not, as I had believed, a diplomat but rather a CIA case officer: a spy. He had taken me to see the office where he humbly carried out his duties, a bleak and uninviting strip mall in suburban Detroit where the sign on the door read ACME INSURANCE. In practical terms, his revelation was an act of forced complicity. It meant that from then on, I had to lie about what he did. At his direction I told people that he worked for the

U.S. Department of Commerce. As a child I performed the deception required of me with a certain pleasure, or what I mistook as pleasure at the time. It took a certain skill to navigate this type of illusion, and I enjoyed learning how to hone my abilities. Along the way, however, the task of deception became something more like an identity: I *was* someone who knew things other people did not, and it was my job to keep them to myself. Over time, the act of perpetuating the lies became more seductive than the lies themselves.

Childhood is full of innocent deceptions, of course. Children pretend, they play make-believe and all manner of games that allow them to become, however briefly, somebody else. In my case, it wasn't really a game, or if it was, it was a very adult kind of game, and there were real-life consequences, one being a risk of getting lost. Deception is a labyrinth.

We like the idea of being somebody else. I was once at a bar in Cape Town, South Africa, with a French friend, speaking French, when a woman joined in our conversation. No sooner had I said hello than I realized I had started speaking to her in English, but with a made-up French accent. I have no idea why, other than that I thought it might be fun to see if I could pull it off. We sat side by side on the floor of the bar's outside balcony, looking down on the carnivalesque atmosphere below as I carried on the ridiculous farce, amusing myself perhaps but no doubt becoming tedious to her. Eventually she asked me something that revealed a genuine curiosity on her part, the kind of curiosity that demanded real honesty, and I had no choice but to drop the act: to do otherwise seemed cruel. She accepted my apology but soon excused herself to go to the bar.

I had recalled this moment more than once when I had thought about the Con Queen scam. A constant refrain among the victims was how much they had enjoyed their conversations with their fake avatars, how impressed they had been with the level and depth of their knowledge, and how seemingly well attuned their Amy Pascals or Wendi Murdochs had been to the circumstances of their own lives. In a thousand small ways, the scammer had breached that wall separating consideration from cruelty. Again and again he had made the choice to continue with the deception. These small, incremental choices were the building blocks of sadism.

We all lie, of course. Several times a day in a multitude of ways and degrees of severity, if the experts are to be believed. Lying, fibbing—there are degrees of deceit, but all within a spectrum we decide is acceptable. Yet we're fascinated by those who make the choice to go *beyond* that spectrum, breaking the social contract, reminding us that it's just an artificial construct. Putting the whole enterprise in doubt.

THE APPEAL OF DECEIT REVEALS a paradox about being alive: even as we strive for consciousness, we also often shun it. What, after all, had propelled Greg's family, the Mandarano clan, to tumble so completely into the absurd alternate reality of Anand Sippy's world? Alice Pleasance Lidell, another kind of traveler from long ago, had followed a White Rabbit down a hole because she was bored and curious—about the creature's waistcoat, its pocket watch, its ability to talk—and wound up in Wonderland. In the strictest Carrollian sense, these travelers fell down a rabbit hole and went mad for a time in an alternate reality; just like Wonderland and the tunnel that led there, the destination was as illusory as the journey was distracting. Their only guide was a mirage; that floating grin of the Cheshire Cat taunting the Queen of Hearts comes to mind. The end, for everyone, was sudden and disorienting, the return to reality somehow less real than the dream from which they had just woken. Some went much further into this dream than others. So far did the Mandarano family travel, however, that their journey nearly destroyed them.

It was no surprise that the China Film Group executives told Greg's family they were the "dream team." From the scammer's perspective, they were. But all good things must come to an end, and after siphoning tens of thousands of dollars out of the Mandarano family coffers, the Con Queen eventually began to wrap things up. One day toward the end of 2015, several months after their first trip to Indonesia, Anand Sippy called a series of emergency meetings with Greg and Jay in Jakarta. "I need to see the boys one on one," Sippy wrote to Greg's mother. "I need to discuss the process with them so there will not be anymore [*sic*] snide remarks, unnecessary personal comments and a pure focus on the project."

By now, the constant haranguing from Huilang, Greg's chief contact at the China Film Group, had taken its toll. In addition to concerns about the money they had spent, Greg and Jay and their families had begun to wonder whether something more insidious was under way. A few weeks earlier, in October, Huilang asked Greg and his sister Melanie to travel to Hong Kong for a meeting, but when the siblings arrived Huilang didn't show up and Melanie, who along with Greg had begun to grow skeptical, wondered in a panic if she had been lured to the city as part of an organ-harvesting operation. That night, Huilang called sounding drunk and happy, almost euphoric, proffering excuses for her absence. "They wanted us to go all over the place," Greg said. "They wanted us to travel as much as possible."

As the end of the year approached, the Mandaranos began to wonder if they had possibly been ensnared in some sort of illegal operation whose ultimate purpose remained unknown to them. The family had agreed upon a secret code, to be sent by text, in the event that something went wrong so the others would know to call the police. This was the mood as the meetings with Jay and Greg got under way. Alternately playing Anand Sippy and Huilang Jing, the Con Queen confided to each of the two screenwriters terrible insights about the other. During a three-and-a-half-hour meeting, Sippy told Greg that Jay thought he, Greg, was a terrible writer. Greg had trouble believing this of his friend and instead spent the time worrying about Jay's physical safety; perhaps they had been separated so that one or both of them could be killed. As hour four approached, Sippy finally told Greg that while CFG wished to continue working with him, Jay had been fired.

Later that same day, in a meeting that lasted only twenty minutes,

Sippy told Jay that Greg wanted to cut him out of the project. None of that was true, but by telling Greg and Jay different stories, the Con Queen set them up to destroy each other all on their own. The Mandaranos and Shapiros stopped speaking to each other. The years-long friendship ended in bitterness and resentment. Greg's mother, Lisa, fell into a major depression. The scammer had fed her what she wanted to hear about her son, and then played her for all she was worth. She doubted the family would ever recover. Greg's sister Melanie found herself thinking about the darkness in her own life: Were people good? Greg tried to alert the FBI but the agency ignored him, as did Interpol. "The only one who cared," said Lisa, "was my accountant." In 2018, three years after the dream team discovered the truth, Greg's father died after being hit by a car, having never regained the money he had lost, or any clarity about the scam.

Why did the scam work so well in this instance? Why did some people return again and again to Indonesia? As a friend pointed out to me, "Some people went once and said fuck it, pay me back, right?" Right. But people, some people anyway, wanted to believe in something more. Occasionally this desire can take on elements of a contagion, extending to an entire collective, like those cases of mass hysteria that have throughout history consumed entire communities: a clown panic in Canada, the witch trials in Salem, recurring episodes of grief at schools in Nepal. The scam, too, had its own beautiful architecture, its own logic. One entered at the largest, most accessible point and traveled in a circular fashion along a steadily constricting path of sealed chambers, as if inside a nautilus. Until the strange creation's intricate workings crumbled, or were crushed, they held firm.

Some of the victims claimed that they had figured out it was a scam but went along with it anyway just to see what would happen. Why? A poker analogy might be helpful. They told themselves they had been dealt what is known as a "gut-shot straight draw," a hand that will very often win if you chance to hit one of the three remaining cards in the deck that will make your straight. The odds are very low, but every now and again people do get lucky, though people tend to bank on their own luck more than they should.

And sometimes discovering the truth is scarier than remaining inside the fiction.

When faced with a tale of deception, people tend to count themselves among the wise. Those who skirt the dangers of a con linger on the foibles of the duped, the contradictions, weaknesses, and logical fallacies of the fraud or the fraudster, and tell themselves that they would have done otherwise. As much as I sympathized with the victims, I had also struggled sometimes with their accounts. How *could* they have fallen for such an obvious ruse?

But, as it turns out, the rules of human behavior tell a different story. The grift is a fundamentally human experience, ages old, tested and retested in every epoch and every civilization. The trickster is a human constant, as ubiquitous in myth as in current events. There was nothing especially new here. But as in every other case of true deception across the ages, it *felt* entirely new to the people upon whom it fell. There were, according to Nicole and the FBI, hundreds of victims, and there were also just as many explanations for why the experience of being trapped in somebody else's lie had felt so real to each one of them. These explanations were as diverse as they were contradictory, but in the end, a simple and poignant refrain broke through: the human need to believe in stories.

This very human impulse helped propel centuries of religious development and patterns of human migration that shaped Indonesia.

I sometimes thought of Harvey as a drifting archipelago. Beyond the crimes themselves, beyond even the victims, I wanted to understand why he had fragmented in the first place. My curiosity had gotten the better of me, and it forced me to ask a question of myself: Why did these kinds of liars interest me? An image kept intruding into my mind: a lone traveler on a horse, meandering down a deserted road. A memory flickered, but for the time being, I set it aside.

Chapter 9

I filled in the gaps in Amisha's account as best I could. Harvey, I soon learned, had one friend in childhood, a Sindhi boy named Atik. Like Harvey's sisters, Atik was a prefect at the Gandhi School, a six-story building whose atrium-style courtyard and imposing entryway resembled a Manhattan art museum. The student body drew from the Sindhi émigré community to which the Tahilramani family belonged. Harvey tried repeatedly to gain acceptance to his sisters' fashionable set, but his attempts went nowhere. His thick black hair dyed with orange-tinted henna, he found himself mostly alone.

Harvey was "kind" and "full of life," Atik recalled during an hour-long phone conversation, but his most marked trait lay in his performative abilities, and in the "really interesting stories he shared." But as much as Harvey told stories—and perhaps precisely *because* he told stories—he became one about whom stories were told. In the halls of the Gandhi School, some of the students whispered that Lal had been abusive toward Kavita, but offered no evidence to support the claim. Some chalked this up to the times in which they lived, and the paternalistic culture that surrounded them. Other families faced similar struggles.

The one place Harvey felt comfortable was onstage, and in those moments, it was as if the gears of his personality clicked into their proper alignment. He was preternaturally gifted with accents, a British one in particular. By his teens, he alone among his peers could speak American English without inflection. But what really distinguished him was a flair for performance. "He had it," Atik recalled. "He could capture the audience. He saw a room and delivered." During recess he and Atik often stayed indoors while their classmates kicked balls in the yard. Atik studied while Harvey regaled him with stories of the latest Hollywood awards show. His encyclopedic knowledge of movies, along with an aesthetic sophistication that eluded his peers, set him apart. While his classmates were trading basketball cards, he was in the Gandhi School's movie room studying VHS tapes of Vivien Leigh's portrayal of Blanche DuBois in *A Streetcar Named Desire*.

Every once in a while, if he felt particularly stung by rejection, he let loose with a verbal barrage that left even his harshest critics shaken. Like a veteran stagehand, he would deliver the withering critique as if he wanted Atik alone to hear it, but of course—*wink, wink*—it would be just loud enough for the intended recipients. Atik sometimes alerted the teachers to Harvey's struggles, and sometimes the teachers listened, but the fundamental dynamics did not shift. Harvey might be gay, Atik thought. There was certainly plenty of talk in that vein among the boys; but they were young and ignorant, and what did it matter anyway? It seemed to him that Harvey had something to offer, if there were only a platform to accommodate him. It wasn't that he was hated. Atik remembered a few times, such as the field trip to the Hill Station, where a classmate's family owned a bungalow, and the boys on the bus had played music from the silver boom box Harvey had carted along, when it felt for a brief moment like they were all rowing on the same team. But in the end, they weren't. Then one day, Harvey was simply gone.

HARVEY HAD LANDED IN LA in 1997 and enrolled at Los Angeles City College. One of the first people he met was Ken Sherwood. Sherwood had been directing the speech and debate program at Los Angeles City College for four years. LACC was the most ethnically diverse college in the United States; the majority of its students came from disadvantaged and troubled backgrounds. Many of Sherwood's charges struggled with mental illness. A few had been homeless. Sherwood believed that his program could provide kids a way out of cycles of poverty and despair. Most American presidents had competed in college speech and debate, he told them. Right here in California, where more law students failed the bar exam than passed, Sherwood had never known a debater who didn't have a cushy job lined up before graduating from law school.

Sandwiched between the Hollywood Freeway and Santa Monica Boulevard, LACC was situated on Hollywood's bleeding edge. Sherwood's kids were more interested in the big screen than the bench. The school had a feeder program that funneled aspiring actors into its prestigious Theatre Academy, which had over the years produced an astonishing array of talent, including Clint Eastwood and Morgan Freeman. Competitive speech fit into this ecosystem nicely as a way for these dreamers to hone their performative skills and improve their chances of gaining admission to the academy.

From the moment he joined Sherwood's team, Harvey Tahilramani stood out as a unique talent. He was a decent "persuasive" speaker, a genre that required both logic and intuition. He showed particular aptitude and enthusiasm for dramatic interpretation, or "interp," which required a performer to inhabit multiple voices and characters, toggling back and forth between them. Harvey was especially skilled with female voices. His natural register was already a little higher than the typical male voice, and he had an ability to inhabit diverse characters that Sherwood rarely saw. Mimicry and authentic impersonation skills were naturally occurring phenomena, like musical or athletic talent; they could be taught, but only up to a point. Some people had it; most did not. Other debate veterans who encountered Harvey agreed. As one of them put it, "He could do anyone he wanted."

Debate could be competitive. In such a high-pressure environment,

Harvey was a rare presence: compelling to watch, but also nonthreatening. He was a polished speaker, with crisp diction, and while the secondhand suit he wore, half a size too big, lent him a hangdog air, he was always impeccably groomed. His favorite category of all was oral interpretation, a combination of poetry, drama, and prose bound together by a unifying theme. He advanced to state finals in his first year, earning accolades and a bronze medal for a series of performances about cutting, a form of self-harm.

Harvey was "coachable." He adapted easily and without ego to the suggestions of his fellow student Amber Wormington. Amber was among the few people whose experience of Harvey seemed to penetrate to a deeper level of friendship. In exchange for math lessons, Amber was helping him hone his performances. One night, their lessons complete, Amber offered to take him to his car. They drove around the dimly lit streets of the Hollywood Hills past secluded mansions and palm-lined canyons as Harvey looked glumly out the window until, finally, he admitted to her that he didn't actually have a car, that he had taken the bus to get to her house.

Eventually Amber began to wonder whether Harvey's facility with performances, the ease with which he slipped in and out of everything, masked a darker desire than an ambition to excel as her apprentice. It was almost as if he wanted to *become* someone else, or even to replace them. Sometimes she caught Harvey studying her. Harvey, she knew, had always wanted to be more *like* her—bold, confident, take-charge. But later she realized it was more than that. Maybe what Harvey actually wanted, what truly animated him, was a baser and in some ways more childish kind of envy—to *be* her.

Harvey was also, it turned out, a lot of trouble. Sherwood had pulled him aside more than any other student over petty rumor-mongering and personal squabbles. With so many kids facing emotional challenges, it wasn't surprising that they all didn't get along that well, but Harvey pushed an already stressed spectrum to an extreme. After one tournament, Harvey giddily told Sherwood that he'd just had sex with the opposing team's coach, a man Sherwood knew. It was certainly unethical behavior, but not, technically, illegal. He never learned if it was true.

The next year, 1999, Harvey wanted to up his speech game. "You can't just be sweet," a coach told him. "Do something fucked up." The resulting piece was inspired by the account of a real death row inmate, convicted of killing her own baby. He opened in the voice of a boy whose busy mother had given him a doll. In the performance's next sequence, Harvey slipped into the character of the condemned baby-killing mother, who held a doll in her hand until the moment of her own execution. Only then did the audience learn that the mother was actually innocent; it was the sister who had committed the murder. Six finalists were announced in descending order, until Harvey was standing victorious before five admiring judges and an amphitheater filled to capacity. The crowd rose in a standing ovation for the gawky kid with the floppy ears in the too-big suit who had tears streaming down his face. In the audience no one cried as much as Amber.

The next year Harvey transferred to Bradley University, in the flatlands of Peoria, Illinois. With thirty-two national championships, Bradley had the very best debate team in the entire country, "the Death Star of Speech," in the words of one former national champion. The gold standard was nothing short of utter dedication. In the pursuit of that excellence, the world cleaved neatly into two very distinct groups: future politicians and lawyers who wanted to give good speeches; and theater kids who wanted to become other people.

Harvey arrived in January 2000, when the average low temperatures hovered in the midteens. In a community that prided itself on its acceptance of society's outcasts, more than a few people were weirded out by the Indonesian guy from California. He always seemed "on," as if every encounter was a performance. Harvey talked about picking up older men; he liked "to smooth out their wrinkles." Many former teammates described his constant attention and unwavering enthusiasm as more akin to that of a "mascot" than a teammate.

The team spent a lot of time at a library that housed a large collection of audio recordings, which they studied to perfect accents, characters, and intonations. They learned that mimicking an accent required breaking speech patterns down into their constituent parts, studying how those linguistic changes felt within their own vocal tracts, and devising workarounds to mimic particularly challenging accents. One of Harvey's teammates recalled using the library's tapes to polish a British cockney accent, and learned that by swallowing quickly between words he could reproduce the tortured inflections that confounded nonnative speakers.

Harvey's best friend at Bradley was Alison Fisher. Bubbly and playful, Alison sometimes thought of herself as Harvey's "beard," even though he wasn't closeted. She drove him everywhere; he paid for gas. They practiced speech at night until they passed out from exhaustion, sometimes falling asleep wrapped in each other's arms, cuddling. They went shopping and Harvey often brought her little surprises, a 7-Eleven Slurpee or a Twinkie, and she appreciated how he paid attention to small details that made her feel good. But he also played weird mind games. After a long night spent practicing, she woke one morning to find that the diamond stud earrings she had left on the coffee table were missing. During one tournament, Alison suddenly couldn't find her favorite lipstick. She slayed the performance anyway, but afterward, Harvey slid the tube out of his pocket. "See?" he said. "I told you that you didn't need the lipstick." Sometimes Alison overheard Harvey having long and emotional telephone conversations. He missed his mother, he confided; she wasn't doing well.

As the announcement for State Finals approached, Harvey and Alison speculated excitedly about who would make the cut, and what pieces they would perform. On the day the finalists were to be posted, the pair made their way to the Communications building. For Alison, the news was great: she had qualified for the tournament. Harvey had not. On their way out of the building, Alison was celebrating, perhaps even gloating a little. They were standing at the top of a set of wide stairs when suddenly Alison felt a hand grab the handle on her backpack and yank her forcefully backward. She stumbled, momentarily losing her footing as the same hand shoved her violently forward. Down the stairs she tumbled, landing hard on her wrist. She looked up to find Harvey staring down at her with a smug, self-satisfied half smile that seemed to say: *Who, me?*

"You must have fallen!" he said coolly, unconvincingly, but a small crowd of people had witnessed the incident: Alison hadn't fallen down the stairs. Harvey had pushed her. Doctors performed surgery on her broken left wrist—the one she normally used to hold her speeches—and she underwent physical therapy for weeks. She had been looking forward to participating in the upcoming State Finals but that wasn't going to happen with her left wrist in a cast. Harvey was ostracized from the team, but Alison never got the State Finals back, and that bothered her far more than her broken wrist. If other people hadn't witnessed the pushing, she would have concluded that she'd imagined the whole thing. Weeks later, she saw a picture of Harvey and spotted one of her missing diamond studs in his ear. It would be years before she learned that Harvey had lied about his mother "not doing well"— she had died years earlier.

Around this time, back in Indonesia, Lal received a call from a lawyer in Los Angeles. Harvey was locked up in a sheriff's office, accused of running up a $10,000 bill on a friend's credit card during a shopping spree. Humiliated, Lal paid the lawyer's fees and the merchandise was returned.

As the academic year wound down in the spring of 2000, Harvey approached a former teammate named Marianne LeGreco, who had been one of Bradley's star performers. Harvey asked LeGreco if she would help him prepare for an event called Rhetorical Criticism, a ten-minute performance analyzing an important communication event, such as a documentary, social protest, or book. LeGreco agreed, and provided Harvey with a speech she had written, and told him he should use it as a model as he went about crafting his own work. LeGreco's speech was about Rigoberta Menchú, a Guatemalan activist who in

1992 was awarded the Nobel Peace Prize for her work on behalf of Guatemala's indigenous people. In 1998, the American anthropologist David Stoll published a book revealing that Menchú's stories of persecution at the hands of Guatemala's right-wing regime had been at least partially fabricated; Menchú had presented the experiences of her besieged community as her own, or in some cases made them up out of whole cloth. The ensuing controversy became the centerpiece of LeGreco's rhetorical piece, which revolved around a singular question: Was it ever okay to make up stories—and present them as truth? Among indigenous communities in Guatemala, LeGreco argued, storytelling was often a collective affair, with members of a community recalling their experiences and then funneling them to a designated storyteller whose rhetorical skills were up to the task of conveying everyone's perspective to a larger audience. LeGreco instructed Harvey to practice on his own speech over the summer, in time for competition beginning that fall, when he would again be attending a new school, California State University, Long Beach.

When school began again in the fall of 2000, Cal State Long Beach cohosted a Swing Tournament featuring back-to-back competitions. LeGreco, who had since accepted a coaching position at Arizona State University, wasn't at the tournament, but two of her new ASU students, Jennifer Lahoda and John Parsi, were. After the first day had concluded, Parsi and Lahoda called LeGreco and delivered some surprising news. Harvey had won several first-round events, including one for a speech he had given in Rhetorical Criticism. "You coached him a little too well," they chided. After round two, Lahoda and Parsi called Marianne again. "You better sit down," they said. Among the unwritten rules of speech was the taboo on "stealing topics" that other people had already tackled. It did sometimes occur, but it was considered unseemly. When told that Harvey had stolen her speech, Marianne assumed it meant he had stolen her *topic*. "No," her students told her. "Harvey is doing your speech—verbatim." Harvey was disqualified and stripped of his ranking and previous wins.

Almost overnight, Harvey disappeared from the circuit, replaced by a digital version who fired off a series of emails containing dire messages about what *horrible* people Lahoda and Parsi were for having denounced him: They had *destroyed* his life! How could they live with themselves? The emails were soon followed by voice messages, some of which seemed to have been filtered through a voice distortion program that produced a deep and alien timbre, more robot than human. Parsi received the messages on his parents' home phone, Lahoda on her home and cell phones. Then one day a new kind of message appeared; the content was similar, but the messenger had shapeshifted. Here was none other than the Oscar-winning Australian actress Cate Blanchett denouncing Lahoda as "a *terrible* person" for doing "something so horrible to such a *sweet* nice person."

One morning in November, the school's speech director called Lahoda and Parsi into his office. He shared devastating news: Harvey had died by suicide. He had left behind a letter, in which he identified Lahoda and Parsi as bearing responsibility for the destruction of his dreams and aspirations, the note said. Parsi and Lahoda began to second-guess themselves. Maybe they should have given Harvey a warning? Or not said anything at all?

Parsi had grown skeptical. Why, after all, would Cate Blanchett harass a couple of college debaters? Perhaps all of it, the phone calls and the suicide letter, was actually just . . . Harvey, who wasn't dead at all. The Tempe police soon confirmed his suspicions. After investigating, they determined that the emails had come from Indonesia. Unbeknownst to the debaters, on January 26, 2001, a few months after Harvey's disappearance from the debate circuit, two undercover Las Vegas police officers arrested him at the Venetian Hotel on suspicion of check fraud. He confessed to stealing $3,000 and consented to a handwriting test. In a delicate, childlike script full of swoops and curling flourishes he transcribed names—"Miss Queen Roberts"—and words: "dollars," "shut up," "her cash." He told the police he had stolen the checkbook from his aunt Cora, who lived in San Diego and whose family had hosted Harvey when he had first arrived in the United States two years earlier; then he took the detectives to his lodgings at the Town & Country Manor II on Boulder Highway, where they recovered the stolen checkbook. A few weeks later, this latest offense still hanging over his head, Harvey returned to Indonesia. Four years had passed—years during which he had obtained no degrees but had instead racked up an arrest record for theft, physically assaulted a teammate, and been caught in a blatant act of plagiarism. Not to mention the lawsuits and the threats and thefts that hadn't been reported.

The annual Nationals tournament was scheduled to take place that coming April at Bradley University, and as the date approached, the campaign of terror against Lahoda and Parsi intensified as the mysterious calls and emails turned into outright threats. Alternating between a series of distorted voices and Blanchett, who had become particularly venomous, a caller threatened to kill Lahoda, Parsi, and the whole team. "It'd be really unfortunate if something terrible happened to you!" the caller said. "Harvey told me what the speech circuit is. I'm going to be at Bradley in a couple of months. Wouldn't it be *awful* if a bomb went off? Wouldn't it be *unfortunate* if you died in a mysterious accident and someone jumped out with a knife or a gun? I know what you did to Harvey, you're the reason he got kicked out of speech, you ruined his life."

The Nationals tournament that opened at Bradley in April 2001 was unlike any in the school's history. Lahoda's entire family flew out from California to assist as her personal "bodyguards." Police assigned Lahoda and Parsi extra protection and prohibited them from walking freely around campus. Family and friends patrolled the hallways and competition rooms to look for suspicious people and packages. No bombs exploded but the event was marred by an atmosphere of fear. The psychological damage was done.

Dr. Ruyandi Hutasoit performed his first exorcism when he was twenty-seven years old, in 1977, in Jakarta. His subject was a woman who claimed to have been possessed by a demon. The whole ordeal took two days to complete, but when it was over, the woman, seemingly freed of the evil spirit, thanked him. Over the coming four decades, Hutasoit, a square-jawed and handsome man, went on to perform more than two thousand exorcisms across Indonesia and in other countries. Exorcisms could be performed in a few hours, but in extreme cases, he and his team might spend two or more days on a single individual. He reproduced for me the sharp, high-pitched cries he made when performing the rite: *Argh, argh, argh!* "Everywhere I cast the demon," he said, "they go out."

Raised as a Christian, Hutasoit experienced a profound conversion experience in 1976, in which he was born again into the Presbyterian faith. With the help of the American evangelist Bill Bright, Hutasoit established Doulos (the term derived from the Greek word for *slave*), which advertised itself as a rehabilitation facility for drug addicts. There were beds for seventy patients, a well-manicured lawn and courtyard, and a large staff. Hutasoit told me that Harvey had spent roughly six months at Doulos as a "mentally ill patient." Harvey had made an impression on the staff, Hutasoit said, because he was "ladylike," by which he said he meant that he was "a man behaving like a woman, very feminine." Hutasoit, who has no formal mental health training, nevertheless described Harvey as having a "mild psychotic illness" though he never explicitly described what the illness was. Hutasoit took a dim view of homosexuality, a perspective that was in keeping with fundamentalist Christian orthodoxy. Within certain religious communities of Indonesia, and elsewhere, including the United States, gay conversion therapy is a favored form of "treatment" for the perceived "sin" or "illness" of being gay.

With the exception of Aceh province, where Islamic sharia law prevails and gay sex is punishable by one hundred lashes, homosexuality is legal across Indonesia.

Even so, exorcisms and other forms of conversion therapy remain commonplace, particularly among conservative Muslims but also within certain fundamentalist Christian communities. I had asked Hutasoit if Harvey had been the subject of an exorcism. "I think no," he said, not altogether convincingly. Of the possibility that he had tried to sway Harvey from his sexual preference, Hutasoit didn't say. But he had remembered him because Harvey was of Indian extraction, and Doulos didn't have many Indian patients. Typically, patients admitted to Doulos for mental illness stayed between one and two years, but Hutasoit said that after six months at Doulos, a resident doctor had deemed Harvey "cured" and released him to his family.

Between interludes of care, abortive and ineffective as they were, Harvey had managed to land a few jobs. He worked at the advertising agency FleishmanHillard and later at EMI, the music company. But he never lasted long in one place, and in each a trail of suspicion followed in his wake. He allegedly tried to embezzle several million dollars from the public relations firm Publicis, and when the firm threatened legal action his sisters swooped in and managed to fend off the litigation. Harvey fled. For weeks he stayed in hotels across the Indonesian archipelago: the Santika, the Four Seasons, the Shangri-La, allegedly defrauding each of them in turn with a fake story about a Chase Manhattan bank bond. The hotel complaints piled up and eventually the police arrested him. One of Amisha's closest friends, a woman named Sandra Djohan, paid the hotel bills and then arranged for a flight for Harvey. After his arrest, she visited him one day in 2005 at the South Jakarta police station where he was being detained and brought him *nasi Padang*, rice with curry.

"You've been kind to me," he told her.

"No," she said, "you did this. The way I see it, you lied to me. You used my money to bail you out. You didn't intend to pay me back." She now revealed that she had filed one of the many police reports that led to his arrest.

"I put you here."

Eventually he was released. But his crimes eventually caught up with him, and he wound up behind bars again in early 2007, convicted of embezzlement. Throughout that spring and early summer, while awaiting sentencing, he allegedly conducted at least five elaborate psychological terror campaigns targeting Americans thousands of miles away. These included bomb threats, resulting in large-scale evacuations of buildings across the United States. In Los Angeles, the occupants of the E! Entertainment building were evacuated from their offices on Wilshire Boulevard after security received two bomb threats from an overseas number. *American Idol* producer Ryan Seacrest fled the site in his Aston Martin. Also evacuated was the staff of EMI–Capitol Music Group, which had offices in the same building. Meanwhile, in Las Vegas, hundreds of people poured out of the Hard Rock Cafe after Harvey, using his own brother-in-law's name, threatened to blow up the concert venue and said other bomb threats were being planned for San Francisco and Jakarta. In New York, police evacuated the Viacom building on Broadway, home to the Minskoff Theatre, where *The Lion King* was running.

As the embezzlement case moved through the court system, Harvey was eventually transferred to Cipinang, a maximum-security penitentiary on the far eastern edge of Jakarta. A massive structure built during the Dutch colonial administration, Cipinang was a nasty place, a gulag for the political foes of two successive autocratic regimes and, more recently, for dozens of convicted terrorists, too. But even Cipinang's walls didn't contain his phone habit and he continued his campaign of bomb threats against targets in the United States. In June, a bomb squad was brought in to clear the premises of an LA blood clinic that he threatened repeatedly. In one of those calls, Harvey told a terrified receptionist that he knew the police had been notified, and he demanded that she contact the detectives in charge and patch them into the call. For the next forty minutes, a pair of Los Angeles Police Department detectives spoke at length to Harvey. He claimed to be of Middle Eastern descent and said he had ties to terror cells across the region. He named several well-known terrorists and boasted that he had "taught them all" and "worked with them all."

The LAPD and the FBI assigned teams to track and find Harvey. Agents and detectives fanned out across LA searching for him and interviewing former classmates and teachers. Based on the evidence they gathered, the LA County district attorney filed five felony charges of "malicious informing of false bomb" and the court issued a warrant for Harvey's arrest. They set bail at $200,000—$20,000 for each of the five bomb threats against the LA blood clinic, plus an additional $100,000 on top for good measure. The court, unsure if Harvey was still in the United States, identified him as a "flight risk" and the warrant noted that he was a "probable illegal alien." The boxes indicating possible mitigating circumstances, including "mentally disturbed" and "suicidal tendencies," were left unchecked. Instead, the charge sheet pointed to the "unlawful" and "malicious" intent of the bomb threats.

Not all the calls were malicious. From Cipinang, he also called the Four Seasons hotel in Jakarta and ordered $7,500 worth of food, including Wagyu beef burgers and bottles of Hennessy cognac, and booked a hotel room for two nights. He convinced the hotel staff that he was a VIP and explained that his bodyguard would be staying at the hotel with his family. Two days later, the "bodyguard," who turned out to be a prison guard whom Harvey had befriended, picked up the food and returned to Cipinang, where he distributed it among the inmates.

Harvey's dwellings were spartan, a cell in a massive three-story edifice that was divided into blocks, each of which contained three to four hundred people. One of those people became Harvey's closest confidant. A handsome man with a wide grin, Rudi Sutopo arrived at Cipinang in 2004 along with a governor, a minister, and the director of the central bank, Bank Indonesia, all former Suharto cronies convicted on corruption charges. He and Harvey lived on the same corridor and spent time together every day. A businessman, Rudi enjoyed a privileged position as a mentor and coach to the other inmates. As he saw it, his job was to improve their mental habits, to help them become, as he put it, "good" through a daily routine of exercise, conversation, and moral support.

The man with the chortling laugh and the buggy, roving eyes whom Rudi knew as "Hargobind Lil Punjabi" was skilled, smart, and cunning—even, at times, helpful. As far as Rudi knew, "Hargobind" was the son of the well-known Indonesian movie mogul Raam Punjabi. When other inmates needed a hand with more advanced arts, like writing, he stepped in. He helped one of Rudi's friends make a personal diary about his life. Hargobind had undeniable talents. But the young man was also unstable. According to Rudi, his young protégé took medication for a bipolar disorder diagnosis he had received from the prison's medical staff. As long as Hargobind could control himself, Rudi thought, he would be fine. The problem was that Hargobind didn't control himself, and neither could anyone else. He became quickly and irrationally furious, shouting and raging, interrupting people and speaking over them. "Hey, Gob," Rudi would snap. "Take your medicine. Please, be focused. Calm down."

Just before midnight on the evening of April 21, 2008, Harvey asked to borrow a cellmate's cell phone, a black LG, and made his way into a hallway where he called the general number for the U.S. embassy in Jakarta. The U.S. Marine on duty answered the call and heard what sounded like a woman speaking in a hodgepodge of accents—Middle Eastern, American, and Eastern European. "There is a bomb inside the embassy and it's set to detonate seventy-two hours from now," the woman said. Two more bombs had been planted inside the Pentagon and the FBI headquarters in Quantico. Both were "set to detonate in one week."

The Marine reported the call to his superior, and a sweep of the grounds was conducted but nothing was found. The next day, Tuesday, another call came in. The same woman, using the same patchwork of accents, informed another Marine guard that "the American embassy will be bombed immediately within forty-eight hours." Security conducted another sweep but again found nothing. Nevertheless, the next morning, the embassy reported the calls to the Indonesian government, which immediately dispatched ten bomb squad units from Gegana, an elite antiterror detachment.

From the American perspective, the bomb threat was not just idle chatter. In 2002, Islamic extremists attacked a nightclub on the popular resort island of Bali, killing 202 people. Three years later, terrorists attacked Balian tourist sites again, using suicide and car bombs, killing twenty and wounding more than one hundred. By then, the Indonesian government had formed an elite special forces counterterrorism squad. The soldiers of Special Detachment 88, or "Densus 88," were top of the line. Trained by both Australian and American special forces, with help from the CIA and the FBI, they were Indonesia's equivalent of the Navy SEALs or the U.S. Army's Delta Force.

U.S. officials tracked the bomb threat to Cipinang. Carrying M4 carbines, a Densus 88 detachment followed the warden as he moved down the hallways, searching for the source. Eventually he stopped before the cell of a dark-skinned man. Slightly chubby and balding, he had a disarming cleft in his chin and a wide, toothy grin. Densus agents took Harvey to an interrogation center somewhere in Jakarta, where he confessed. During his trial the following year, prosecutors alleged that Harvey had "intentionally used threats of violence with the intention of causing widespread terror or fear of people or causing mass casualties, depriving freedom or loss of life and property of others." A judge sentenced him to five additional years in prison for "a criminal act of terrorism." In the court sentencing documents, Harvey listed his occupation as "entrepreneur."

HARVEY HAD MADE THE PHONE call to the U.S. embassy. But . . . did Rudi know anything about it? When I asked him, Rudi deflected. "When you are inside you cannot use a phone," he told me. "No, no, no, no, I have no idea about that, no." Rudi Sutopo left Cipinang in 2010, after having served six years. Harvey followed not long after, on April 11, 2011, released for good behavior three years to the week after the bomb threats to the U.S. embassy. He made his way to Rudi's house, bringing a cake and flowers for his wife. "I'm proud of you,"

Rudi told him. "You can control yourself now. You must be like this in your life." Harvey convinced the couple that he had a licensing deal involving the production and distribution of a TV series in Indonesia based on the popular Marvel character the Black Widow and asked for Rudi's financial support. Rudi forked over $29,000 plus additional money for expenses. A few weeks later, a local outlet covering entertainment published a short item titled "Black Widow Sets Her Sights on Indonesia," in which the rights to the series were said to have been sold to a production company "under the scripting and illustrations of Gobind Lal and Rudi Sutopo."

"He failed," Rudi said. "I'm not saying he cheated us—but he failed. He told us that he failed—that he failed to arrange for the licenses. And we lost the money." Rudi wasn't too bothered, he said. He knew what he was getting into with the lonely man from Cipinang. "I pitied him," he said.

HARVEY RAN OTHER SCAMS WHILE still inside Cipinang—and then still more in the years immediately after he was released. In 2011, the Spanish singer Enrique Iglesias posted a Facebook message alerting fans to a scam surrounding that year's Miss Teen Indonesia, calling it a "big fraud which was set up by crooks" and identifying one of them as a certain "Harvey Taheal." Half a dozen photographers claimed that he stole tens of thousands of dollars' worth of camera and computer gear from them over a period of months in 2012. They eventually found each other on Twitter and Facebook and posted his name alongside epithets and warnings: "sociopath," "psychopath," "criminal." By 2013 he was impersonating an Indonesian cigarette magnate named Michael Sampoerna, offering Indonesian filmmakers and actors job opportunities with DreamWorks and Paramount Pictures. One of these fake auditions led to an Indonesian actor stripping naked for a photo shoot with an Indian "producer" who spoke perfect American-accented English.

Word began to spread within Jakarta's artistic community. After his humiliation, the actor who had stripped naked told his cousin, Joko Anwar, a celebrated Indonesian director, about what had happened to him. Joko began asking around and soon learned that the imposter shared a last name with one of his friends, Yara Tahilramani. He called her in hopes of finding out more about the mysterious "Gobind" who had been tormenting his friends. "That person no longer exists in our family," Yara told Joko. She explained that he had committed crimes and alienated his family. He was an outcast. She refused to discuss it further. Then one day, Joko himself received a call. Gobind was apologetic and even solicitous. Joko was a powerful figure in Indonesian culture, celebrated as the first director who put a gay kiss on the big screen. But as soon as Joko mentioned that he had spoken to Yara, Gobind exploded. It was *he* who had cut *her* out of his life, Gobind said, and threatened to sue Joko for the transgression of calling one of his family members.

By 2013 Harvey was running the Huaxia scam that brought London-based makeup artists to Indonesia, followed by the China Film Group con that hit screenwriters from New York to Johannesburg to São Paulo. At the root of all of these many schemes was one unifying principle: impersonation. In early 2016, his bank account flush, Harvey left Indonesia again and embarked on a round-the-world vacation, visiting Thailand, Cuba, and other countries. Later that year he washed up in London on a tourist visa using a passport with the name Gobind Tahil. He told people that his name was Gavin Ambani. He didn't need to say, Yes, *that* Ambani family, whose net worth of roughly $100 billion made them the eleventh-richest family in the world. People usually figured it out on their own.

One day Gavin went to lunch with Cabin Yim, whom he had met in Thailand during his travels. Yim had also recently arrived in the United Kingdom to pursue his studies in Bristol. At thirty-seven, Gavin was roughly twice Cabin's age, and yet the younger man felt oddly paternalistic about this curious Hollywood executive with the tuft of bleached-blond hair, big ears, and the hammocking, rabbity grin. Over lunch one day at Trishna, arguably the best Indian restaurant in London, Gavin told Yim that he wanted to find a way to tell stories about food, and life, and his many adventures. Together they came up with the idea for an Instagram account. They would call it Purebytes and it would showcase Gavin's ability to tell a good story, a skill that had always impressed Yim. "Every time I have a meal with you, Gavin, there's a story for each dish," Yim said. They settled on a tagline: "Every Meal Has a Story." Purebytes debuted in August 2016, with a photograph of a fillet of smoked salmon on toast garnished with lettuce and a slice of lemon. The hashtags were crafted to lure viewers: #foodporn and #instafood. In the few pictures of himself that he posted online, Gavin looked to be in his mid-thirties, but he offered up no name or other identifying biographical information. He was a ghost, a single, pure "byte" of the digital ecosphere, one among countless millions in the great city's extravagant food culture.

Many posts revolved around food, but some images hinted at other lives, as if they had seeped in through an invisible membrane, and were haunting, even beautiful. One black-and-white photo portrayed an adult and child holding hands, dancing on an empty beach bathed in a brilliant white light, while far in the distance a nub of indistinct darkness rose like a creature from the deep. "You want to be the exception, the one to whom the rules do not apply," Gavin wrote on Purebytes one day, beneath a picture of himself in the Warrior One yoga pose. "We all do. But this boy—the one who is not governed by the rules—is already way up the road because he never noticed the rules, never wondered about them."

Gavin revealed a bit more about himself to Cabin and his girlfriend, Tania de Gomery, who had grown up with Cabin in Bangkok and was now also studying in Bristol. Gavin had attended an international school in Jakarta as a boy and then put himself through college in the U.S. He hinted that he had been taunted and shamed for being gay and teared up when describing bullying by former classmates. But America he *loved*, and his employer, Warner Bros., especially, though he couldn't say too much since "it was confidential." "I'm good at my job," he told the impressionable Cabin, who harbored his own career dreams. Throughout the winter, they saw each other often. Gavin enjoyed taking Cabin to new restaurants and when they did Gavin always picked up the bill and always paid in cash.

For a few weeks, Gavin went dark. Cabin worried that he had left London without telling him. Then one day Gavin texted from an unknown number. Where had he been? Gavin was solemn. Cancer, he replied. He was scheduled to have surgery, and might not live long. "You're my little bro," Gavin said. If things didn't work out, Cabin would inherit all his possessions. When they met up for a walk in Hyde Park, Cabin, skeptical of the story, asked to see his friend's surgical scars, but Gavin shrugged him off. "I'm fine," he said. For his birthday in May, Gavin bought Cabin a Samsung virtual reality headset. "No one has ever cared about me like you have," Gavin said. "I can trust you."

Purebytes began attracting a smattering of regular followers. Gavin tagged high-end London restaurants he frequented, like Granger & Co., Trishna, and Balthazar. Cabin, helpful to a fault, wasn't one to ask too many questions. He understood that his friend worked in Hollywood, and so it came as no great surprise when Gavin said he needed some help setting up a domain for a friend of his in LA, the producer Amy Pascal. By mid-October 2017, while the photographer Will Strathmann was stumbling blindly through banyan tree groves in Indonesia, Gavin had settled into comfortable dwellings at 3 Cyrus Street, a temporary corporate housing establishment tailor-made for the on-the-go business executive in the heart of London's tony Clerkenwell district. The spacious rooms, where "corporate travelers will want for nothing," were fully furnished, with kitchens, Wi-Fi, and unlimited nationwide telephone service.

By 2017, Purebytes was hitting its stride, giving internet foodies a glimpse into the privileged life of a London gourmand. Just three days after Will Strathmann had received his first email from his Amy

Pascal, Purebytes posted a picture of a book. On the cover, etched in energetic black and white lines, was an image of a father and his young daughter strolling hand in hand along a city sidewalk. The only spot of color was the little girl's coat—a splash of bright red. "Whether the act of kindness can be noticed or ignored, both giver and recipient are transformed by the encounter," the post read. "Explore this little girl's act of kindness through 'Sidewalk Flowers' in the #newyorktimes best illustrated children's book."

Three days later, Will Strathmann's Amy Pascal pitched him the idea of a project based on *Sidewalk Flowers*. Two weeks after that, on the same day that Will was picking up traces of vanilla in the air of Kawah Putih, a lushly forested crater lake three hours south of Jakarta, Purebytes posted a picture of Gavin grimacing under the weight of an unwieldy piece of CrossFit gear. The caption read: "Train so you can take it to a level of violence their nightmares are made of."

Gavin had more than a few quirks. He didn't use credit cards. Instead, he asked his friend Cabin to conduct commerce for him, ordering items online, which he later reimbursed via a PayPal account. By the fall of 2017, Cabin had become the de facto administrator of Purebytes. Managing the posts, and managing Gavin, had become something like a part-time job. Tania balked at Cabin's friendship with the Indonesian, or American, or whatever Gavin was—Tania wasn't quite sure. In fact, she thought there was something distinctly wrong with Gavin. His smile, a huge "plastic" ear-to-ear grin that never seemed to leave his face, even when he spoke, felt fake to her. "He's psycho," she told Cabin several times.

Dissatisfied with his limited exposure, Gavin wanted to hit the kind of epic follower count that other, more well-known food influencers in London were achieving. Cabin hired a Kathmandu-based coder and social media expert. Gavin agreed to pay him three hundred dollars a month. The coder hired third-party vendors that offered "boosts," essentially paid endorsements in the form of "likes" to the site.

When Gavin subjected one of these vendors to a screed of abuse over the phone, the vendor backed out, citing Gavin's volatility. Completely understand your coward terrorist behavior, Gavin texted him. Your mom is a terrorist and so is your fucking religion. Go fuck your mom which is common in your Islam. All the best.

In the final two months of 2017—when Will Strathmann's journey was ending and Caleb Kotner's was just beginning—Gavin went on a shopping spree. He placed multiple online orders through Cabin, reimbursing him in cash via PayPal. On December 21, he bought a "Detachable-sleeve, down-filled Puffer jacket" in cerulean blue from Burberry for 750 British pounds sterling, or roughly $1,000. He also ordered a thirteen-inch MacBook Pro, in space gray, and a one-year subscription to Microsoft Office for just over $2,300. Cabin paid for the items with his credit card and had them shipped to 3 Cyrus Street. More purchases followed in the coming days. A virgin wool and cashmere-blend roll-neck sweater, and wool-flannel trousers, both ordered from Mr Porter, followed on the twenty-second, for a total of $620. Five days later came a much larger Mr Porter order including Nike Flyknit sneakers, woven drawstring trousers from Burberry, and a tan double-breasted camel-colored and cotton-blend suit jacket from Camoshita. Cabin put that day's $2,000 bill on his card. Two days later he bought a Prince of Wales check bouclé field jacket, for close to $800. He rounded out the year with a Galiano jacket, purchased on the thirtieth. December's purchases totaled close to $7,000. Online, Gavin had continued to peddle his cancer narrative. His chances at life, he told viewers, "looked bleak."

For his part, Cabin had begun to push back a little. He told Gavin that his work for Purebytes was interfering with his relationship. In response, Gavin told Cabin he would make *sure* that the next time Tania set *foot* in London the immigration police would come knocking at her door. Cabin responded, coolly, "Don't you dare bring her into this."

There was something else: an investigator in the United States had started asking questions about Purebytes. When Cabin told Gavin about his communication with Nicole, Gavin exploded. "What did you do!" he fumed. "What did you tell them about me?"

"Look," Cabin said, trying to calm him down, "I don't get involved in other people's personal stuff."

No, said Gavin, *you* look. "You have to understand, the FBI have no jurisdiction outside the U.S.," he said. "So don't say too much. You have nothing to worry about."

But Cabin had grown worried. Disturbed by Gavin's increasingly belligerent behavior, and his refusal to pay the Nepalese coder the thousands of dollars he was owed, Cabin withdrew from his friendship with Gavin. As Cabin faded into the background, Gavin began cultivating a broader array of acquaintances, and similar patterns of lies and manipulation surfaced. The following years in the United Kingdom were marred by theft, threats, and abuse. He hired a professional photographer to shoot an elaborate cooking event and then failed to pay him the 4,000 pounds he owed. He invited himself to a cooking event but, once in, proceeded to torment the other attendees, all up-and-coming chefs, many of them immigrants or refugees, who were looking for a break. He threatened to slap and beat some of the women, prompting one of them to file a report with the Metropolitan Police, who issued a warning. The Israeli chef Yotam Ottolenghi banned Gavin from entering any of his restaurants. To one London-based Indonesian chef to whom he had promised a show that never materialized, he wrote a series of threatening messages. "You defame me in London, my solicitors will have the law chase you," he wrote. "Or I'll personally do it. Don't ever underestimate me! Go fuck yourself." He told people that he worked for Netflix and promised to secure them a deal, or that he was the chief writer and also a top executive on the TV show *American Horror Story*, or that he had just purchased celebrity chef Jamie Oliver's $11 million house in Primrose Hill, or any of dozens of other lies. At the same time, he began taking steps to cover his tracks. He stopped eating at restaurants and asked that waiters bring him his food in a takeout box instead. He didn't want to be recorded on their CCTV cameras.

JULIAN LOVICK, AN AUSTRALIAN SOMMELIER, was treated to an intimate view of Harvey, whom he knew as Gavin Ambani, that few others had. A thirty-two-year-old with bright red hair and a slight frame, Julian was an expat worker who enjoyed theater and movies. Gavin was a familiar presence at the Goodman steak house in London's exclusive Mayfair district, where Julian had worked as a sommelier for six years. One day, Gavin told Julian that he had "amazing plans" and suggested they meet. Gavin said he needed help with the photography and videography on Purebytes. Julian wasn't a professional photographer by any stretch, but it sounded fun, and he would be paid, so he agreed.

For the next two weeks, Julian and Gavin went everywhere together. Their walks around London became a confessional space. Over lunch one day, the American—Gavin told people he had been "born and raised in LA"—showed Julian naked selfies as a much larger, less fit version of himself, with one hand barely covering his crotch. They visited adult stores where Gavin perused the gay DVD section and browsed the sex toys on offer. He told Julian he was ostracized from his family because they had forced him into gay conversion therapy. Alongside a deep insecurity about his own body and his fluctuating weight he expressed a paradoxical admiration for Harvey Weinstein, with whom Gavin claimed to have interned as a younger man. Despite Weinstein's alleged crimes, Gavin looked up to him still and viewed the producer as a tragic victim of the #MeToo movement, rather than a principal cause of its inception. Gavin's entire being felt, to Julian, so strangled by the "burden" of a conflicted sexuality that it became hard to disentangle the various motives and manifestations of his behavior. On one of their first excursions to a string of restaurants on Brick Lane, in a scene that would repeat itself many times, Julian filmed Gavin as he took a huge bite of a sandwich and began to vigorously chew—only to spit it out a moment later, after the initial moment of rapture had faded.

Gavin's real home, he told Julian, was a Georgian manor in Clerkenwell, on the Cut, an artsy lane south of the Thames and behind Waterloo Station. While it was being remodeled, they spent the hours inside Gavin's temporary flat, shooting food videos and talking. With its ugly rainbow rug and pinewood coffee table, the place was spare and contained few personal belongings: a Mac laptop, an easel and whiteboard, and, in the bedroom, a wardrobe full of expensive clothes from Mr Porter. On the table in the lounge were hardcover copies of *Grimm's Fairy Tales* and *The Arabian Nights*, the latter of which Gavin said he was turning into a series for Netflix. "That's NDA, by the way," he told Julian. In the bathroom cupboard, Julian found boxes of detox teas, dietary supplements, and bottles of what looked like prescription mood stabilizers. One morning, as they lounged around the kitchen, Gavin prepared a red velvet cake from a premade box. Watching it bake in the oven, he could barely contain himself and no sooner had it begun to cool on a wire rack than Gavin tore into it with both hands, stuffing chunks into his mouth as crumbs spilled onto the floor.

One day, Gavin confessed to Julian that he no longer wished to be a virgin and asked for Julian's help in finding a suitable escort who could carry him across that threshold. Julian emailed him links to several possible candidates, and after a few dismissals Gavin eventually settled on a hirsute, broad-chested go-go dancer who worked at a local bar. Gavin told Julian he called the man but got no response, and the matter was soon dropped. What Gavin really wanted, Julian surmised, was a bit of companionship.

Gavin was not his real name, he told Julian; he used it for anonymity. One Gavin was gregarious, charming, and conscientious. He could be playful, even frivolous. And while he laughed easily, his "Jokeresque" smile stretched and faded quicker than a rubber band in a child's hand. He gave Julian clothes, including a pair of wool sweaters. Despite his fantastic wardrobe, and a pedantic habit of visiting a barber once a week, Gavin rarely wore his nicer outfits, choosing instead to don the same soiled pair of Lululemon leggings and puffy black parka. One day, as part of an ostensible photo shoot, Gavin undressed in front of Julian in his bedroom. "Don't worry," he said. "I'm not going to rape you." He stood there sullenly, clad only his underwear, waiting for Julian to photograph his clothes.

The other, more frequently seen Gavin was angry and vengeful. Strolling through London's East End, home to a large Indian population, Gavin sniffed at the darker-skinned Indians he saw around him and, under his breath, called them *kaala kaloota*, a vicious slur referencing their dark skin tone. On Chinese New Year, about two weeks into their working partnership, the pair walked into a store in Chinatown. Gavin wanted to stage a picture for Purebytes, and purchased an iced pink cake shaped like a pig whose face was scripted in delicate black frosting. But when the pig's face got smudged and Julian offered to pay for another one, Gavin's mood darkened and he took Julian outside. As they stood in a dark alleyway, with Gavin holding the iced pig aloft, he proceeded to dress the Australian down. "You're fucked!" he shouted. "You're never going to work. I'm going to ruin you. I'm going to *destroy* you!" No sooner had the storm erupted than it seemed to pass. "That's not me," Gavin assured his friend. "Don't worry, we won't talk about it again."

Julian had been half-expecting the outburst. Two months earlier, he had traveled home to Australia for a wedding and while there he had arranged to have a reading with a psychic. At first the psychic, using a deck of Tarot cards, had foretold a generally rosy outlook for the sommelier. Then she turned to the third card in the lineup, a horned and clawed devil holding a naked man and a woman in chains, and her tone shifted. She sensed the imminent arrival in Julian's life of a dark and manipulative presence, a "person who is a bully, who is a narcissist" proffering attractive work opportunities as a way to ensnare Julian in a potentially dangerous trap. "Avoid this person with the narcissistic dominant personality," she said. It was possible that he, Julian, would find ways to work amiably with this figure, but other, less fortunate souls might be taken advantage of. She warned him to be mindful.

The devil, she noted, was "coming in upright," which indicated a type that played "nasty games" and "twisted everything around," she said.

Shortly after the kerfuffle over the iced pig on Chinese New Year, Gavin told Julian he wanted to put him in touch with a Hollywood producer he knew, Patrick Markey, an executive at Escape Artists. An email introduction soon followed, but Julian grew suspicious when Gavin seemed to know about the contents of his communications with Markey despite having been removed from the email chain. The Indonesian man's strange behavior became a constant topic of conversation among Julian's friends, and they speculated endlessly about whether Gavin was "sociopathic." He told Julian he had cancer—testicular, liver, and pancreatic—depending on the day, and his occasional talk of suicide, which landed somewhere between a sob story and a power play, felt to Julian just inauthentic enough that he was comfortable dismissing it. Gavin's need for Julian's attention was constant but also temporally defined, ending every day around 2 p.m., when New York and Los Angeles were waking, and Gavin began to pay more attention to his iPhone.

His workday, he explained, had begun.

Julian still hadn't been paid, even though Gavin had sent him receipts from HSBC bank that purported to show wire transfers. One day as they sat in Gavin's apartment, Julian demanded payment. Gavin balked and, later, sent a flurry of texts. Julian, he wrote, was "abusive" and "not worth a single bit of cash." He urged him to drop whatever ambitions he had of becoming an actor and to pick up his dog's "poo" instead. You are absolutely shit, Gavin wrote. I don't need u. Never did!!!!! When the wire transfers failed to materialize, Julian called the police. Two officers took his statement but told him that without any evidence of physical assault, there was little they could do. Then Julian filed a claim against Gavin in small claims court for roughly $3,600. Gavin responded in writing to dispute Julian's claims, but when the court ordered an arbitration process he never showed up and a judge ultimately ruled in Julian's favor. Gavin never paid him.

By the fall of 2020, the many layers of Gavin's, aka Harvey's, life were falling away, leaving him exposed and increasingly unstable. Earlier that year he had messaged an American woman he had met twenty years before in Jakarta who remembered him clearly as the guy who had once scammed her out of some furniture. "I apologize for what I did," he had written, blaming his past behavior on his poor treatment at the hands of an uncle whose kids, he fumed, were "fat, useless and soon to be deceased." By October, as his forty-first birthday approached, his tone with her changed. "You're an idiot," he wrote. He called her a slut, accused her of "fucking" her way to the top, and vowed to bring her and her family down. "I'll shut up for now," he wrote. "But this is my focus. . . . Nothing," he concluded, "[n]o one can stop me."

The world around him had also changed. A year and a half of Covid had largely shut down international travel, depriving him of a significant share of his revenue stream. The virus had decimated the restaurant business, which, while it didn't translate into money for Harvey, was nevertheless the lifeblood of Purebytes, the excuse for his hovering presence on the food scene. A lawsuit and a possible criminal investigation by the Metropolitan Police had driven him out of London to Manchester. Thirteen years after Harvey first popped up on the FBI's radar, followed by years during which the same agency repeatedly dismissed a mounting series of complaints about him, the G-men were now, once again, close on his heels.

Chapter 10

Stories unravel. They fray and tear, and the lives they hold come unglued. But new stories always emerge to replace them. Since her time on the debate circuit in Southern California, Harvey's former tutor Amber Wormington had married and was living in Hastings, Nebraska. Four years passed. One day in 2003, her husband told her that someone "really weird" had repeatedly called her, a woman named Alison Fisher, who she had since learned was Harvey's friend from Bradley, the one he had pushed down the stairs. When the phone next rang, Amber answered. "Hargobind," she said, using the given name of which he had been so ashamed, "why are you pretending to be Alison Fisher?" There was no answer and then the line went dead. Shortly after, "Alison Fisher" started calling Amber's sister. For months, the phone rang every day at 11 a.m. The calls were so regularly timed, and so consistent, that there could be only one explanation, the sisters concluded. Harvey must be living in some sort of an institution, permitted to call the most important people in his life only at a certain hour.

At this point, Amber still thought of Harvey as a "little broken baby bird." With time, however, the story of his daily intrusion in her sister's midday routine grew into a different kind of story, a tale to be told at parties to great effect, the "spooky story of Alison Fisher, a true-life ghost story."

ONE OF THE REASONS THE story the screenwriter Gregory Mandarano had been sold was so convincing was that it was embedded within a long tradition of *other* stories. And not just any stories, but the centuries-old origin stories that undergirded much of Indonesia's history. The Ramayana and the Mahabharata, for instance, were two of Hinduism's foundational, epic Sanskrit texts. Written by the Indian poet Valmiki somewhere between the fifth and first centuries BCE, the Ramayana tells the story of the fourteen-year journey of a stately prince, Rama, who, having been banished from the Kosala Kingdom by his father and stepmother, travels the forests for years before embarking on a heroic return to claim the throne. Composed of some 24,000 verses, it is one of the longest poems in world literature, alongside other sagas like *The Odyssey* and *The Tale of Genji*. The story is set in what is now Uttar Pradesh, where the Ganges and Yamuna Rivers join in northern India. As Hinduism grew over the centuries, extending its reach eastward, the poems wound their way into the fabric of other East Asian societies, including Indonesia's, evolving but also cleaving along the way.

Perhaps because Indonesia is a fragmented land of several thousand islands, the mythology morphed repeatedly. On the island of Java, another version of the Ramayana story took shape. It was called the Kakawin Ramayana and recounted the tale of a massacre by Ravana, a demonic Hindu deity. This Javanese story also incorporated much of the island's preexisting mythology, including the powerful Javanese demigod Semar, a *punokawan*, or wise clown, who appeared in bas-reliefs and sculptures as a flat-nosed man with a lazy eye and a bulging belly who doles out counsel and spiritual advice to peasants.

Ninth-century artists carved elaborate scenes from yet another version, called the Ramakavaca, on temples at Prambanan in the Javanese city of Yogyakarta. The story unspooled by Balinese *kecak* dancers showcases the original Ramayana characters, now two millennia old:

Rama and his wife Sita; her ravaging by Ravana; the Hindu monkey god Hanuman burning the deity Lanka in a sacrificial fire. More than a thousand years later, the same vivid traditions that shaped the moral world of these ancient societies are still practiced today.

This was the world that the grinning, green-haired American producer Anand Sippy wanted Greg Mandarano and Jay Shapiro, "the boys," to understand. He encouraged them to explore the mythology on their own, so that they could create more authentic characters. Their script would in a sense be a retelling of those ancient myths, just as the writers themselves would be modern-day channels for bards long dead. What did this mythical exploration look like? In a few short months, in 2015, Greg and Jay traveled from New York to Indonesia six times and took another thirty-six internal flights. Bali's Ubud Monkey Forest, a set of stone ruins now home to a community of more than a thousand long-tailed macaques, became the setting for one story line of the sci-fi extravaganza; a trip to the Buddhist temple at Borobudur became another. Greg relayed his thoughts about how specific plot points could be paired with certain locations. "We see the ideal 'front' for Vivian's boarding school as buildings in the Batavia Old Quarters," Greg wrote. "Especially the Red Shop which is quite visually striking." In another email, Greg observed that "the monkeys from the Ramayana were builders, so it stands to reason their architecture would be striking, from bridges and treehouses, to their village center." Shaped by these excursions, and informed by the myths, *Shadows Beyond* began to take shape. One action sequence referenced the Mendut Temple, a ninth-century Buddhist site in Java.

Even as the myths of Indonesia were winding their way into *Shadows Beyond*, another kind of myth was taking shape within Gregory himself. When he was still stuck inside the scam, and blind to its existence, the story he told himself was that he was a screenwriter on a fantastic creative journey. After completing *Shadows Beyond*, he wrote another script, *Chameleon of the Mind*, a biopic of the criminal mastermind who had duped him. If that wasn't meta enough, he also broadcast the writing of it, live, on the gaming platform Twitch. In the years to come, he spoke about the deception at every opportunity, participating in news shows, a documentary, and two different podcasts. In the story of his life, the scam became an orienting pole, as important as other major milestones. He was someone who had been deceived, a victim of an elaborate ruse, but ultimately a storyteller who could turn tragedy into gold.

In the beginning, Mandarano had expressed admiration and even awe at what his deceiver had been able to achieve. It had been a feat of spectacular creativity, a virtuoso display. As the years went on, his view began to change and, in the end, he felt disappointed—not so much by what he had suffered, but by what the scammer had failed to achieve. As a character in one of Gregory's screenplays, Harvey could use his grifting talents to perform some truly ingenious, worthy crimes. If only the truth had been different, he might have created "something of value."

IT WASN'T JUST THE SUBSTANCE of the myths that provided ballast for the scam. The scam fed off the precepts of myth itself. These were heroes' journeys, epic adventures. The fantasy of ancient tales wasn't always the bait. Some of the stories had a more contemporary hue. For one photographer—her name was Jessie Evans—it was the promise of adventure that captured her imagination. *She* was to be Odysseus, venturing across wine-dark seas and into the heart of Indonesia. *Her* Wendi Murdoch had identified right away that Jessie's hard-won self-image as brave and intrepid was also her greatest vulnerability. Jessie wanted to see herself as a daredevil and Murdoch obliged. To cement her position as Jessie's mentor and advocate, Harvey-as-Murdoch created another alter ego named Aaron, Wendi's assistant, who served to reinforce Jessie's trust in Wendi as well as her own self-perception.

Wendi Murdoch did seem to *get* Jessie. "You're such an adventurer," she told the younger woman. "I feel like the age of the explorer has changed so much. The magic of just going and getting lost seems to be gone." She admired Jessie's bravery; it was why she wanted to send her into the wilds. Murdoch, like Jessie, lamented that the romance of the wide-open world and its lost places was an evanescing dream; with such few wonders left to discover, perhaps Jessie would be the one to find them. Jessie, who *is* in fact adventurous, found her own, well-deserved self-conception confirmed, and in the luster of Murdoch's endorsement, it glowed even brighter. This trip to Indonesia was an audition of sorts. If it worked out, her photographs would be showcased in an exhibition. Jessie reminded Wendi of herself, the older woman said, bold and intelligent, a risk taker, drawn to history's grand dramas. Aaron lived in a bubble, she lamented, and didn't understand how the world really worked.

Jessie was not yet thirty years old and her life until that point hadn't been particularly conventional. She had been an orphan. Her adoptive parents were David and Jeanie Evans, close friends of Rupert Murdoch and his second wife, Anna. The family owned a home in the Hollywood Hills, nestled at one end of a huge yard where scorpions lurched amid the sun-blasted rocks and coyotes yipped at night. Every summer day, she and her father swam and frolicked in the pool, but most hours she spent at Jeanie's side. Her parents entertained frequently and on those nights the dreams that overcame her, in a bedroom at the top of a set of winding stairs, were infused with the scents of candles and the sounds of carousing adults below. When she was eight her parents moved, purchasing Steve McQueen's house in a Malibu cul-de-sac bordering a concrete hill. On the other side lived the actor Michael Madsen, who would later star as "Mr. Blonde" in Quentin Tarantino's *Reservoir Dogs*. At the time David was CEO of the Hallmark Channel and traveled for work constantly; Jessie, too, longed to travel, and read Philip Pullman's Northern Lights books, which kindled a passion for the Arctic and the fantasy of far-off lands. Often, at the Malibu house, she and her mother eyed Madsen with fascination and fear, wondering if the stories they had heard about the Chinese loan sharks were true. Madsen called Jeanie to tell her she'd be sorry if she touched his house, so Jeanie kept her daughter inside. One day the girl watched from a window as Madsen walked a leashed tiger on the beach, the snapping paparazzi close behind.

But Indonesia tested her in new ways. In a village at the top of a mountain, Jessie stepped into a heat-enveloped world that seemed to stretch back in time. Young women wove baskets alongside a river system lined with thatched huts. Nearby was a tidal pool in which there sat a goanna, a large and ancient predatory scavenging lizard whose poisonous saliva, sharp teeth, and curved claws were perfectly suited to rip and tear at carrion. On another day, Mr. Rusdi took her to a wet market. She hoped it might be like the Seguchi Fish Market in Tokyo, and was disappointed to find a run-down commercial fishing dock. In ankle-high Converse sneakers she scrambled around rubble to a break-water swarming with mangy kittens and a hut where seawater lapped at the bare feet of the men and women eating inside. It looked like a war zone. Rocking gently in the waters were huge wooden vessels painted in fading reds and blues like the boats that, when they weren't sinking or running aground, had brought refugees from Indonesia to Australia.

Looking around at the crumbling jetties, she was overcome with a visceral sense of darkness, certain that human traffickers had stood where she now stood, that someone fleeing for safety had passed by this very spot. Later, in a garage-like market, Jessie watched chain-smoking men behead chickens with *golok* machetes and fling the bodies into a pile, covering the floor with blood and guts. On her last day, Mr. Rusdi took her to a Chinese cemetery filled with ornate headstones. "Dead Chinese, dead Chinese," he said, pointing to every single one. "Chinese people think you take money when you die. You cannot." He laughed, that same awful hack—Jessie called it a "cackle"—that Will Strathmann, the drone operator and photographer, had remarked upon.

On the way to the airport, Mr. Rusdi asked if he could show her something. It was a Sunday and there was no traffic. They drove over a long bridge to a housing development, newly constructed but abandoned. It was the Chinese, he told her glumly. For weeks, pursuing

Wendi Murdoch's vision, they had been driving around looking at artifacts and cultural sites that were, ostensibly, also Chinese: a cave in Buniayu, a cemetery, an archaeological dig. But the bleakness of this abandoned housing development, and Mr. Rusdi's solemn insistence on showing it to her, felt more authentically Chinese than anything else she had seen thus far. Rusdi drove very slowly, and when they reached the middle of the bridge again, he stopped the car and they both got out and walked to the edge. He pointed at the city, and then at a plane overhead, and then at Jessie. "Take you home," he said.

Once again she left, but within days she was on her way back to Indonesia. During a layover in Singapore, she opened her email and saw that a friend had sent her a blog post written by another photographer. It told of an elaborate scam targeting photographers traveling around Indonesia. She took one look at the pictures accompanying the post—of Mr. Rusdi, of the permits, of emails—and knew right away. She sank into a chair in the Qantas lounge and drank four Old Fashioned cocktails one after another, straight down the hatch. She called her boyfriend. It was 3 a.m. in Newfoundland.

"I'm fine," she said. And then she broke down.

Jessie remembered her travels as an epic journey because taken together they had been. She would return home broken, but in time she would rebuild.

Most scams are designed to allow a grifter access into a victim's home—and usually their bank accounts. It is the grifter who enters, while the victim remains passive. But the Con Queen worked in reverse. He lured people into his mind, but *out* of their own homes, and ultimately halfway around the world to his homeland, Indonesia, a country and a culture that the vast majority of them had never much thought about. There, suddenly and unexpectedly, the myths and legends of Indonesia's 17,500 islands, along with the physical landscape itself, became the arenas for their personal journeys as well as their exploitation. He had lured them out of their own story and into his own.

The farther afield they roamed, and the longer they stayed lost, the better this spell seemed to work. Again and again victims told Nicole about the myths and folklore they had been asked to explore, be it the Chinese tradition of window flowers, the ancient Hindu myths, or the proliferation of Chinatowns around the world. The mythical tableau available to him was immense.

Long ago, even before Hinduism and Buddhism had begun to spread across the archipelago, the animist people of the Sundanese empire who inhabited the southern shores of modern-day Java lived in awe of Queen Kidul, a goddess who ruled over the demons and deities of the sea. Over the centuries, her powers became associated with natural fertility and agriculture. In later Sundanese folklore, she was reanimated as Dewi Kadita, a princess from the ancient fortified city of Pajajaran. Having been struck down by a ravaging skin disease, the result of a witch's curse, Dewi Kadita fled to the sea, where she was rejuvenated and crowned as a spirit of the tumultuous deep, purveyor of tsunamis and storms.

As myth spread, this once and future queen would respond to many other names and appear in multiple forms, a spindly grandmother, a bewitching daughter, each a reflection of a time and place, each the result of a distinct origin story. Across the archipelago, deities often gained or lost influence among worshippers as beliefs changed or new strains of thought emerged. They morphed into other gods, or were subsumed by more influential stories and traditions. The queen, whose "ambiguous, vacillating nature," as one scholar described it, contained both demonic and benevolent aspects, also adapted.

With time, the name for all of these divine beings was distilled into one all-encompassing honorific, Nyai Loro Kidul, the Queen of the Southern Seas. It was said she could take the soul of anyone she wished, though she had a special fondness for visitors, particularly handsome young men. She appeared in different forms, and was able to shapeshift multiple times in a single day. Frequently portrayed as a mermaid, she had also been associated with snakes, self-rejuvenating old women, and the underworld. The ancient cities that had given rise to the Queen of the Southern Seas became, in Harvey's hands, waypoints for travelers whom he had coaxed into the open. He transformed the cities that Nyai Loro Kidul had at times called home—Bogor, Yogyakarta, and Solo, as well as the many fishing ports along the southern coasts of Java where she is still worshipped today—into traps, just as the Queen of the Southern Seas had beckoned visitors, whose souls she coveted, to her underworld kingdom. At Harvey's direction, Will Strathmann and many other victims had visited every one of Nyai Loro Kidul's spiritual domains.

The fake work projects Harvey designed enabled him to exploit people's genuine interest in the intricacies of the world: Greg Mandarano's mythical sci-fi extravaganza; Will Strathmann's journey of the lost girl modeled on *Sidewalk Flowers*; Jessie Evans's pursuit of China's historical influence. The list went on and on. Not everyone became a traveler, but those who did soon found themselves lost to these tides of history, drifting in a dream not their own.

PART III

The Entity

What is dark within me, illumine.

—John Milton, *Paradise Lost*

Chapter 11

For more than two years, Purebytes had been a roving, restless enterprise and Harvey hopscotched all over the United Kingdom. He spent time in Edinburgh, Scotland, and then Leeds; in Manchester, and of course London. He went for weeks and months without visiting the same city, much less the same restaurant, and often pretended to be places he wasn't. Whether that was a deliberate attempt to foil would-be snoops, or whether he just enjoyed the deceit, was hard to say; more than likely, it was both. For a long time, I tried to establish contact with him via telephone, WhatsApp, and emails, but he never responded.

Then one day in the fall of 2020, Harvey resurfaced in a very public way. As was the case with so much about his life, a clue emerged from social media. In early September, an Instagram account belonging to an Indonesian influencer named Haseena Bharata published a fresh video on her Instagram Live video feed. Wearing a blue and pink floral-patterned dress and holding what looked like a cocktail in one hand, she told viewers that a "very special, special guest" would soon be joining her. She described him as a "survivor" who had overcome great difficulties. Her cohost then read aloud from the guest's prepared statement. Viewers learned that it had taken a lifetime to summon the courage to plumb the painful memories of his childhood, but he was now prepared to share his darkest secrets with the world. Describing Harvey as a "family friend," Haseena was midsentence when suddenly his video feed connected and he appeared on the bottom half of her split screen. Dressed in a black baseball cap and a loose black T-shirt, Harvey looked trim and fit. His wide grin bisected a beard flecked with gray. He was seated in front of a window with a view onto a cityscape of high-rises, parks, and apartments, but his face took up most of the screen. She asked him how he was doing. "Fabulous!" he crowed, in an American accent.

Haseena had a complicated past with her former schoolmate. They had grown up together, attended the same schools and gatherings. Their families were friends, and yet Haseena was cautious. A few years earlier, Harvey had asked her to arrange a driver for a "friend" who was coming to Indonesia. It sounded sketchy and she refused. When he asked if she needed anything from London, she sent him some money for cosmetics. He kept the money but sent her nothing. The truth was, Haseena wanted something from her old classmate. Harvey had privately confided that he was gay, and she hoped he would come out publicly on her show, which she was trying to position as a progressive voice in an otherwise conservative landscape.

The interview lasted thirty minutes. Haseena asked about his struggles as a young man. Harvey told her he'd been bullied, smeared, ridiculed—for being fat, or uninterested in sports, for being effeminate— but he had escaped Indonesia and, thanks to an immigration attorney, was thriving as a newly minted citizen of the United Kingdom. When she asked if he had ever sought out therapy, he returned to his youth in Indonesia, and said he'd been subjected to forced gay conversion therapy, even though he himself wasn't gay. "I'm not *banci*," he said, repeating the antigay slur he said his classmates had called him. "I'm not gay, there you go." Toward the end of the interview, Haseena asked how he liked London and he gazed at the skyline behind him. He loved it, he said.

"There was a lot of bullshit," Haseena said later.

I HADN'T LEFT MY HOME for months by that point. The pandemic was raging, with seemingly random global spikes. India was in the grips of a Covid meltdown, with thousands of deaths every day. In the United States, 200,000 people had died. The United Kingdom was particularly hard hit, with more than 40,000 deaths. Not a single vaccine had been produced, and while the pharmaceutical companies were hard at work, even by the rosiest estimates I would have to wait for at least another nine months before I would be eligible to receive one. I had started feeling a little panicky. In February, the very same month the first Covid cases began to spread in the United States, I had lost my job. I had a mortgage to pay and a family to feed. I couldn't go anywhere or do much of anything to further the reporting of the story I was pursuing. I was stuck. What I needed was to talk to Harvey. And suddenly, there he was—that is, there he was on a screen.

Searching for him five thousand miles away in the middle of a pandemic seemed like a terrible proposition. It was unlikely that I would ever locate him, and even if I did, it was even less likely that he would talk to me. The risk of infection from Covid was serious. When I began to read about the rules the United Kingdom had implemented, my heart sank further. Travelers had to quarantine for two weeks upon arrival. Anyone caught violating the rules was subject to deportation and a hefty fine. Without an address, the only option was to traipse around looking for Harvey in a crowd of masked people. I had never before gone in search of a person under such circumstances. Nevertheless, I began to toy with the idea. I considered telling Nicole, and then thought better of it.

Harvey had participated in the interview using a cell phone that he held up, selfie-style, and the washed-out sky behind him cast him into shadow. He was seated in front of a window in a relatively tall building.

Just behind him, if one looked carefully, was a balcony with several black wicker chairs and potted plants. In the far distance there was a tall white building with what looked like a large black stripe running down one side, while the closest buildings were shorter, in an older style, with red brick and gabled windows. I took screenshots of the most clearly visible background features. I also grabbed several screenshots from Instagram Stories he had posted from what looked like the same location. In the background of one of those pictures there was a silver skyscraper with the words CITY TOWER emblazoned across the top. He had told Haseena that he was in London. I spent a long time looking at maps to see if any of the views in my screenshots matched the London cityscape. But the City Tower London looked nothing like the one in the picture I had. Then again, Harvey was an inveterate liar. So I looked for City Towers in other places Harvey had visited and the only building that matched was the thirty-story skyscraper that rose up from the heart of the Piccadilly Gardens district, in a city that lay more than two hundred miles to the northwest of London, Manchester.

Over the years I had gathered dozens of pictures of Harvey—some from Purebytes, others from people who knew him. I sent a few of these to a friend, Jon, who had grown up in Manchester. I had chosen recent ones in which the background was visible. After university, Jon had spent several years working in Manchester's Northern Quarter, a once-gritty neighborhood that had begun to gentrify in recent years. Jon thought one of the buildings in the photos looked familiar, but he couldn't quite put his finger on it. We agreed to talk again later.

When Jon got back to me the next day, he sounded excited. It had hit him: in the lower right-hand corner of one picture was a small but distinct patch of grass bordered by wrought iron fencing. For six years, Jon had worked in a building directly across the street from that very patch, on Dray Street. He hadn't recognized it at first because the perspective was backward. Harvey had taken the video as a selfie, which had reversed the orientation; what appeared on the right in the picture was actually on the left.

There was only one building in the vicinity tall enough to offer the perspective seen in the photos, one that included the tall white tower, the park, and the red building. That was the Light Boutique ApartHotel, at 20 Church Street. Accommodations like these were to be found all over the United Kingdom. Part hotel, part apartment, they were equally suitable for the needs of a short-term visitor or the corporate client.

I felt like I was at a crossroads. I had stumbled across as solid a location for Harvey as I was likely to find. Given Harvey's peripatetic nature, there was a chance he was no longer at the Light ApartHotel; the one advantage of Covid, however, was that everyone's movements had been circumscribed. I hemmed and hawed until finally Ali said, "You have to go." She gave me a 20 percent chance of success. (She actually put it at closer to 10 percent.) I booked a room in the Light ApartHotel and in the final days of October 2020, I boarded a British Airways flight bound for London.

The airport was eerily quiet. Covid rates were spiking in the United States and the situation was equally dire in the United Kingdom. After an eleven-hour journey on a nearly empty plane, I touched down at Heathrow on the morning of the twenty-ninth and took a train to Manchester. I checked in that afternoon around 5 p.m. To my surprise, the city's streets were full, the shops mostly open. The Light ApartHotel offered me a suite, with Wi-Fi, a spacious kitchen, a bedroom and lounge area, each with a TV, and a small balcony. I recognized the interior from the photos Harvey had posted. It might have been the exhaustion, but it felt sad and lonely. What I hadn't expected was the hotel's most striking feature: wall-to-wall glass in every room, a fishbowl perched seventeen stories above the city.

HAVING COME ALL THIS WAY, I had locked myself into a search that I wasn't sure I even wanted to undertake. I had to face the possibility that Harvey was a dangerous person. Confronting someone who doesn't want to talk to you is never pleasant; the idea of confronting a suspected criminal with a known potential for violence was nerve-racking. I felt sick to my stomach.

That first night, I went for a walk. I recalled the conversations I had had with Lia, whom you'll hear more about in a few pages, an old acquaintance of Harvey's in Jakarta who believed he was spiritually precocious. Whatever gifts of human perception he possessed were eclipsed by a more elemental force. "He has a story in his head and he cannot define what is true and what is wrong," she told me one night in a wandering conversation that lasted more than an hour. "He is lost in his own story." In response to my questions, she had tried again and again over many months to describe his effect on people. He was, she believed, a dark malignancy in semi-humanoid form, glomming on to souls and retching in their dreams.

"You know Gollum," she said at last.

"Who?"

"Gollum."

She sighed, and it was as if she had finally found the words, the word, she had been looking for. I imagined the slinking torturer of Hobbits from *The Lord of the Rings*, whose garbled exhortations and huge, wild eyes mapped fittingly onto the man I was now chasing. I pictured the iconic scene from the *Lord of the Rings* trilogy in which Gollum talks to his former self, the Hobbit known as Smeagol, as they conspire to seize control of the all-powerful ring. It was a depiction of utter insanity, a cleaving of the psyche.

Rain sliced through the air and store windows glowed in luminous emptiness. I wandered into a corner shop for food. Security guards were stationed at the entrance, next to hand sanitizers and mask dispensers. In this landscape, where everyone was already half-disguised anyway, the threat of the virus seemed to be making all of us even more suspicious. All of this was strange.

I awoke to a gray and cold morning. I spent some time trying to figure out where I was situated in relation to the perspectives I had seen online. My suite, 1701, was located on the west side of the building, with a partial view of the City Tower. If the calculations Jon and I had made were correct, Harvey's room was on the opposite side of the building. Looking out a hallway window, I saw that just two floors below there was a balcony with similar décor to those in the screenshots and in Haseena's video interview with Harvey. Still, I had to find the east-facing rooms, which I had learned were reserved for long-term guests. After studying the pictures and comparing them to the view from my own suite, I figured that Harvey wasn't on the seventeenth floor, or on the two floors above me, either. He was likely to be lower down. The fifteenth floor was too far down, it turned out. It had to be the sixteenth floor. There, on the other end of the hallway, was a door: room 1603.

The elevator doors pinged and a member of the cleaning staff emerged. Dragging her cart of supplies, she headed for room 1603. I waited in the elevator bay with my ear to the wall. From around the corner, I heard her knock and a voice, indistinct, but to my ears male and nasal, ushered her in. I crept closer. Though I couldn't make out the words, the two appeared to be holding an animated conversation, like old friends. As I inched my way along the wall, heart pounding, I marveled at the preposterousness of my situation. I saw the whole scene as if from above, a skulking, masked figure lurking outside a hotel room. If he had suddenly opened the door at that moment, I wasn't sure what I would even say.

I was in the sort of choose-your-own-adventure story that I sometimes invented for my children while lying on the floor in the dark of their room, listening to their shallow breaths and innocent questions as they tried hard not to fall asleep: *How big was the dragon? As big as our house?* As a kid, I had played Dungeons & Dragons with abandon, and in some ways, it felt as though I were right back there, chasing a monster. I knew that I was tempting something, placing myself so close to the door; I was acutely aware of the potential danger and transgression of prying into the deep recesses of someone else's life.

But I also realized that I wasn't yet ready to knock.

For one thing, I didn't know what he was truly capable of. He had pushed at least one woman down a set of stairs. He had threatened worse to others: death and maiming and bombing. He had been convicted and sent to prison on a terrorism-related charge. His own family was terrified of him. What would prevent him from attacking me? Or—and this prospect felt even more devastating—slamming the door in my face? Better to confront him in public, where either of those options would be much harder. Harvey would have to leave his room eventually. I quietly retreated to my own room.

MANCHESTER WAS AN ODE TO the damp. If it was not raining, it had either just done so or would again very soon. I sought shelter among the twenty-five thousand volumes inside the Portico Library, on Mosley Street, whose archives chronicled Manchester's rise at the height of the Industrial Revolution and England's colonial expansion over more than four and a half centuries. Harvey had visited once and posted about it on Purebytes. In an exhibit called *The "Strangers Book"* were handwritten records of "mountaineers, paleontologists, Irish cavalry officers and Napoleonic war luminaries." One library visitor, in 1840, was the "Storm King," James Pollard Espy, a controversial American meteorologist who believed that the pollution caused by Manchester's factories was in part responsible for its mighty rainfall, a conclusion that wound up in his book, *The Philosophy of Storms*. Espy also recommended burning six hundred miles of oak and hickory forests in Appalachia to produce rain along the Eastern Seaboard of the United States, prompting an American senator to wonder that if Espy "possesses the power of causing rain, he may also possess the power of withholding it." When eventually I wandered outside, the crowds seemed indifferent to the downpour. In that flow of human traffic, where a call to prayer for Allah mingled with the Muzak emanating from Boots or Primark, the incitement to buy might just as well have come from a drug dealer, a silver merchant, or a snaggle-toothed, bell-tolling vampire on early Halloween charity duty.

The throngs on Market Street surged, blowing by in the streets like embers from a great bonfire. Humans in streams, sometimes holding their breath, dodged each other in both directions, rushing toward life and away from each other, and then back again the other way just as fast.

LIA ANANTA, A SUCCESSFUL FASHION designer, was one of Harvey's oldest acquaintances in Jakarta. She had been on the receiving end of his vitriol, but had maintained a cordial distance and had even encouraged him when others seemed not to, somehow unruffled by his verbal onslaughts. He seemed to hold her in high regard while she had concluded that the man she had always known as Gobind was possessed of a dark prowess. She described him as an "indigo."

The term *indigo children*, coined by a self-described synesthete and psychologist, Nancy Ann Tappe, was first popularized in 1970s-era New Age circles. It referred to children who were purported to possess unusual and sometimes paranormal powers, such as telepathy or mind-reading. Adherents believed that an entire generation of children with these unusual skills was being born as a sort of cosmic antidote to a sick human society. The idea enjoyed a resurgence with a series of books and films in the late 1990s even as it was dismissed as junk science.

Like so many others, Lia had heard the lies about Harvey's famous film producer father, his house in London. He had bragged to her about his bomb threats to the U.S. embassy, which she told him were "crazy" and about which he had laughed, because the whole thing had been a "joke." When his mood darkened, she described it as a "black cloud and then there's thunder everywhere, and when it becomes rolling, he can't stop." Somewhere from within that vortex there emerged what Lia described as a sixth sense, some ability he possessed to "see the future" and to "create vibrations." What this translated to, she tried to explain to me, was an ability to read people's emotions, to see when they were angry, or calm, or scared. "He can feel it," she said. "It's scary, of course, because he can terrorize anyone anytime."

Her characterization felt vague and ill-defined, at least at first. To "terrorize" was to act within a very specific set of parameters; only the bomb threats to the U.S. embassy in Jakarta seemed to clearly fit the bill. It took me time to understand the complexity of what Lia was describing. But her words were prescient. Dozens of people removed in space and time by decades and thousands of miles, and with no knowledge of one another, repeatedly reached for the same words to describe the damage Harvey had wreaked on their lives.

An in-law of Harvey's whom I managed to reach in Singapore became so upset that he hung up on me. Several expressed concern that I was somehow in league with Harvey. One of his cousins, in New York, said he believed I might even *be* Harvey, and needed proof otherwise before he would speak to me. He never did. I had yet to find a single person who called Harvey a true friend or spoke lovingly of him. The kindest among them, like his high school friend Atik, pitied him. Most were scared of him.

Now the terrorist was essentially on the lam. Though he had raised his head briefly, he remained in hiding—hiding from his victims and hiding from his trackers, from the law and from his own past. His passport was no longer good. Certain countries and certain cities were now unavailable to him. And while he may not have realized it yet, he was not only hunted but trapped.

I RETURNED TO THE HOTEL around noon and sank into a lounge chair in the lobby. Two receptionists discussed the ravages of a Covid peak seventeen hundred miles to the east, in Romania, where a few days earlier scientists had captured six Eurasian wolves on camera in the Tarcău forest district of Transylvania. Several times the elevator dinged or the entrance to the street swung open and I glanced up; a young couple exited and strolled past, arm in arm. Eventually rain began to fall again. I had been sitting near reception for over an hour when the elevator sounded again. Before I had a chance to look up, I heard a voice. It was upbeat, slightly nasal, more middle American than not, and punctuated by a high-pitched and forceful laugh. "Yeah, let me know," he said. "Yeah?" Like a scent, the voice hung in the air. I still hadn't looked up but there was no doubt who was speaking. I glanced over and saw a man wearing a black baseball cap, black leggings, black athletic shoes, and a dark green overcoat.

On his way out he looked in my direction. I watched him go, then swept out the door after him. By the time I spotted him again, he had already reached the corner of High Street. I stayed back, not wanting to get too close. He was close to six feet tall, with broad, sloping shoulders; a green and white Marks & Spencer shopping bag dangled from his left hand. His feet splayed slightly outward and his gait was even and measured, the pace of a man of purpose. He seemed to be moving just a fraction slower than the crowd, as if waiting to gauge its intentions before entering its fray. He moved west along Church Street past the outstretched hand of a homeless man and the Northern Soul's Grilled Cheese shop playing Beak and Donald Byrd, on toward the T-junction where the train passed by, and there he stopped for a moment.

It was one thirty in the afternoon, past lunchtime, and the day was as bright as it would get. Sunlight refracted in pale sprays off the city's glass, and water sluiced down drains and pipes, onto windowsills. After looking both ways he crossed the street and headed west. I stayed on the east side to parallel him, the way it's done in spy thrillers. But then to my dismay I saw that he was heading into the entrance of the Arndale mall, an enormous building with hundreds of shops. I tried quickly to cross but as I stepped out into the street a bus crowded into the lane, forcing me back onto the sidewalk. By the time I ran around he had disappeared inside. The giant red building had swallowed the Con Queen whole.

I spent two hours scouring the mall, circling it three times—twice on the upper floors and once on the lower—but he had vanished. The window of opportunity was shrinking. That night, carousers on the eighteenth floor kept me awake and littered the roof's astroturfed terraces with McDonald's wrappers, chicken nuggets, and soda cans. I

lost myself in the doom of the BBC and successive episodes of *Law &
Order: Special Victims Unit.*

The next morning, I took up my position on a wooden bench under
the awning of a sandwich shop to watch the entrance. Harvey appeared
just after 1 p.m., as he had the day before. This time I managed to stay
on his tail and followed him through the mall and out the other side
to a Marks & Spencer on Main Street. As I waited, trying to remain
inconspicuous, Amisha's words of caution rang in my ears. "Please,"
she had written, "it is very important to stay away from this individual.
Don't fall into his trap of superficiality and pity. He's like a riptide that
comes at you and just when you think you can swim, you drown." Ten
minutes later, having purchased some groceries, he retraced his steps
to 20 Church Street and disappeared.

Inspired, I returned to the mall and bought myself some groceries
and, while I was at it, a white orchid and a tiny, barbed succulent. It was
Halloween, his birthday. That night, I again considered knocking on
his door. The scene from days prior now recast itself as a horror flick:
a masked man with a white flower in one hand and an oversize thorn
in the other finds himself alone in a hallway as a large and hollow eye
fills a peephole on the other side of a door. Maybe he didn't like flowers. I played a game with myself: Which of the two would he choose?
The delicate bloom, embodiment of innocence, symbol of virility to
the ancient Greeks? Or the tenacious thorn, whose pot was no bigger
than a clenched fist? I couldn't decide and it didn't matter anyway; the
pots sat on the kitchen table all night, and I spent the time wondering
how he was bringing in his forty-first year. Alone in his room just one
floor below me. Possibly on the phone, talking to a victim somewhere,
someone I wasn't yet aware of. Or browsing through the Drafts folder
of his Gmail account, where he kept detailed notes of all his targets.
Or, like me, gazing through the glass to the glittering lights below, the
slashing rain, the milky sky that faded so quickly into blackness.

On the television the next morning, a reporter announced that
Covid infections were spiking across the United Kingdom. The

country was going into full lockdown soon. With three days remaining, I had nearly despaired of catching him. I headed into the rain at 7 a.m., alternating lookout perches between the sandwich shop and a lunch counter inside the mall with a view to the door. The hour of his usual appearance came and went. It was raining harder than it had on previous days and I had begun to wonder if I had missed him. What if he had left and gone to London? Or disappeared underground? Or somehow spotted me and fled? The lunch counter was spattered and smeared, a Covid petri dish.

And then suddenly there he was.

THE NIGHT BEFORE, I HAD asked my father: What advice can you give me for a situation like this? Here is what the spy said: Compliment him on his success and accomplishments. Play to his vanity. "Many people, particularly those with overly healthy egos, can't stand for somebody to think they don't know everything there is to know about whatever," he said. But of course, it went deeper. I wanted to understand him, didn't I? Tell him that. His side of the story was important. These thoughts played in my mind as I stood outside, staring at the entrance of Marks & Spencer. About ten minutes later Harvey reemerged. I could feel my heart thumping in my chest as I approached him from behind.

"Excuse me . . ."

He stopped, and though the rest of his body remained immobile, he swiveled his head toward me. Above a blue surgical mask, two dark eyes pinned me with a look of utter fury.

Chapter 12

In more than two decades as a journalist, I have found myself in some disturbing situations. I once interviewed a child soldier in South Sudan who had been abducted by the Lord's Resistance Army, a militia run by a madman named Joseph Kony that has been terrorizing huge swaths of east and central Africa for decades, kidnapping and killing thousands along the way. Kony had forced the boy, no more than twelve or thirteen at the time, to slaughter his family and then cannibalize their remains. There was no way to independently verify this account of savagery, but the dull manner in which the boy told the story bore no trace of deception. And by then I had heard enough similarly depraved accounts that I saw little reason to doubt him. Not yet a man, the boy had long been broken, and the methodical way he swallowed spoonful after spoonful of green soup while recounting the ticking evil that had befallen his family was chilling.

But evil wasn't limited to barbaric extremes. The lives of child soldiers and the African bush was not my world, in any case. I had lived there for a few years, but I would always be an outsider. A world of casual deceit, however, of masks and betrayals and manipulation? That was a world I understood. Which is not to say I had much explored it, at least not in this context. With me, my mother had obscured the details of her own story of abuse at her father's hands as much as possible. Until I told her about Harvey and how his story reminded me of the "dark oil" in her parents' house, neither of us had ever broached the subject of opening that door. But now she said, "It's the elephant in the room, isn't it?"

I hadn't been able to shake the image of Amisha floating in a glass-bottomed boat, staring through its underside, where a creature clung and drifted with her. Now I began to question who I had actually had in mind. A terrible crime lay at the heart of my family, staring at me from the other side of a glass pane. I could not see one story without now seeing the other.

Not because the crimes of these two men were similar; they were not, or at least not in substance. But the impulse to take advantage of innocence, the remorseless egotism that drew one to disregard another's pain, sprang from the same dissociative and self-poisoning root. On that morning in Manchester when I found myself standing outside Harvey's door at the Light ApartHotel, something in my childhood was lurking on the other side. My apprehension of this was dim at the time. I had not set out to find this connection, and even after it appeared, I had not welcomed it. Yet it did appear, and like the pale face in the painting that hung in my grandparents' dining room, I could no longer not see it.

My mother remembered that, as a child, I was often fearful of her parents' house. And because she didn't yet know that I *knew*, her fear became misplaced: she thought I was scared of her. And now, some thirty-five years later, she asked me: Did I ever feel shame about being connected—she didn't say "about belonging"—to a family in which such things had occurred? In the moment, I told her that I thought it might have shaped whatever sense of empathy I did possess.

In any event, it was a difficult question to hear. In our family, her abuse was acknowledged in the most general way, but she had never really discussed it with me. Everyone was more or less satisfied with this arrangement. On the rare and brief occasions when it came up, we foreshortened it, eliding what my mother called the "gory details." No one had any desire to go there. But when, in the spring of 2021, I explained how I had found my way back to the old painting in her parents' house, she suggested we do so.

She discovered that I had learned about her abuse much earlier than she had ever known, when I was about ten and a snooping stepbrother had found her journals. I absorbed the revelation, bastardized no doubt, then tried my best not to think about it ever. When my mother asked whether I would want to dissociate myself from them— "them" being her, and her family—the answer was yes, I would. And I had.

I hadn't been my grandfather's victim, at least not in the strictest sense. But for all my life, the question had been lurking: What is this evil that dwells so close by? Is it in my blood, my inheritance? There is no denying the allure that the dark holds for me. I am fascinated by the evil things people do. Was my mother's experience the source? It was with that question in mind that I now turned back to the question of Harvey's own actions.

I MADE AN INVENTORY. IT began with a simple statement of fact: Harvey had hurt a lot of people. He had allegedly punched Amisha and pushed her down a set of stairs, breaking a collarbone. He had gone after his other sister as well, pulling her hair and slamming her into walls. He had also pushed Alison Fisher down the stairs, breaking her wrist. This much was clear: Harvey seemed to take pleasure in hurting people.

His behavior followed a clear pattern of exploitation. He cast himself alternately as a wild success story, a tycoon from a wealthy family responsible for the success of a company, or, in other cases, as a helpless victim to be pitied. He researched his victims thoroughly, learning their routines and hangouts and hacking their private information. He used people he knew to find new victims. He was frequently verbally abusive and demeaning, attacking people's character and mental stability while simultaneously portraying himself as the real victim. He repeated these patterns over and over again.

John Parsi and Jennifer Lahoda, the two Arizona State University students who had been referenced in Harvey's "suicide letter" and later became the targets of "Cate Blanchett's" bomb threats in the run-up to the Nationals Tournament at Bradley, had to grapple with the fact that he had singled them out. I'll return to Blanchett soon, as her story isn't quite done. Lahoda thought about it for years. For those few weeks in the winter of 2000, she found herself at the mercy of a sadist who faked his own suicide and then blamed her. He had placed her at the center of a bomb scare involving thousands of people at a time in her life when she was pursuing, and realizing, long-cherished dreams. To what end? The only possible outcome for him was a kind of infamy, and what she described as "the dark personal satisfaction" to be had from having caused another's pain. Hurting people physically was one thing, but for Harvey, "these dark, terrorizing things" had been equally satisfying. People were his "playthings," Nicole had observed.

A disparate assortment of people found their way to a similar kind of language. Parsi, Lahoda's friend and teammate at Arizona State, believed Harvey had carried out a campaign of escalating violence with one clear objective: to "destroy us psychologically." As far as Parsi was concerned, Harvey was a "torturer" who sought to destroy the good in others, a fine definition of spite and contempt. If Harvey couldn't see his own dreams fulfilled, no one else would, either. "I think he just thought, if I can really get at them at this one moment, I will really ruin this thing for them forever," Parsi said.

OTHERS HAD ALSO MADE INVENTORIES. Amisha had lost track of the hours spent researching various disorders in the *Diagnostic and Statistical Manual of Mental Disorders*, the standard diagnostic reference book. If she could sum up the constellation of psychological symptoms that described her brother in one word, that word would be *psychopathic*.

The specter of mental illness seemed to hover around Harvey, but

it also seemed unlikely that mental illness alone had propelled him into a world of criminal misbehavior, manipulation, physical assault, and pathological lying. Those elements of his character felt more like the result of a malignant personality. But so many people had described him or his behavior in the same way that I felt I had to explore the idea.

Traditionally, the category of people known as psychopaths have been thought not to possess human emotion, but more recent research suggests that is not the case. They do experience a range of what one clinician described as "feeling states," but they tend to be pre-socialized. Somewhat like the emotional states of small children, they are immature and ill-formed, narcissistically focused on the maintenance of their own grandiosity and sense of entitlement. Amisha believed that Harvey had used mental illness as a recurring excuse. "A crime is a crime," she had observed. "The intent is to harm."

We think of psychopaths as the serial killers, the cold, emotionless machines who single-mindedly destroy. In many instances, the destruction of other people was a literal descriptor. Serial murderers, mass killers, dictators who deploy the machinery of genocide. But in another type of psychopath, satisfaction could be found in less dramatically violent ways. "You know what you're going to get with a serial killer," a friend of mine said: death. He was right. It was the more subtle mechanisms that interested me, and I was beginning to think I knew why.

THE EMOTIONAL LANDSCAPE OF PSYCHOPATHS is generally antagonistic. Power and hierarchy are important to them, and lie at the heart of the disorder. They possess prodigious amounts of aggression toward others, but that aggression can also be turned inward. Contemptuous of others, they derive a certain satisfaction and even pleasure in the deliberate degradation and devaluation of other people, and set out to engineer situations to bring this about. The happiness or success of other people stirs in them a related sensation, envy, which functions like an accelerant on the tinderbox of contempt. They might be overcome by an overwhelming desire to harm and damage another,

to degrade them in order to enhance their own sense of self. In other words, their wish to destroy the goodness in others also disfigures them. The destruction of another frees them from the envy of wanting to be that person or, as one doctor put it, of wanting to be "what they once were." I was reminded of the story of O. J. Simpson, facing prison a second time not for murder, but for armed robbery, after attempting to steal memorabilia of his exploits as a football star and actor.

Psychopaths can be skilled and analytic observers of human frailty. They enjoy a sense of impunity, and bait people into increasingly complex scenarios whose ultimate purpose is known only to them, a kind of predetermined endgame in which the lines between predator and prey are clearly demarcated, yet largely invisible.

More than most, psychopaths are pretty good at adopting other personas. The creation of a convincing mask is integral to this process of deception, the fabrication of an elaborate persona and the systematic persuasion required to convince the world of its truth. The data on how often people fall for impersonated voices is inconclusive, but a successful impersonation is a difficult act to pull off consistently. Even those who are not drawn to impersonation as part of their criminal profile are nevertheless often skilled imitators. A psychopath might want to convince other people that he possesses the emotions that other people have, and so will read people closely and imitate them. The serial killer Ted Bundy often acted like he had a broken leg or arm; it was how he lured people to his car before killing them. Such facades are immensely pleasing to psychopaths, creating a feeling of unrivaled attraction and power, which they then strive to replicate. One psychiatrist I spoke with had spent some time with the notion that psychopathic behavior was possibly adaptive, and even beneficial for a certain type of human interaction. Psychopaths could be seen as "interpersonal cheaters, enabling them to benefit cheaply from their interactions with others." He suggested that psychopathy might be an adaptation for social predation and wondered whether psychopaths mentally represented other people as part objects rather than whole, real, and separate human beings.

EVEN WHEN DISCUSSING PSYCHOPATHY IN a specific diagnostic context—not just "Oh, that person is psycho"—the assumption is that we're talking about people who are beyond the pale and beyond redemption. Yet as far as I knew, Harvey's scams never depended on physical violence. He seemed content with sowing the implicit *threat* of violence. That undertone—you might say an *atmosphere*—of psychopathic violence seemed to linger, even when he wasn't the one doing the threatening. After Jessie Evans had left Indonesia and was safely back in Melbourne with her parents, she and her mother, Jeanie, huddled. They decided to call Wendi Murdoch's assistant, the man they knew as "Aaron." Jeanie held her phone's recorder close while Jessie dialed. It went to voice mail. They called again. No answer. On the third attempt, Aaron answered. "Jessie," he said flatly, sounding bored.

Jessie did her best to sound casual, too, but her voice betrayed the anxiety that had been mounting since she had discovered the truth: she had been conned. She began with a lie of her own this time, that she had fallen sick and missed her flight. At first, Aaron indulged her patiently. Then she segued into the question of the money she was owed, $103,000 by that point. She and Aaron bickered over details for another minute or two and then Aaron interrupted her abruptly. He said Jessie's father had threatened to kill *him*, Aaron. When Jessie protested, Aaron grew angrier. He had recorded it, he said, and would share the recording with her.

"You need to explain, why would your dad call me just to threaten to kill me?" Again she pushed back, this time more vehemently: no, her father had done nothing of the sort. Aaron dismissed the denial with a contemptuous sniff. He continued to build on the fiction that her father, whom he now described as a "thug" who would "kill someone for money," was the out-of-control aggressor, the true menace of the story. He wouldn't entertain any of her questions until she acknowledged her father's murderous impulses. His voice took on an even slower, more menacing cadence. He told her how she must address him. "*Nicely*," he spat. "*Respectably* . . . Then, I'll answer your question."

Hurting other people. The childlike simplicity of the phrase itself belies its potential depths. In truth he seemed always poised on the edge of psychopathic violence. Sometimes he was rather blunt about it, such as a call in which he had threatened to castrate a man and go after his family.

Medical terminology aside, it was pretty simple. He seemed to want to hurt people; he threatened to hurt people; and in many cases, he did hurt people. As a result, he had spent years in prison. He was a wanted man. "He can be incredibly charming, and very complimentary," Nicole had said. "He talks in a way that is interesting to listen to. But I think he has an incredible ability to push things out of his head. I mean you have to—to not feel remorse, and to do things like this to people, to hurt them, and to manipulate them, and then just go out to a restaurant in London and take a little video about a hamburger."

HAD THE CRIMES AGAINST MY mother been discovered today instead of sixty or seventy years ago, the perpetrators would have likely faced very different consequences. Gardner would have gone to prison. His wife, guilty of shielding him from proper scrutiny, could have wound up there, too. This, more than anything, seemed to haunt my mother. "That whole thing is pretty scary," she said.

She had tried to confront her father but he had always found ways to deflect. Which is to say, the question of whether he was evil or ill was never resolved. He went to his grave that way. It was his wife's fault; she was frigid and critical. His crazy daughter was to blame; she pushed his buttons. He was to be pitied; his childhood had been really rough. And anyway, he was a hardworking man. Didn't that count for something? If ever you did manage to breach these well-worn defenses, Gardner and Helen changed the subject. They looked out the window, where a calliope hummingbird might be sucking on a plastic teat.

My mother wondered: If someone acts in what you might call an "evil" way, does their intention count? The question straddled what seemed to me an impossible line. I had told her about Harvey and it was she who placed him side by side with her father. I waited for her verdict—less because she knew the ins and outs of each and every circumstance—she did not—but because I wanted to hear how she, of all people, would choose to weigh what she did understand. Harvey, she concluded, "wanted to hurt people, he was consciously aware." She was, strangely, less sure about her father, and wondered whether he was conscious of what he was doing. "He was very sick," she said. "Very, very sick."

One person's sick is another's evil. What is distressing for one might in some cases be merely character-building for another. How much does the context of our lives define how our actions are understood? People, after all, do act out their unconscious trauma in a thousand twisted ways. Gardner, an exceedingly accomplished person in every other aspect of his life—a graduate of the Ivy League, a renowned economist, a scholar, inventor, and, in many ways, a man full of small kindnesses—wound up hunched over his bone-secret at the end of a very long and dark road. He was conscious in every aspect of his life; why not this one? It struck me as a cop-out to claim, as one of Harvey's victims had, that he was compelled to manipulate people. As though he had no choice in the matter.

To call what happened to my mother a con is to deeply understate the reality. Gardner's unfathomable violence was not the same thing as Harvey's wanton cruelty. But I could see the lines that tethered them. The tactics used by my grandfather and by Harvey were similar. They both stole something valuable and even irreplaceable: dreams, trust, self-confidence. My mother wondered whether Gardner was a manipulative psychopath who used love and loyalty to groom her. Others had posed the same questions about Harvey—who used charm and guile to, as Nicole had described it, "groom" his victims and then exploit them.

In another household the oil painting might tell a different story, that of a benevolent guardian keeping watch over the itinerant traveler. In the mouth of a simpler man, Gardner's casual invitation to search for the hidden figure could have been amusing. But this was not that house. And Gardner was not simple or benign. Our story was not that story. It could only ever be this way. An abuser of children, and a sadist, he invited his guests to speculate on the monster hiding in plain sight. I have wondered whether this invitation was his way of offering his guests a glimpse at his secret truth.

Many years have passed since then. Only now do I see him clearly as the pale face in the belfry, the soul of the painting, facing down his human form in our world night after night.

It was an afternoon in the mountain country north of Seattle, and I was watching a group of young boys play with a frog. They had dug a small pool in the mud next to a river and placed the frog inside it. It wasn't deep enough, they decided. It needed to be deeper, so the frog couldn't get out and find his way back to the river. They wanted to "adopt" him, take him away from here for a day, maybe two.

My son was one of the boys on the riverbank that day, and these were his friends, but he balked at the shenanigans with the frog. He was six at the time, younger by a couple of years than the other boys, and every now and again he wandered over and asked in a quiet voice—so quiet that it seemed as though he was talking to himself—for them to let the frog go, to let it be. I could see he was in pain: unable at that age to hide his emotions, his face betrayed his angst. But when I asked, more out of curiosity than a desire to intervene, if anything was wrong, he just looked at me and chirped, No. His natural instinct to survive as a social animal, to be accepted and liked by his peers, was stronger than the will to become the guardian of all things living. But I knew that he would have preferred not to touch the frog, or disturb it, but rather to watch it simply and slowly progress. Eventually I wandered over and held the frog in my hand for a moment, so my son could see what it felt like. Both of us were happy when it slipped away. I held him in my arms and said nothing, but I was grateful for his discomfort, and for the quiet grace of his words.

These boys were just children discovering the world and learning how it works. They didn't harm the frog, nor would they, at least not intentionally. But my son's reluctance struck me in the moment and has stayed with me since. I have never particularly enjoyed fishing, and so perhaps because he is my son, I have projected my own feelings where they don't belong, but it's also possible that because he is my son, I understand the look of discomfort I saw on his face. I didn't want to intrude upon the life of the creature in this way. But there are those among us who insist on it, who take pleasure in the transgression. My grandfather was one. Harvey is another. Discontented, furious, he wanted to play with his toys, his little people. Of course, I realized, were someone to go after my children, I would have no qualms about destroying them. I swore an oath that *my* children will be free of this.

Chapter 13

Y ou've been following me," Harvey said, his voice shaking with accusation. Indeed I had.

I shook my head. No.

I steeled myself. His eyes seemed to grow much larger as he looked at me. I apologized for scaring him, and as he scanned the crowds, looking for signs of further trouble, I told him I was writing a book and needed to give him an opportunity to present his side. This seemed to disappoint him. I offered to buy him coffee. His expression softened, but he shook his head, glancing at the two police officers who were standing nearby. I thought he might run at any moment and I wouldn't have blamed him. He was the subject of an international FBI investigation involving law enforcement authorities from three continents. My heart was still hammering as he turned back to me, as if to assess this challenge more fully. He glanced down at my hands, in which I held a notebook.

He demanded to know how I had found him. I deflected and tried to stick to what was true. I had seen the interview he had done with Haseena, and the rest had just happened. He said he was nervous that I knew where he lived, that he wasn't in a good frame of mind, and didn't want to have his name out there in the public. But then he dropped a crumb. "I promise you this, Scott," he said. "I promise you this. I will tell you everything you need to know, no lies, whatever you need to know when I have the ability to do so." In the wake of the promise, he promptly delivered several lies. His "aunt" and his "lawyers" would have to be alerted about this intrusion immediately. He would be going to London the next day anyway, so it wasn't a good time. Nevertheless, he began to walk and, with a nod of his head, invited me to accompany him: "Shall we walk?"

As a journalist, I aim to tell the truth to my subjects and my sources. It's not always a straight line: people sometimes want to know things you cannot reveal; they want assurances of a predetermined outcome; they long to hear you say something you can't say. I have tried to be straightforward, and mostly I have met that challenge. But in that moment, I felt, more acutely than I have ever felt before while doing my job, a fusion of his world and mine. I shoved the discomfort aside. It was only months later that I was able to recognize it for what it was: the moment I stopped being merely an observer and became a character in his story.

My father had been right about one thing: my quarry would struggle to resist a confessional urge. It began in those first few steps. I didn't know his story, Harvey said, or what his sisters had done to him, how he was "kidnapped" and swept away to a mental institution. "I can't even have . . ." He let the sentence trail off, leaving the word *sex* hanging in the air between us. These dramatic first lines in his Portrait of a Victim as a Young Man had obviously been drawn before, and seemed even then like a ploy, yet I found myself enjoying the sensation of being swept along.

He directed me along the side of the Marks & Spencer building, toward a pedestrian footpath that led to an open square, talking all the while. He interrupted his story frequently with short, panicky asides about his fears—that I now knew where he lived, that I had spoken to people in Manchester who might know him—which in fact was a rhetorical trick to elicit information from me. Elicitation was my father's preferred method of gathering intelligence, the one the spymasters at the CIA's Langley headquarters or their training facility known as the Farm taught every new generation of disciples, and also the one he most often accused me of failing to grasp. But I had certainly learned enough by now to know when it was being used against me, and I didn't bite. So Harvey grew more blunt, which was, historically anyway, *my* preferred method: How did I find him? How long was I going to be in Manchester? Where was I staying? I deflected and dodged. I couldn't remember the name of the building, but it was over there, and I waved my hand dismissively in the general direction of the Light ApartHotel. However, this intense focus on his own vulnerability raised another question.

He had been living in the United Kingdom for close to five years by that point, and in all that time never once had anyone confronted him directly about his impersonation schemes. His own surveillance powers were, if not diminished, at least matched, as the lens was turned back on him. From here on out, it seemed things could go in one of two directions. Either he acknowledged that he was caught in a moment of reckoning, and took the opportunity to deal with it. Or he found a way to twist this to his own advantage. That remained to be seen, but in the meantime one fundamental shift was already under way: I was now a part of Harvey's story, just as he was a part of mine. I had observed him, and the observation itself altered everything. I half-wondered if he welcomed it. I didn't know if I did.

As we headed toward the paving stones of Exchange Square, I told him I had no interest in scaring him, and while he seemed to appreciate this, he didn't extend me the same courtesy. Instead he quietly threatened to call his lawyers to inform them that I had followed him. There was a law against that sort of thing in the United Kingdom, he assured me casually, in the way of a friendly piece of advice. When I told him I was doing my job, he just returned to the recitation of his life story, as if I hadn't spoken at all. (It was a pattern that would come to be very familiar in the weeks ahead, as he found ways to ignore what I said so that he could continue on with his own train of thought. I would have to learn to insist, sometimes even to shout, to make myself heard.) The name I had for him—I had called him Hargobind—was wrong, he went on. He had legally changed it as soon as he got out of prison. His sisters had neutered him in a thousand different ways, by having him declared "dead," by arranging for him to be "beaten" and "kidnapped" and "injected" with the drugs that would keep him sedated, all while they stole a house and a fortune that was by law and by rights every bit his as it was theirs.

We had begun walking—a halting progression along the gray stones. A light rain fell and he declined my offer to share an umbrella. Every few steps he stopped, and it was in these interludes that he tried again to frighten me away by warning me about the danger I was skirting. I could find myself in real trouble, he explained, because while I might be a journalist, I was "tapping" him. I wasn't tapping anybody, I said. However, and this I didn't say, the camera on my cell phone, which I had placed in my shirt pocket facing out, was turned on, in case he decided to resort to violence. He kept talking. He had rights, he said, he was not to be forced, he had been electrocuted. At the behest of the fanatics in his family, one unscrupulous religionist after another had tried to dissuade him not just from his adopted faith, Catholicism, but also from his homosexuality.

But how could I possibly understand any of this? He said I had never been bullied; I countered that I had. He tried to flatter me, and I laughed in a way I hoped showed that it worked, which probably meant it didn't. He asked me who else I had spoken to, and I told him I wanted to tell his side of the story. He knew that whatever I wrote would be bad, he said, and that he could sue. Around and around we went. I was alone, whereas he had advisers. His "aunt" was one. Haseena, who had conducted the Instagram interview, was another. But, ultimately, I had a trump card: I wanted to know what had happened to him, and this, in the end, was the invitation he would not be able to decline. But before he spoke further, he wanted to know more about my role in all of this. He had appreciated that I had been polite, though he was sure I wanted to kill him, or at least slap him in the face. I knew plenty of people who would have taken him up on this offer, but I told him I wasn't one of them. "One minute, your life is taken away from you . . ." he mused.

By this point, we had wandered down into Exchange Square, where we stood close to the entrance of a coffee shop. The initial moments of terror I had felt while confronting him had faded. I had a chance to really look at him. His hair was cut short and groomed stylishly to one side. He had a long, oval-shaped face with a large forehead, punctuated by thick, bushy eyebrows. He moved and morphed with great expressiveness and verve, the puzzle of his face torqueing like a set of gears. He opened his eyes to their full orbital capacity when speaking, which gave an unsettling feeling of being stared at. Just as he seemed to be warming up, he was now also retreating. He had squirreled away the important documents that would prove his story, he told me, the ones necessary if ever he needed "to arm" himself. We had been standing in a light rain for more than twenty minutes by then, and he didn't want to talk anymore. He needed time to think things over. He said he would send me a message. I nodded, and turned to go, but then thought better of it and turned back.

"You promise?" I said, smiling with what a friend of mine had once called a "jackal punk grin"—the one my mother-in-law had silently shaken her head at, the one that could get me in real trouble—and Harvey laughed with what felt like genuine mirth.

"I promise," he said.

But for Covid he would have shaken my hand. We fist-bumped instead, which I later realized was just as risky as a handshake.

"Please don't follow me," he said.

"I'm just walking this way," I said. "Here we go."

As I left, it occurred to me that I was walking into a trap. I had little confidence I would ever hear from him again. It was enough, I thought, to have found him at all.

As I WALKED AWAY FROM that fist bump in the middle of Exchange Square, I was overcome with adrenaline. Resisting an urge to turn around and look for him, I swung left onto Main Street and merged with the pulsing crowds. I thought I might lose myself in the anonymity there, but instead the human thrum only sharpened an acute sense of individuality within me. For a long time that afternoon and into the evening, I wandered aimlessly through the Northern Quarter, waiting for darkness. I lowered my mask and let the cold air nip at my face. At the time, I was relieved to have found him. For months I had been feeling trapped—by Covid, by my own inability to understand or talk to him, and even by my sources, whose concerns I had adopted. Now I was liberated to some degree; we had an open line of communication. He had teased me with fragments of a story I longed to understand, a story of exile, torture, and alienation. Perhaps I had completely misjudged him. After all, I wouldn't wish for anyone to be dragged kicking and screaming into a mental institution for gay conversion therapy. Then again, maybe it was all a lie.

Alongside these musings about Harvey's motivations was another feeling, which had less to do with him, and everything to do with me. Prior to confronting him, the nervousness in the pit of my stomach stemmed from fear—of failure, or rejection, of the possibility of physical violence; now a sensation of triumph flooded into me. Journalism is in many ways an act of possession, even, perhaps, of conquest. Journalists speak of "getting" or "scoring" or "bagging" an interview. You *get* someone; or you don't *get* them. A lot—everything, in fact—hinges on this. Ours is the language of the hunt. Anyone who tells you otherwise has misunderstood.

For years it had been Harvey who had been the intruder, the hunter. It was he who had been peering into the lives of his victims from the safe remove of the internet. I had been chasing him, to no avail. I had known his name for a long time, but it wasn't enough simply to possess these few biographical details, or the brief contours of his life. I had needed to speak to him, to hear his real, unfiltered voice. I had longed to be able to sit down with this person. Even if his story was a fiction, I wanted to hear him tell it. That evening, as I walked, increasingly invigorated by the cold and the dark, my confidence grew. The tables had been turned. He was no longer in my crosshairs, no longer a mere specter. He was mine.

THE NEWFOUND FEELING OF POWER lingered long after I returned to the hotel. The glass walls, which before had left me feeling exposed and vulnerable, now offered expansive views over the world's first industrialized city, a former Roman enclave where, nearly two thousand years later, the atom was first split.

I got him, I messaged to a friend that night, another journalist.

Excellent, he replied. Again, the language of hunter and prey. How'd you approach?

I felt almost ecstatic with the sense of freedom this one act had bequeathed.

Just one floor beneath me, at the other end of the hallway, sat Harvey. Now, however, instead of imagining him as a plotter wantonly sowing destruction, I began to see him as a prisoner, a creature in a cage of his—and now my—making. Whereas before it was I who hoped for contact, the power imbalance had been inverted, at least temporarily. That evening he messaged me on Instagram. His tone was plaintive.

Scott, it's me—Let's just chat here! Is that okay?

Yes. It most certainly was.

Later that night I left the hotel and treated myself to dinner and a large glass of wine.

The following evening, he called using a video feed within the Instagram application. His face appeared briefly and then disappeared, leaving only his voice. "I want to fulfill one thing before anything happens to me," he said. "Because you know, I don't know what's going to happen. But I want to do good in the eyes of people that I've done bad to—you know who I'm talking about."

How quickly he broached the crime and its punishment! Until I realized that he had left it vague enough that it could conveniently be misunderstood. In any event, I should have realized that it was just a prelude; he had something more specific in mind—a podcast he was calling *Motherland*, which was to be modeled on *The Arabian Nights*. Shahrazad, the narrator of that classic work of literature, tells a thousand and one tales to her tyrannical husband, Shahrirah, in order to stave off her beheading. Now, facing a virtual beheading of his own, Harvey, like Shahrazad, would spin a thousand and one tales drawn from his own life "only to survive and to fulfill something that I've always wanted."

"You may laugh at me and say it's not going to happen," he added. "But, sir, I'm going to try and make it happen."

Sir. Such a self-conscious, reflexively submissive word, and odd coming from the mouth of someone who so enjoyed being in control. Perhaps he was just being respectful. But why? *I* was the one who had intruded upon *his* life. It belied a deeper set of motivations. I wondered if he was in some sense pleased that I had found him. We spoke for nearly two hours that night, twenty-four hours after our initial encounter. He knew I was a journalist, and the person most responsible for the moniker that had come to define him: the Con Queen of Hollywood. He also seemed aware that forces of accountability were being marshaled, that around him there now existed watching eyes, invisible entities preparing his fate, the next phase of his life's journey. In the face of that coming storm, would a modern retelling of *The Arabian Nights* lead to redemption? How could a podcast about escaping the wrath of a murderous tyrant enable him to "do good in the eyes of people I've done bad to"? In a mind thus deluded, it was possible to believe that the suffering of victims wasn't really suffering at all; rather their experiences were simply context for the grander tableau of his own life, that the hundreds of people who had sought help from Nicole were extras in a drama of his own creation, in which he played the central role. Were the elaborate fictions he used to trap these people, in some sense, stories about himself? Or was there also, concealed in the life story he began to uncoil for me that evening, a pathway to the truth?

Harvey had few personal possessions; what he did own, he carted around with him on his wanderings across the British Isles. Though he claimed not to read, *The Arabian Nights* was one of his treasures (the other was *Grimms' Fairy Tales*), and it's worth noting how these stories may have resonated with Harvey, both because of what they offer, as well as what they do not: they are visceral and concrete, and at the same time fantastically untethered from reality. *The Arabian Nights* is drawn from multiple sources, including old stories told in Greek, Turkish, Arabic, and Persian across much of Asia, India, and North Africa. One of its sources is the *Kathasaritsagara*, a Sanskrit text that has been translated as "The Ocean of the Streams of Story," first compiled in India in the eleventh century. The influence of the *Kathasaritsagara* on *The Arabian Nights* is suggested in the title's allusion to the ocean, a landscape in which stories move like waves in an endlessly refracting vibration. The English novelist A. S. Byatt, in a story called "The Djinn in the Nightingale's Eye," compared the tales of *The Arabian Nights* to the reproductive cycle of the Surinam toad, wherein offspring emerge from the backs of their mothers. The eighteenth-century English poet Samuel Taylor Coleridge had described his own creative process using the same unruly metaphor. The scholar Robert Irwin had argued that the "Chinese box" structure of the tales in *The Arabian Nights* had parallels in real life, "wherein we are all of us the stories we carry within us." The end of the story signals death, what Shahrazad describes as "the destroyer of delights." The heads of countless princesses, less skilled in the art of the tale, had preceded Shahrazad. By putting Shahrazad in the position of having to weave these fantastical tales, does the prince ruin her life, or give it eternal meaning? With a heavy emphasis on cunning and deceit, each story serves as a stepping-stone to a new world. A reader rarely knows whom to trust; everyone is an unreliable narrator. As a template for living, the book offers uncertainty and doubt, the possibility of endless regeneration.

HAVING COME ALL THIS WAY in the midst of a pandemic, I had hoped Harvey would agree to meet with me in person again. Instead he informed me that we would be communicating only by telephone or video, even though from my balcony I could have shattered the glass of his apartment with a well-tossed stone. Like the victims who had come before me, I was beholden to his caprices. The open streets had been too hazardous. It was only here in the obscurity, comforted by the static of technology that Amisha had described, that he could consider further communication.

To hear Harvey tell it, his life was born of legend and blessed by the gods. It began in the aftermath of war, when his father single-handedly shepherded his family across the Pakistani border into India. And while he hadn't been able to prevent the border guards from raping several of the women, Lal had nevertheless prevented their deaths and ushered them to safety, and for that they saw him as their hero.

I was drawn to this tale of refugees and depredation, and the lingering effects of the British colonial enterprise. My father had lived in Pakistan as a boy and attended a missionary school in the years just after Partition, when his father had been posted there as an adviser for the U.S. Department of Agriculture, and the remnants of the fading empire were still visible. Many years later, I was born in India, and had also lived in Pakistan, six years on the subcontinent as a child, and another year much later as a journalist. No wonder Harvey's refuge in the Victorian airs of the Portico Library, with its monographs and maps detailing the exploits of colonial captains and ethnographers, felt like mine as well.

When Lal arrived in Indonesia, he had no more than a few dollars in his pocket. He met and married Kavita, and she bore him two daughters, but Lal was desperate for a son. The couple sought guidance from the Maharaj of the Gobinddham Manjhand Darbar temple in Mumbai. To their great disappointment, the Maharaj touched Kavita's belly and foretold another girl. If they wanted a boy, they would have to pray. The next day, the Maharaj touched Kavita's belly once more, and found the future altered. They called their son Hargobind, and in that name the echo of the Gobinddham Manjhand Darbar temple still lived—proof, Harvey told me, of his "miraculous" birth.

What surprised me was how comfortable he was speaking to me, knowing full well what I knew about him. Eloquent and confident, he spoke in a bland, American-accented English, and sometimes slipped into other cadences and inflections that sounded to my ears more Indian or Indonesian. Eventually I would hear British English and American Southern. He switched to Bahasa Indonesian when recalling a word or phrase or place. All of this he did effortlessly, without drawing attention to the transitions.

I soaked up the details of his childhood, the house in Bungur—gated, with two doors, one for guests, the other for the maids who traveled a staircase to their quarters on the second floor—because it reminded me in some ways of my own childhood, in the G-6/3 district of Islamabad, Pakistan, playing in the rose garden under the pepper tree, in sight of the mustachioed Sikh sentry who stood watch at our gate. I pictured Harvey in his room with the balcony from which he could see the golden bulbs hanging off the angel fruit tree and the spiky leaves of the Indian tulsi. Across the way lived four Chinese brothers. Behind them was the old film studio and a house that had burned years earlier, and ever since the fire the plot was overrun with shrubs and trees, and it was said that an old lady whom everyone knew as Nenek, a chatty, screechy woman, had died in the blaze. The maids spoke about it in hushed tones. He avoided the balcony after the sun set and the Maghrib prayers echoed out across the city because that was when the Gates of Hell were opened and spirits evil and otherwise roamed free. His father considered purchasing the land but a visiting clergyman warned him that to invest in the detritus of fire, where death so clearly lingered, would bring only misfortune, and so it was left undeveloped and unnurtured, a forlorn thicket of weeds. Now Nenek, the "black grandmother," as the maids called her, emerged at night to haunt them all.

As children, I thought, we all longed for a certain exoticism that was not ours. Whereas I played dusty cricket with the local boys in their *shalwar kameez*, and custom-ordered mixed cassette tapes of Jackson, Diamond, Denver, and Rogers at the Jinnah Market, Harvey escaped to his parents' attic to watch Miss Universe pageants. When he wasn't in the attic, he watched Disney movies. He loved *Aladdin* because he thought he bore a striking resemblance to the genie, and he felt a kinship with the villainous, soul-stealing octopus Ursula in *The Little Mermaid*. I felt a pang of sympathy. Maybe when you were, as he had described himself to me, "overly fat and notoriously effeminate," you needed a competent villain on your side. Because no one else seemed to be, least of all his classmates at the Gandhi School who bullied him, called him *banci*, a slur that translated to "half man, half woman" or, more colloquially, *faggot*, and scoffed at his adoring predictions about the soon-to-be stardom of Mariah Carey. Many years later Harvey would write that Ursula and other malevolent women who had so captivated him in childhood—Maleficent, the Wicked Witch of the West—were actually "misunderstood angels," forced to defend themselves "by doing the opposite of what was deemed good."

Still, Harvey's life as a gay man had been a closed book. So it came as a surprise when he opened up so readily about this aspect of himself, not only because he had kept it so private but because his self-portrait was more openly flamboyant than I had expected. Even in the telling, it was as though the change of venue from Jakarta to Los Angeles allowed him to speak about it with more freedom. Venturing out from his residence at 4108 Marathon Street, he took West Hollywood by storm. You might find him clad in leather at Faultline or steaming in a bath at Flex. "I wasn't like *all* that," he said. "But my *God*. I had *appeal*, I had *persona*. Something was *there*." He remained a virgin but he was active in every other way. Yet it was a secret liberation—at least he secreted it away from his father, who handwrote him long daily letters with stories about his own childhood in the Indian village of Sukher, the long-ago camaraderie among Hindus and Muslims that had since descended into acrimony, and the riots against Sukarno that were sweeping across Indonesia at the time. In every letter, Lal had tucked in a twenty-dollar bill.

A Bukowskian squalor permeated Harvey's stories; it was a land-scape populated by rough characters with hard-won lessons to impart—lessons, moreover, that would serve him well in the years to come. He told me about the weeks he had spent helping a Salvadoran madam run a Hollywood brothel, and the men who patronized it; about the raspy-voiced janitor, Earl, and the elderly Black secretary with whom he "cuddled" after eating takeout from the local Korean convenience store, and the single mothers, and their mothers, who came from Guatemala and took him to outdoor food markets to show him how to really eat.

But of all the figures who had important life lessons to impart, there was one who stood head and shoulders above the rest: Harvey Weinstein. Harvey—*my* Harvey—claimed that during an internship at the Weinstein Company, the famous producer had taken him aside to tell him he was his "favorite" and that he had "a future in this business." His fascination with Weinstein was intriguing to me. Weinstein was the ultimate Hollywood insider; he was also a predator. Was it really, as Harvey argued, Weinstein's unquestionable skills as a producer that made him so appealing?

Harvey had been scamming people for years, but it was only in the fall of 2017, when the furor around Weinstein had erupted into the public, that he began aggressively targeting the prominent women of Hollywood, beginning with Amy Pascal. The timing of this up-tick wasn't just coincidental, I realized. Now I wondered whether one Harvey, *this* Harvey, was enacting a kind of revenge by piggybacking off the infamy of the man he claimed to so admire—the *other* Harvey.

My Harvey, after all, noticed everything. And in the autumn of 2017, the downfall of Harvey Weinstein was the biggest, ugliest story out there. It seemed inconceivable that he would not try to involve himself in the chaos that had resulted and find ways to twist it to his advantage. What better way to simultaneously invert the narrative and inflict more pain than to capitalize on Weinstein's crimes? He might not ever be able to be Harvey Weinstein, but hidden behind the mask of Weinstein's female counterparts, he could be a version of the man.

I would eventually learn that Harvey—my Harvey—kept copious notes and research about his victims: details about their work history, their contacts, the projects they had created and those they still longed to do. He kept the information safe in a Gmail account. But that wasn't the only lesson he learned from the Salvadoran madam Elsie's dark rooms. There was something else: it was men who were too emotional, men the weakest sex.

Talking to my Harvey was exhausting. Imagine a room in which a television broadcasts a Miramax movie, conservative AM talk radio blares, a YouTube influencer scrolls through TikTok videos, and an actor performs a never-ending series of monologues all at the same time. Harvey was a room of voices, lucid or raving, frantic somehow to escape or hold me hostage or both. It felt like a static of lies, distortions, and exaggerations. Hyperbole, drama, and volatility were in constant tension and came from every direction. I tried hard to listen to him, tried to understand him, while also challenging him, but whenever I did, he backed away or changed the subject. As skilled an embellisher as he was, he just as easily eliminated inconvenient facts, like the plagiarism that resulted in his expulsion from the circuit. His coach, he told me, had written his speech for him. But Marianne LeGreco, the true author, had done no such thing. If he was circumspect about the precipitating events, he was silent about the fake suicide letter, the menacing emails, and the bomb threats that followed.

It wasn't always easy to reconcile his versions of events with the stories I had heard from others. You'll recall that "Cate Blanchett" was Harvey's staunch defender and the one making the threats against his former teammates, but in Harvey's version of those years she was nowhere to be seen. And why would she have been? The real Cate Blanchett had always been busy with her own life, yet his obsession with her had endured; he'd kept her in his sights the whole time. A year before Harvey met me, Blanchett made her debut at London's National Theatre in a performance of *When We Have Sufficiently Tortured Each Other*, a play about "the messy, often violent nature of desire and the fluid, complicated roles that men and women play," according to the program. Harvey finagled a ticket to the premiere, and when the audience spilled out into the street, he was right there in their midst, jumping up and down and clapping his hands like a child. His companion that evening later told me Harvey had understood "nothing" about the play, which surprised me. Harvey had told me he had won a spot at Juilliard on the basis of a monologue from *A Chorus Line*, and a section from Eugène Ionesco's *Rhinoceros*, an absurdist play in which all but one of the residents of a small French town are turned into rhinoceroses. If the detail about *Rhinoceros* was a lie, and I was pretty sure it was, he was still telling me something. Among other themes, *Rhinoceros* examined the notion of metamorphosis—of the individual, the collective. Was he telling me about his own transformation—or perhaps his own violent vanishing? After all, if you have become a rhinoceros presumably you have disappeared from your own life. Because after searching, I found no record of an internship with Harvey Weinstein. I found no record of his Juilliard audition or subsequent acceptance. I might have asked my grandmother to look into it, but Helen, my Helen, who really had studied at Julliard, had been dead for years.

I REMAINED IN THE UNITED Kingdom for a week. The day after I flew home, abandoning the white orchid and the tiny succulent on the kitchen table of my Manchester apartment, the British government announced a complete Covid lockdown. If I had waited any longer to find Harvey, I almost certainly would have missed him. As it was, I had stayed in Manchester for three extra days, hoping that he might change his mind and meet with me in person. He didn't.

Back in Seattle, I sent him a message on Instagram. He said he would call me in a couple of days.

We spoke dozens of times in November. Our conversations sometimes lasted for several hours, other times only minutes. There were days when he called eight or ten times, from early in the morning to late at night, the time of day Shahrazad, his muse, deemed best for the weaving of tales, or *asmar*, "things of the evening." I had set up a special Instagram account to communicate safely with him, and he responded from his own Instagram account, "saysomethingthatmatters." The site, as he described it, was "an endless quest to discover my identity." He always called from a blocked number that appeared on my phone as NO CALLER ID.

Harvey hammered away at the victim narrative. He didn't dispute that the years following his return to Indonesia in 2001 were troubled, but he blamed his sisters, casting them as homophobes unwilling to accept the sexual being who had blossomed in the United States. He turned again to the phone for comfort and resumed his old habit of cold-calling people and inducing them into having phone sex. Occasionally he called 1-800 sex numbers. To placate his sisters, he said, he reluctantly agreed to an inpatient stay at Doulos, the rehab facility run by the Christian preacher and exorcist Ruyandi Hutasoit. In Harvey's telling, his treatment consisted of medication and forced gay conversion therapy.

One day, he said, seven staff members took him to a prayer room, locked the doors, and began singing and chanting. The men held his hands behind him and pushed him against the wall while worshippers touched his body. They commanded him to sing and pray to God. He sang. *Hallelujah!* Louder, they commanded. Louder! "The devil is coming out!" they shouted. "The devil is coming out! Look at your eyes, your eyes are red!" In the presence of three or more people, they said,

Christ the Lord would make his own existence known. Every day for three weeks they took him back to the prayer room for thirty to forty-five minutes for another session; eventually they scaled it back to once every other week. "They didn't make me less gay," he said. "They just made me who I am." He called it "the Dark Ages." It reminded him of *The Hunchback of Notre Dame*, adding, "The animation, you know, it's very dark."

He left Doulos but soon found himself institutionalized again, this time very much against his will. He had been alone in his room upstairs at the house in Bungur when his sisters and several relatives asked to see him. Downstairs, five large men held his legs and hands as he screamed and lashed out. He claimed he broke a vase trying to escape but they overpowered him. He felt the stick of a needle, and as they shoved him into a waiting car, the sedative began to wash over him. Drifting off, he heard his sister Yara say, "We got him."

He woke to find himself in a medical facility surrounded by beds filled with people screaming, and learned he had been asleep for a week, like Rumpelstiltskin. A doctor told him he had been admitted here—the place was called Dharma Graha—for bipolar disorder and homosexuality and asked him, "Well, from one to ten, how gay are you?" Ten, Harvey said. His hands trembled and he felt stoned. A doctor gave him Mellaril, which is used to treat schizophrenia. Two weeks later, his family visited. He would be staying in Dharma Graha "for some time." He underwent several sessions of electroshock therapy, and as he had while a student in Los Angeles, lived among people whose hearts had been broken, like the woman who believed a microchip that allowed Al Gore to watch her naked had been planted in her head. He spent nights locked inside with his roommates until the doors were thrown open for exercise and breakfast, followed by conversation or the watching of television. He said the heavy doses of medication he received there permanently neutered his libido, leaving him impotent. He remained inside for a year and four months. And then he was gone, having fled, or been released, it was never clear.

I HAVE A STACK OF faded legal documentation detailing some of the crimes Harvey is known to have committed in Indonesia. Some of it is typed, some handwritten in black ink in Bahasa and English. In all, it totals more than two hundred and fifty pages, and includes police reports, trial transcripts, sentencing memos, and sworn testimony, including Harvey's. Even so, it remains an incomplete accounting. In one document, Harvey claims that the Indonesian public relations firm Publicis pursued him for embezzling 200 billion Indonesian rupiah, roughly $13 million. (Those figures seem improbably high. A Publicis employee familiar with the case said that he thought Harvey had pocketed roughly $90,000 that was intended for ad campaigns.) He admits to stealing his father's ATM card and transferring 98 billion rupiah, roughly $6 million, to another bank. In sworn testimony, he excoriates his sisters for cutting him out of his share of a seven-figure inheritance, including houses in Jakarta and Bali and several pieces of valuable jewelry. While some or perhaps even all of that may be true, Amisha contends that his excision from the family stemmed from his own misdeeds. Whatever injuries inflicted on him by family fall short of explaining the studious and determined criminal who appears in the pages of the dossier, however, which someone in Indonesia helped retrieve for me from the South Jakarta District Court and a small, air-conditioned room at Cipinang prison, where Harvey lived for so many years.

His version of those years bore little resemblance to the account the documents presented. As with his other tales, he set the stage for the coming performance with all the skill of a dramaturge. "The moment you entered there, my *God*," he said, "there was an air of darkness. It was like you're entering another *world*, sir." A constant source of fear among the inmates of Cipinang was the threat of transfer to an even more notorious gulag: Nusa Kambangan, known as the Island of Many Flowers, home since the time of Dutch colonialism to nine prisons, four of which were still active. For a time, he lived in a cell block run by a drug addict and trafficker named Boy, who was there one day, gone the next, transferred to Nusa. A feared gang member named Camonte took over. But when Camonte began kicking at the heads of the Muslim inmates while they were praying, his block mates called a midnight meeting and hatched a plot to kill him. After Boy's transfer and Camonte's murder, the cell block was restructured and Harvey was moved to a room with six other men, including a priest, a spindly cook, and the group's leader, a former member of the Indonesian special forces serving a five-year sentence for beating someone into paralysis.

Of all the people Harvey met in prison, it was Rudi Sutopo to whom he was most drawn, and his account of the older man was more intricate than what Rudi himself had told me. Rudi was a force of nature, Harvey thought, rugged like the people of East Java. While Rudi, who had been convicted on corruption charges, loved all the inmates, he spent the most time with Harvey. He liked to call the young man into his room and show him pictures of girls on his laptop. Harvey had never enjoyed a bond quite like theirs before. It wasn't sexual—he had lost those appetites altogether in the mental hospital. Their connection was deep but platonic.

Even with Rudi's protection, Harvey wasn't safe. He was beaten, spat at, extorted by the guards, but Rudi—virile and bold, a leader of men—toughened him up. If anyone could do it, Rudi could; Rudi sometimes left their block to visit a girl in the women's prison who had been convicted of murder. Forget about your sisters, Rudi told Harvey. "After this is over and done with," Rudi said, "after we're both out, you're going to come and work with me! We're going to build an empire together!"

By Harvey's account, a day came when he quarreled with his sister Yara. Should he ever get out of Cipinang, the family would make sure he was returned to Dharma Graha. It was prison or a mental hospital for the rest of his life. "You pick," she told him.

"Do something crazy," Rudi said. "Make another crime."

It was Rudi, Harvey now told me, who had convinced him to

make the bomb threats to the U.S. embassy in Jakarta. Harvey's true captors were waiting outside the prison walls, Rudi explained; if Harvey wanted to avoid the mental hospital he would have to stay in prison.

The story Harvey unspooled bore all the hallmarks of his particular kind of deceit. It sounded just true enough to be believable, while also being shot through with the kind of exculpatory asides that absolved him of any real responsibility. He didn't deny the call but, in his telling, it was more along the lines of a woeful misunderstanding, and not only that but it wasn't even his idea!

Here it is: He had called the embassy and the regional security officer responded. Once he had his mark on the line, Harvey slipped into character using a fictitious name that he had pulled from memory of the TV show *Dynasty*. She was a southern American belle. A "baroness," as he had described the character to me, from Texas. The Baroness said she knew the ambassador and was planning a trip to Indonesia, and would need some protection when she arrived. They got to chatting, and she confided that she was a contributor to certain veterans' groups, which seemed to please him. The RSO loved Texas; he had lived in El Paso! Wonderful place, she agreed but . . . had he ever been to *Dallas*? She had a *beautiful* spread there, where she hosted *parties*. The conversation was slowly segueing into politics when the Baroness put a stop to things. Wait!

Before they went any further—because she was contributing *lots* of money, after all—she said: let's talk about *you*. Well, one thing led to another and before the Baroness knew it, the RSO had disclosed that he wasn't wearing any pants. He even repeated himself: "I'm not wearing any pants." Soon enough it had gotten pretty hot and heavy, and as the Baroness gibbered on, the RSO kept her apprised of his progress. As the Baroness expertly eased them away from their shared intimate moment, she said she had a lot invested in Hillary Clinton, whose candidacy she was wholeheartedly backing. Now there was silence on the other end.

The RSO, it turned out, was an Obama man. They began to bicker, like a couple having their first—and, as it happened, their last—argument. Look at Margaret Thatcher, said the Baroness. She had an iron hand. Or Indira Gandhi, a woman of steel. The RSO was unmoved.

"They don't matter," he said.

"They do matter! If Obama becomes president, there could be dire consequences. The embassy could be blown up, you know?" With that, the love connection was severed.

HARVEY CONFESSED TO THE CRIME soon after. One night, Rudi made sure Harvey got his favorite meal, fried rice. "For you," he said, "to celebrate."

As Harvey concluded his story, I found myself laughing. But then he turned serious. As much as he admired Rudi Sutopo, Harvey wanted me to understand that Rudi had helped him orchestrate the bomb threats, that he had been an accomplice, that the "empire" Rudi had promised was going to begin there, inside the walls of Cipinang. "Rudi wanted women," Harvey said. "He knew the things I'm *capable* of—like I could make a call, from the inside, right? I could make a call to those—you know what I mean—he recognized my skills."

It was the lens through which you viewed the bomb scare that really mattered: the story of his most serious crime to date was best understood as a tale of redemption. Rudi was terribly corrupt, he said, but also kind and successful. And he, Harvey, who had always felt a failure, had been misunderstood and wrongly maligned. All of us, in other words, were flawed beings searching for peace. In Rudi, Harvey had found "someone who accepted me." In return, he wanted to demonstrate to Rudi that he could be "a good son." These two criminals could free one another.

In the moment at least, I fell for his spin. Only later did I reconsider. Harvey said he had made the calls to avoid being dragged back to Dharma Graha. An additional five-year sentence, along with a guaranteed spot on the U.S. terrorist watch list, seemed a high price to pay. He'd had no trouble escaping Dharma Graha the first time, and even if he did wind up back there, which was doubtful, I didn't see why he wouldn't just run away again. It was far likelier that he made the calls on a whim, that the idea of getting one over on the U.S. embassy and causing a mass panic was reason enough. At one point in our ongoing conversation he had admitted as much to me. "It was more about just getting excited," he said, giggling. "I didn't know where the conversation would lead me!" The entire episode had amused him.

Chapter 14

By the time I arrived in Manchester in October 2020, Nicole had been tracking the Con Queen for three years. She had long ago stopped billing clients, or entering names into Victim Tracker. She had delivered her initial findings to the FBI, but the FBI had ignored so many of the victims for so long that Nicole was the only person they trusted. When they asked for updates, she sometimes told them the same thing she told herself: the investigation was continuing; the Con Queen would be stopped.

During those years, her role had morphed into something beyond just a mere investigator; she was more like a therapist. On the way to or from her kids' karate practice or dance lessons, or alone, seated behind the wheel of her minivan, rapping along to Missy "Misdemeanor" Elliott or Ludacris, she answered her phone every time it rang. Victims revealed their nightmares and financial problems. They told her how the scam had affected their relationships; they were having trouble forming new ones or keeping old ones intact.

Her family had grown accustomed to these rhythms. Nicole had assumed leadership of her daughter's local Brownie troop by then, and she took advantage of the extracurriculars that were constantly on offer, helping her daughter earn "Democracy for Daisies" and "Trailblazer" badges, along with a dozen others. All of it took time, but was deeply satisfying. When her children asked about her work, she explained that she helped people find answers, and sometimes uncover secrets, and that now and again she helped catch bad guys. "It's like *Magnum P.I.*," she told her mother, who remained flummoxed about what her daughter actually did. "Or Sherlock Holmes." Nicole's daughter knew that her mother was chasing a man who was pretending to be a woman. "Is he still doing that?" she asked.

He was indeed.

"He's so fresh!" her daughter said, and Nicole had to agree.

The case kept her up late at night and seeped into her dreams. More than once, Anthony discovered her slumped over her desk, like Carrie Mathison connecting her dots on the TV show *Homeland*, and gently urged her back to bed. All roads seemed to lead to the Con Queen. Having found an article about the scam, victims who were still in Indonesia called or emailed her wondering if they were being trafficked, or if their luggage contained hidden drugs. Unable to reach the FBI or in some cases rebuffed by the U.S. embassy in Jakarta, they relied on Nicole to help them get out of the country safely. To that end she had developed a three-step checklist:

1. Don't pick up the phone.
2. Don't bother with the embassy, go to the airport instead.
3. Get home.

There were couples who had traveled to Indonesia together, including some husband-and-wife photographer teams. Different sets of victims occasionally bumped into one another at the same tourist sites. One British actor ran into two other victims at a hotel, each accompanied by their own team. A South African screenwriter from Johannesburg traveled twice to Jakarta with her mother. A Canadian stunt performer based in Australia spent two weeks traveling around Indonesia on a trip that included a five-hour journey outside Jakarta to climb trees in a zipline park, and set him back $8,700. The scam had destroyed friendships. A man in London was suing a friend of his who had referred him to the fake Wendi Murdoch. Soldiers no longer spoke to their former comrades-in-arms. A former American Navy SEAL had traveled to Indonesia with his thirteen-year-old son believing he was scouting locations and offering security advice. When Nicole checked Victim Tracker and an extensive email log one day, she saw that she had spoken to 436 people. She had received emails from at least twice as many. The scammed hailed from six of the seven continents—Antarctica being the exception—every habitable landmass on the planet.

Nicole wasn't just their advocate; she was also a vector to the FBI, but the FBI had few answers. Identifying Harvey as the Con Queen had been a coup, but not enough to arrest him. To do that, the agency would have to demonstrate that Harvey was orchestrating the flow of money across borders; that he had asked the victims to make the trips; that he had been instrumental in getting them to hand over funds; and that those funds had made their way into bank accounts that he controlled. They were tapping his phones and were monitoring his emails, but it would take time. With every day that passed, Nicole's understanding of the scam deepened, and her usefulness to the FBI investigation grew.

Nicole estimated that he was making roughly $5,000 per person who traveled to Indonesia, and calling about fifty people a day trying to find potential marks. Most of the money—the FBI estimated it at over a million dollars—wound up back in bank accounts he could access from the United Kingdom. His technological prowess was fair at best. The domains had been poorly masked, the numbers shoddily concealed. His real skills lay in the human arts of impersonation and persuasion. He worked constantly. His WhatsApp was LAST SEEN ONE MINUTE AGO at all times. He kept his travelers isolated and in a state of perpetual exhaustion; he discouraged them from talking to friends and family. What had appeared to be nurturing advice was soon revealed to be a controlling mechanism. His understanding of Hollywood's inner workings was comprehensive and up-to-date. When news of a deal broke in the Hollywood trades, Nicole would learn that he had referenced it in a conversation with a victim just days later. If a victim challenged him on a particular point—the deal he had referenced had fallen through, for example—he recovered quickly: no, the deal that had fallen through was now being renegotiated. Being targeted by the Con Queen had become a mark of distinction among up-and-comers and the well established alike. Those who had been, it was said, had in some sense made it. Yet another sign of how twisted Hollywood was, in Nicole's estimation.

In all this time, Harvey had never let up. Of course, she thought, laughing to herself when Covid first hit—*of course* it would take a global pandemic to stop him. But she was wrong. He adapted to the virus and even found ways of incorporating it into the scam itself. Soon he was convincing people to wire money for online martial arts classes that never materialized. When at one point lockdown restrictions looked as though they might be eased, he told people that in-person classes would soon be available, pending a Covid test, and demanded they send him their results. But once they had provided a negative result and paid for their classes, he was gone. He began impersonating people who were immensely wealthy and powerful but didn't have much of an online presence, like the Hong Kong investor Christina Ong, the so-called Queen of Bond Street. In the meantime, journalists were hovering, and Nicole worried about what might happen were Harvey's name to get out. Some victims were so angry she worried they might hurt or even try to kill him. If, that is, he didn't flee first.

Her colleagues asked if the end was in sight. Her response varied by the day. It would soon be over; it might never be over. She tried to stay optimistic. By her calculation, Harvey had been scamming people in one way or another ever since he emerged from Cipinang a decade ago. Unable to arrest him but also unable to detach herself from her position at the center of the case, she was growing tired. "It's become horrible and it's my job," she said. In those moments, Anthony tried to reassure her. "They have to arrest him," he said. But in truth Anthony was also tired.

White-collar crime isn't allocated the same resources as other areas of the criminal justice system. Prosecutors tend to focus on the crimes of Wall Street and regulatory abuses. Tangled cases like the Con Queen's tend to slip through the cracks. There were periodic signs of progress, though. The FBI opened an online portal and solicited information from victims, then turned their evidence over to the Department of Justice. A grand jury was convened and returned a federal indictment against Harvey on eight felony counts of fraud, conspiracy, and aggravated identity theft. Nicole, meanwhile, had also tracked him to Manchester by comparing selfies he had taken inside his new dwelling with images she found advertised on Travelocity and Expedia.

On the morning of June 22, 2020, Nicole woke up and, as she always did, reached for her phone to check Purebytes, only to find that the account had been taken down. When she googled it, the only hit was an account called "Imcummin4u." She checked the Wayback Machine, an online log that archives old posts, but found nothing there, either. Harvey, her constant digital companion for more than two years, had disappeared. Overnight, her primary source of information had inexplicably vanished from the internet. She felt oddly destabilized.

From an investigative standpoint, she was now almost wholly reliant on additional victims washing up. Which, of course, they did. Then one day, not too long after her bed of Adriatic lilies had started to bloom, she received a call that showed up on her office phone as "anonymous," each digit corresponding to a letter of the word. She suspected it was Harvey, but the voice on the other end was unlike any of the voices she had heard him use before. He had tweaked it to reflect a nasal inflection that to her ears sounded Persian. The voice introduced himself in stern tones as an unnamed "FBI agent" and addressed her as

"Miss Kotsianas." Nicole had "interfered in an FBI investigation," he said. She "knew too much."

"What do I know?" she asked.

"It's not what you know," he said. "It's what you did."

"What did I do?"

"You know what you did."

He told her to "back off" of her investigation. On one level, it was so preposterous that Nicole almost laughed. But then she noticed her hands were shaking. Was this a prelude to a further escalation? Over the next two weeks, he called her back several times but her company, K2, had decided it was best that she not engage, and Nicole never picked up. In the eighteen months since they had last communicated directly, Harvey had clearly descended into a very dark place. Unfortunately, her window into his world, and her ability to track his whereabouts, had been turned off.

Then, in the late summer of 2020, Nicole obtained the most disturbing audio recording she had yet heard. An LA-based actor had recorded a nine-minute phone call with a man he had initially believed to be Doug Liman, the director. The recording began with a ringtone. Harvey, shouting as Liman, immediately launched into a tirade about another man, a U.S. military veteran Harvey felt had wronged him. "This Hispanic fucker," Liman exploded. "A fucking Spanish guy. Or Italian. Fucking—whose language isn't English! Unless he apologizes, I'm gonna fuck his fucking career. Or his family. You can call the FBI. Whatever. I'm gonna fuck him over." He was apoplectic, rage strangling his words. "If I don't find him, cut his cock, my name's not Doug Liman!" he shouted. "Gimme three days. If his dick isn't cut, call the FBI—I promise you that will happen."

BY THE TIME OF THAT call, however, the FBI had already passed much of what it knew to the Metropolitan Police in the United Kingdom, which was busy conducting its own investigation. I didn't want to involve myself in any way. On the other hand, I had thought about Nicole often when I was in Manchester, wondering what she would make of the strange apartment-hotel where Gavin had holed up, the banal routine of his day-to-day existence, the fact that I had found him. It also occurred to me that my presence there might cause her unnecessary strain, were she to learn of it. In any event, I had my own reasons for being here, only their full contours hadn't made themselves altogether clear yet.

I knew that for Nicole, his sudden disappearance from Instagram was a cruel twist. Just at the moment when Gavin appeared most dangerous, he had crippled her access. Nicole was back where she had begun more than two years earlier: listening to a disembodied voice in the darkness.

Chapter 15

"That woman," Harvey said one day, scornfully. Since my return to Seattle, he had started calling me every day, usually around 8 a.m. my time. Unprompted, he uttered her name for the first time: *Nicoletta*. He launched into a rant so venomous and convoluted I had trouble keeping up. She was a racist and a liar, hell-bent on destroying not only him but his father's good name, and for that she should never be forgiven. If his team of lawyers didn't take care of her, he would do it himself. He had contacts in the dark web and friends in Russia who would wipe K2's hard drives bare. If none of that served to quiet her, he would sue, but not before he "puked" in her face.

As consumed as Nicole was with finding Harvey and having him arrested, Nicole was central to his narrative of victimization: *The Tale of an Evil Huntress!* He claimed that his human rights were being violated, that Nicole had harassed and defamed him. He would fight back, have people "pound at her." The longer he spoke, the more agitated he became. As his mood darkened, his ravings veered off into the supernatural. He communicated with his dead parents every day, and his bridge across mortality would serve him well in his fight with Nicole. "If I have to haunt her, I will do it," he said. Then, abruptly, he turned the lens back on himself. If Nicole wanted him gone, why didn't she just kill him? Just yesterday he had contemplated suicide, and if it would end Nicole's obsession, he would do it. The only thing stopping him was his parents' admonition against it.

But just when I thought he was done he took it one step further: he spoke about Nicole's children. "Nothing will happen to them physically," he said almost coyly, as though he wasn't yet fully decided. "I would never harm anyone physically, but you don't know my talent in another way. You *don't*. You just think, you know, he's just talking. You don't, so—listen well!" He swore to me that he would figure out a way to convince Nicole's children that their mother was a racist whose obsession with her White Gods of ancient Greece would be her downfall. Nicole had grown up steeped in Greek culture, true. As a child she had attended dances, festivals, and ceremonies at the St. George Greek Orthodox Church in Clifton, New Jersey, and later, when the family moved south to Toms River, at St. Barbara. In the summers, she participated in a camp where everyone wore traditional costumes and, *alta voce* under the stars, chanted ancient poems about Greek Independence Day and Grecian heroism during World War II. "The neighbors thought we belonged in a cult," she said. But of the poems she once knew by heart, she remembered only one, "Niaou, Niaou to Gataki," or "Meow, meow goes the cat."

Harvey swore he would systematically turn Nicole's children against her. "I will make that happen," he said. "I've done that in the past." No one, he warned, should underestimate him. I believed him. I didn't doubt for a second that he would resort to extreme measures to execute a plan of revenge. I wasn't only concerned for Nicole. I feared for my own family.

There might be one solution, he now suggested. He asked me to intercede on his behalf directly with Nicole, and hinted that he might be open to considering a mutually beneficial détente. She could do her part to help "clean up" the misapprehension that he was a terrorist, and in return he would "help the people that have been duped." She simply needed to be corrected. He somehow managed to keep from laughing when he said, "I've always insinuated she's a good woman and I look up to her." I declined this particular offer, but it was clear that Harvey was suiting up in full battle regalia, preparing for war.

LET'S RETURN TO THE CHILDREN. Sandra Djohan, the woman who had helped put Harvey in jail after his spree defrauding hotels, had once told Harvey about her own little boy, adopted when he was just a few weeks old. Sandra had sent Harvey a picture of her son and written about her love for her child, the simple purity of her joy. Harvey then sent her back a picture of his own: a toddler dressed in board shorts and a T-shirt with a photo of a walrus. The boy's coffee-colored complexion was just a shade lighter than his own, his eyes the same brown hue. "My baby boy Bodhi," he wrote. "I'm just finalising adoption papers. I love love love him." Whose child was this little boy? Somebody's. Not his. Whose flesh and blood had he appropriated?

Envy: a desire to be another, to possess another's life and all that it contains. He was a Netflix producer, a writer, the scion of a dynasty, the son of a movie mogul, a self-made man, a wealthy investor, a Warner Bros. executive, a real estate magnate, friend to the illustrious and the blessed. But he was none of these things. He inhabited avatars when they suited him. He devoured them whole.

We were in the middle of a conversation one morning when my son suddenly burst into my room and before I had a chance to stop him, he was asking for my help with some small task. Harvey immediately interjected himself. Was that my son? My daughter? He *loved* children. I set about helping my son—I think he needed me to untie something— and asked for Harvey's patience. Instead of sending my son away, I let him linger and for a few quiet moments touched my forehead to his, felt his small breaths, his warmth, and whispered those phrases that parents summon when trying to comfort their children: *Here we go. It's okay.* A great shame descended upon me later when I realized that I had simultaneously been trying to exclude Harvey—in whom I had sensed a weakness, though I couldn't say exactly how—from the intimacy with my son while also using it to cement my advantage. Along with the shame was a fear that this moment might eventually hurt us. In the event, he listened and oohed and aahed while waiting for me to finish. When I had fixed whatever needed fixing, my son turned to go and as he did, he told me that he loved me. "I love you, too," I said. Harvey nearly melted, like the Wicked Witch.

"How do you feel about him playing you?" Ali was curious. It was mid-November. We were standing in the kitchen. It was early evening but already dark. Other journalists had gotten hold of his phone number and had begun calling him, so far without success. During the most recent conversation, he told me their calls bothered him, whereas talking to me was "healing." He asked me one day: Did I know why he chose to speak to me? When I had approached him on the street in Manchester, he had noticed that my hands were shaking. I was as nervous as he was. He had looked into my eyes and liked what he saw. He would tell me everything in due course. "I can see you're being convinced by him," Ali said. I rambled as she pottered, repeating his arguments as if to test them out on myself, and on her. He had shared details, names and dates, that checked out. Was phone sex a crime? Not if it was consensual.

> Ali: But they thought it was a job interview.
> Me: What if he was a pawn in someone else's scheme?
> Ali: It's easy for you to get swept in.
> Me: He's being very forthcoming, opening up about
>   everything.
> Ali: He trusts you. Maybe he realizes the walls are closing in.
>   He could be arrested. He wants to get his story out there.
>   He's a con man.

In between diatribes about Nicole's supposed perfidy and extended rhapsodies about his epic journeys, Harvey had begun to speak about the scam directly. We were on a Zoom video call when it happened. He wore a maroon-colored T-shirt and was seated against a white wall. He had grown a beard flecked with gray. In profile, a prominent, arched nose broke into view. His smile stretched all the way across his face.

In the moment, it felt very much like he was building a case, and because he jumped so frequently from topic to topic, and was so emotionally volatile, I felt disoriented. But I went back later and broke down what he had said.

How, I had asked, had he met Mr. Rusdi, the driver in Indonesia who had ferried so many of the victims around?

"Through Helen."

"Who's Helen?"

"That's the *real* Queen Con of Hollywood." He laughed. "It's not me! *That* is where the money is." When I asked to know more about Helen, he deflected.

"No, I can't, especially not her because I'll be kill—"

"You'll be what?"

"I can't. Never mind."

In another call, he conceded that he *was* involved, but only as an instrument of Helen, a far more sophisticated entity than he. He detailed an elaborate business arrangement in which he and two other people—a man named Joseph and a woman, Shirley, who owned the company that issued invoices for the transportation services—worked for Helen. Shirley organized the logistics and the cash transfers on Helen's behalf. "You think I can arrange all that?" he said, chortling. "*Hmph!* I don't have the street smarts for that."

It was Helen who pulled the strings, sending drivers and bagmen to pick up the "guests" from the airport, to collect money from them after visits to ATMs and to deliver them to the prearranged locations. It got more complicated still. Rusdi, he said, was employed by a car company, now defunct, owned by a man named Kris, who was another associate of Helen's. When victims handed over cash, it went first to Rusdi, then to Kris, and then on to Helen, who disbursed it to the rest of the team. Of the generated income, Helen kept the lion's share, he said. From a hypothetical $6,000 haul Helen would keep $5,000 while he, Harvey, might come away with a paltry $250 or $300. As for Mr. Rusdi, sometimes he received his marching orders from Harvey, other times from Shirley. "I wish you could see the bank account!" he told me. "I wish you could see what I got!"

I asked to see these records, of course. He would show them to me, he responded. In good time.

Perhaps because he was shifting the ultimate responsibility onto someone else, he chose this moment to make what was arguably his biggest gamble. In the midst of blaming Helen, he did something else. He confessed. That is, he confessed to being responsible for a key part of the scam: the impersonations. "It was never [Shirley] talking to the guests," he said. "That would be me. Fine. You want to say that? It's fine. It's true!"

In that instant I understood two things: that he had never admitted his role in the impersonations before, and that he had been waiting to do so for a long time. He was the voice, the disembodied entity, and in that recognition was another. He had downgraded a youthful longing for fame to a more achievable goal: infamy. There was something prideful in the way he said it, as though he relished being able to take ownership over this particular element of the scam. *You want to say that? It's fine. It's true.*

"I may be," he would eventually tell me, "the Con Queen of Hollywood."

In childhood, he explained, his fascination with accents had developed organically. He'd done nothing special to hone the skill except pay attention to his heroes of film and TV. He had culled his American accent from the same place he would later find his victims: Hollywood. "I picked it up from movies," he said. He had a special affinity for Meryl Streep, a "master of accents." Accents opened a window that allowed him to understand other cultures and people. People misjudged the true masters of the craft: Streep's New York accent was superior to

Robert De Niro's; Jessica Lange playing Patsy Cline in *Sweet Dreams* was perfectly rendered.

But the actor who really took it to the next level for him was Glenn Close. His face took on a worshipful expression. "I loved her in *Dangerous Liaisons* . . . the last scene . . . when everyone finds out that *she's* the culprit, she's the con woman, she's the woman who's done everything, and they boo at her! And she goes home. And she faces her mirror. And she takes off her makeup. That . . ." He trailed off.

His description of Glenn Close's performance as Marquise Isabelle de Merteuil was close to rapturous. And wasn't his admiration for her a little like the admiration the duplicitous Vicomte Sebastien de Valmont professed for the supremely cunning marquise? When Valmont, played by John Malkovich, asks Merteuil how she managed to "invent" herself, de Merteuil responds: "Well, I had no choice, did I? I'm a woman. Women are obliged to be far more skillful than men. You can ruin our reputation and our life with a few well-chosen words. So, of course, I had to invent not only myself, but ways of escape that no one has ever thought of before. I've succeeded because I've always known I was born to dominate your sex and avenge my own."

"Yes," Valmont responds. "But what I asked was 'How?'" Merteuil then goes on to explain how, beginning at the age of fifteen, she became "a virtuoso of deceit."

When Harvey was about fourteen years old, he told me, he had called Tommy Mottola, who at the time was the head of Sony Music. He had pretended to be a producer connected to President Suharto, who was interested in bringing Mottola's client, Mariah Carey, to Indonesia for a tour. Mottola told him Mariah's fee was roughly half a million dollars and asked him what he had in mind. Harvey said he would think it over, and hung up, flush with a feeling of success. It was his earliest recollection, he said, of a successful real-world impersonation.

Later, I went back and compared the video of Harvey describing Close's performance in *Dangerous Liaisons* to the scene in which Close describes herself as a "virtuoso of deceit." They had the same faraway gaze, the same sense of wonder at their own will to power. Watching the two scenes side by side, I actually felt a shiver. It was as if he had re-created his impersonation of Close in a private performance just for me.

His interest in Amy Pascal and some of the other women whose identities he had assumed also stretched far back into his past. Ever since he was a boy he had loved Amy Pascal. She was a "hoot." She was "dynamic." While it was unusual for a child to be drawn to the producer of a movie rather than its stars, Pascal's history of generating hit after hit impressed him. He wanted to work for her. Some of these women, like Pascal and Kathleen Kennedy, were to be revered; he said he regretted what he had done to them. Sherry Lansing, with the black hair—he swooped his hand along the side of his head—was the classiest woman in this business. But there were others, like Stacey Snider and Deborah Snyder, both of whom he had impersonated, who "deserved" what had happened to them—what he had done to them. In the course of normal business, all of these women might be at each other's throats, as the Sony hack and the subsequent email dump had amply demonstrated. They were all wealthy and powerful, corporate warriors and captains of industry, responsible for shaping the cultural appetites of millions of people around the world. Feted, envied, and reviled in equal measure, they enjoyed a status somewhat akin to royalty in the insular world of Hollywood. Harvey had united them in ignominy.

As Harvey explained it, initially he was unaware that Helen was up to no good. Then, late one night in the fall of 2015, he said, the American screenwriter Gregory Mandarano arrived in Jakarta on one of the six trips he ultimately took, and handed the requisite payment off to Mr. Rusdi, as he had so many times before. But on that night, it fell to Harvey to collect the money. He showed up at 1 a.m. outside a gas station in front of the Aston hotel and saw for himself how much money Greg was handing over, and how little of it he, Harvey, was getting. It was at that moment that he discovered it was a fraud. He was as much a victim as the Mandarano family was. Helen had been fooling them all!

"It was *her* first client, *her* idea!" he said. Against his will, Helen had coerced him into doing the impersonations, supposedly by holding his previous terror-related convictions over his head. Helen threatened him and told him she knew that he had been convicted on terrorism charges. "If they find out about your past," she said, "Hollywood's not going to associate itself with you." He had suffered terribly as a result. The deception ate away at him. It was killing him, in fact, eating away at his soul. No, worse: it had left him without a soul at all.

He maintained that it was Helen who instructed him to sow discord between the Mandarano and Shapiro families and destroy the years-long friendship between the two old friends. "I loved Gregory's mother the most," he said. "She was like the mother I'd love to have. I remember Gregory's mother was on a call with me, pleading."

I had to sit with this particular confession for a while.

He "loved" Gregory's mother; she was the mother he wished he'd had. So what had he done to this woman he loved? He had listened to her "plead," and then carried right on doing what he'd been doing.

MY FATHER ALSO REMEMBERED THE painting on Gardner's wall. Only he recalled it slightly differently, that Gardner sat underneath the painting, not across from it. It was all the same, I said. And anyway, my father had never made a connection between Gardner and the painting, so it didn't much matter where it hung, or that it was the only piece of art in the dining room. My father did accompany my mother when she finally confronted her parents. She was brave and steadfast, he recalled, and said what needed to be said: they had hurt her when she was young and had continued to hurt her up to that very day. Later, her mother turned on her and blamed her for everything. My father was close to eighty years old when he wrote my mother a letter of apology. They had divorced decades earlier but were still very friendly. He should have severed ties with Gardner at that very moment, he wrote; he should have stood by her in that way. No one cut him off, though, not even my mother herself. She was by Gardner's side when he died in the hospital, after suffering a stroke. My grandparents, Gardner and Helen, are buried in a field near a small New England chapel, just down the road from the scene of the crime, or one of them anyway.

INSTEAD OF BACKING OUT AFTER discovering that he was being cut out of the lion's share of the profits, or returning the money, Harvey decided to double down. Helen—his fictional Helen—was clearly making a mint; there was no reason he couldn't do the same. He would make the fraud his own. "I was intrigued," he said. He cut ties with her and moved ahead on his own. In this account, he had no explanation for why Helen didn't make good on her threat to expose his past. As far as he was concerned, Helen had betrayed him.

In this, the longest of our battles about the truth, the Helen Lam story was his first major volley. When he initially raised the possibility of another mastermind, a second-shooter theory of sorts, I was ready to believe him. Indonesia was rife with scams, many of them involving multiple people and convoluted arrangements. The idea that he was simply a part of something bigger was believable.

Yet, very little squared with the victims' accounts. No one had ever mentioned Helen Lam. Her name had never appeared in any invoices, emails, or NDAs. Nicole had never heard the name, nor had I. Furthermore, Harvey had a track record of inventing people in order to shore up a narrative or to send curious snoops on a wild-goose chase. Harvey had insisted all along to Nicole that the real culprit behind the scam was not Helen Lam but the enigmatic Maggie Ling. So now I asked: Was Helen Lam the same person as Maggie Ling?

"Ah," he answered. "You thought I was becoming Maggie, yes, I was becoming . . ." I could feel the gears in his brain straining. Finally, he settled on his story: Maggie Ling was an alias that Helen used for invoicing. It was Helen and her associates, he said, who had built the China Film Group Corporation website, Helen who had diverted the server to China, Helen who had instructed him to use the phone-forwarding services, and, finally, Helen who had told him to use her credit card to pay for those services while registering everything under a fictitious name: Maggie. According to Harvey, Helen had told him, "You become Maggie, and you talk. I don't want to be in the picture."

But Nicole had never found a Maggie Ling because, as Harvey had just admitted, there was no Maggie Ling. There never had been. And if there was no Maggie Ling, there was likely no Helen Lam, either. He had just invented her, another straw man, to muddy the waters. There was only Harvey. But I went along with the story anyway.

Where was Helen now? I asked.

Singapore, he said.

What did she look like?

Mid-fifties. It was hard to tell. She had dark hair and a flat chest. He laughed.

"You know the Wendi Murdoch impersonation?" he said. "That sounds like her." The most telling detail he provided was just another mirror; one ghost, in other words, resembled another.

No sooner had he finished this story than he moved on to a new argument in his defense: the victims were fame whores who got what they deserved. The schemes that took place after his supposed rift with Helen had been his and his alone. But the people who had come to Indonesia weren't victims. They were "guests." Their safety had always been his first priority and they were willing participants. "Nobody was pointing a gun at them at the ATM," he said. Ultimately, he took a very dim view of them as people. On the whole, they were "obsessed by fame and wealth," he said. He sounded a lot like the other Harvey, Harvey Weinstein: The victims had known what they were getting into. They had wanted it. They were seeking fame and fortune.

He was equally dismissive of the people who, believing they were being auditioned, had engaged in phone and video sex. He told me he had video-recorded them without their knowledge. After studying the comments on my articles that had appeared in the *Hollywood Reporter*, he reckoned that about three-quarters of the reading public believed the victims had been naïve, even stupid. All of this was to his advantage, and he would find a way to spin it. They shouldn't have fallen for it, he said; that they had, meant only one thing. "They wanted it done."

He blasted the victims for returning to him so often. He tried to cut them off but they chased him, endlessly, tirelessly, consumed by a hunger for fame. All of this was in the past, in any case. He had paid some of the victims off after court proceedings; his lawyers had entered secret negotiations with Lucasfilm and Kathleen Kennedy; he had tried to open a dialogue with Marvel. As far as I could tell, none of this was true.

HE WAS A HOUSE ON fire; he was also the fire hose. The inferno roared nonetheless. After a lifetime of abuse from dolts and zealots, impersonating someone else was the only path to survival left to him, he insisted. "Maybe when I was talking to those people, I felt like someone was listening," he said. It was so hard to be wanted, to be accepted. In all of this, Harvey blurred the lines of whatever we were discussing. If I asked him about the impersonations that drew people to Indonesia, he might answer as if my question had been about a phone sex call. More than once he had attempted to pursue both tracks with the same victim, and occasionally succeeded, so perhaps the boundaries were as blurry in his own mind as they appeared from the outside. If he admired these women in Hollywood so much, why had he impersonated them? Was it a strange kind of tribute? Did the process make him feel successful? "No," he said. "Empty. When I made those phone calls, I felt dead. I couldn't ejaculate. You have to believe me when I say I'm impot—"

In this fey and pitiful version of himself he was a powerless vacuum. Because when he spoke to people as himself, as poor Harvey, he was nothing more than a freak, a terrorist. But the voices of other people, powerful people, powerful women, were contained vessels, and once he inhabited them, he was liberated. Was there not something to admire in all this? Not only was Wendi Murdoch his favorite person to inhabit; he believed his impersonation of her was the closest to the real thing. Yet his palette was broad, his tastes catholic. There was hardly a powerful woman left in Hollywood whom he *hadn't* impersonated, he said, only half-joking. The victims' pain didn't matter. What mattered was his own satisfaction. "When I had to put on a mask as someone new," he said, "I was accepted. It wasn't just one person. It was *all* of them. And they felt great."

Chapter 16

Not only did the voices feel good; they offered a path to redemption. Thus did he now begin to unfurl the final leg of his battle plan. He would use the voices to clear his name, make up for his transgressions. He returned to the idea of his podcast, which he wanted to call *Motherland*. Within the last twenty-four hours, he had finished five episodes. He held up all five fingers on one hand and began to describe an episode that would begin in "the land of crows" who had their headquarters on the summit of the compound stratovolcano known as Mount Lawu. He would entrance listeners with his stories. A marketing genius in the mold of his idol Harvey Weinstein, he could turn a dirt floor into gold. He would make a killing. He would donate 95 percent of the podcast proceeds to three or four victims and expand the pool steadily as the inevitable profit margins bloomed. He acknowledged more of them by name: Gregory Mandarano, the screenwriter whose family lost $100,000; Jessie Evans, the photographer whose father he had accused of being a thug. "Of course, they were heartbroken," he said. "They were put in a puzzle. Those two I'm going to pay back first." If, on the other hand, he wound up in prison, no one would get a single red cent. He would face what came, "like a man, or a woman, it's the same thing to me." What he had done was "fucked up," and he thought a hard-hitting documentary might help sway future criminals from the path he had followed. He wanted to start clean, and he wanted to do it all "for Nicoletta." At the end of the day, he said, they would become good friends.

Didn't I understand? As much as the victims had been put, as he put it, in a puzzle, so, too, had he. Had I ever been a patient in a mental hospital? I had not. Had I been subjected to an exorcism? To a washing of my sins by devotees of a faith to which I had no allegiance? Again, no. Had I been incarcerated in any setting against my will? No. His logic seemed to be that what he had done was justified by what had been done to him. But really, there was no logic. "I am not my past," he said, as though this explained everything.

AND YET, HE WAS PERSUASIVE; I had to constantly remind myself that I was dealing with a con man, and a successful one at that. Even as he professed to be coming clean with me, he continued to play games. He once began a call with me while pretending to be speaking to his attorney on another line. He called her Marsha: *Yes, Marsha, I've got Scott on the line now. Yes, I'll tell him. Don't worry. Thanks, Marsha.* In 2017, when the photographer Will Strathmann had asked *his* Amy Pascal about money, Pascal had suddenly been interrupted by . . . Marsha. Marsha didn't exist; maybe I should say "But Marsha almost certainly didn't exist" just to be on the safe side. She didn't exist with Will and she didn't exist with me. Similarly, his "aunt," a recurring character in these conversations, felt like a fiction, as did his "best friend" who lived in New York and also happened to be called "Amy." He told me that his aunt, his attorneys, and his "reputation managers," another echo of what he had told Strathmann, were hectoring him about talking with me. He dismissed their concerns; it was none of their business whom he spoke with. Another Escher-like puzzle: he said he told these people, who turned out to be imaginary, that they should think of *me* as "imaginary"—a pure fiction that he, Harvey, had "made up."

FOR A FEW OF THE victims, these impossible mental gymnastics created a sense of distortion. One day in the late fall of 2017, the photographer Will Strathmann received an email. The sender was one Amy Pascal.

Will didn't respond right away. He didn't even open the email at first. When, a few days later, he did, the first lines hit him hard.

Dear Will, the email began. This is the actual real Amy Pascal.

The "actual" Amy Pascal. The "real" Amy Pascal.

He stopped reading, and lingered on the sentence. The name. The idea of a person. The idea of *that* person, wandering into his mind once again, and wondering who she was to him anymore.

I am so sorry about everything you went through . . . , Pascal wrote. What a horrendous situation. I feel terrible about it for you and your family.

A short message—perhaps too short. But it was to the point, and honest.

Best Regards, she had written. Amy.

Eventually he responded.

I'd be lying if I said it wasn't a little strange getting this email from the real you, he wrote. But I am glad to receive it and appreciate your condolences.

He thanked her for reaching out and expressed his sympathies for what she, too, must have endured.

If you ever need storyboarding help for a travel show throughout Indonesia, he concluded, I know someone who has quite a few visuals and is currently unsure of what to do with them.

HARVEY'S ATTENTION WAS EXHAUSTING. HE peppered me with questions and, if I hesitated or paused, accused me of lethargy or disinterest. Once he told me I reminded him of his sister Amisha and thanked me for listening to him. When I failed to respond immediately, he threatened to cut me off: "No more being nice and opening up." I had to apologize before he would call me back, but when I did the phone rang instantly. I had heard one recording when his suggestion that someone was gay caused that person to have a complete meltdown. Now he tried it with me. "I don't know why I'm talking to you," he said. "I usually prefer straight guys."

This barrage of feints, lies, and attempts at manipulation takes an unusual toll; by "unusual" I mean both *large in degree* as well as *strange*. From my home in Seattle, I had been talking to him every day, or nearly, for three weeks. His attention consumed my days and my family. One day he called me "my dear." A week later it was "my love." I knew he enjoyed getting straight men to engage in phone sex with him, and I wondered if he was trying to lead me in that direction. "Listen to me," he said coyly. "Sounding like the Con Queen!" He laughed. He called four and five times a day, talking for hours. Sometimes I was at home but often I was not, and so I wound up talking to him in the park, at the grocery store, in the car, with my kids. He jumped between topics: his childhood, Nicole, a grievance. He was lucid and then incoherent, often manic. He was angry. And hateful. And then ingratiating. He spoke of suicide and revenge; of his own glory and frailty. One day he called me to tell me he had spoken to his best friend Amy in New York. They had discussed the possibility that he could flee to Iran or Qatar or China, where extradition would not be possible. He had decided against it. "I don't want to keep running," he said. I struggled to know what was real, or what his endgame might be, or if there even was one. One night he called and asked that I not record anything. It was late and I sat in the dark on the floor of my living room and listened. In a subdued voice, he returned to the question of his fate: What was going to happen to him? Did he have any talent? He began to sob. I no longer had any idea what to believe. And I had no good answers for him.

He was responsible for his own entrapment. No one had forced him to plagiarize or steal, to impersonate or make bomb threats. So why did I find myself feeling sympathy for him? I began to worry about his health and, after talking with a friend, considered trying to find him some help in the United Kingdom. Harvey insisted I include his childhood friend Haseena on one of our Zoom calls. But overnight, while

I slept, they had a huge fight. In the morning, I woke up to messages from both of them. She felt deceived and thought he was an evil person. She wanted nothing more to do with him. His affection for her of twenty-four hours earlier had also vanished: she was an opportunist out for money, capitalizing on his recent notoriety. A fool! Now he issued an ultimatum: I had to convince Haseena to take down the Instagram Live interview she had done with him. If I didn't do him this favor, he wouldn't speak to me again. I told him this was impossible, but he insisted, and so to placate him I caved. I wrote to Haseena and did as he asked, citing Harvey's "mental health."

He had played me, clearly. In an earlier conversation he said he thought he might suffer from bipolar disorder. But people who suffer from bipolar disorder don't generally behave in the ways he had. He didn't fit the profile at all. They don't go out of their way to steal, deceive, lie, defraud, and manipulate people. They were also unlikely to be inclined toward—or to be able to sustain—a pattern of deliberate deceit over long periods of time, as Harvey had. One psychiatrist told me that psychopaths often used other disorders to mask their behavior, and that I should be "skeptical" about labels like schizophrenia, bipolar, or psychosis. A smart psychopath would soon recognize if a mental disorder diagnosis would serve his interests, and would imitate the behaviors surrounding that diagnosis. Unlike "normals," psychopaths tend to be less driven by punitive threats, focusing instead on rewards. Nicole thought she had observed behavior that matched that description during their brief conversations in the winter of 2018, though she never ventured so far as to make any kind of diagnosis. "When he was on, it was all the razzle-dazzle stuff that he does with victims, and he was trying to do stuff like that with me. And then he would occasionally switch into 'Oh, I'm just a very depressed person, I don't have control of my own finances because I'm 'mentally ill,' like this pity sort of thing." In the end, Haseena quite rightly refused the request I had transmitted—as I had hoped she would. But I had lost all perspective.

ON THE ONE HAND HE struck me as a broken figure. There were times when his pain felt real, and I pitied him. Despite his protestations to the contrary, he seemed to have nobody. His sisters had disowned him. He had no friends. The characters who peopled his world were fictions. He lived in a world of unreality. It was sad and even tragic. Yet a small voice in my mind kept reminding me that all of his suffering might be a lie, a performance and nothing more. As I vacillated between these alternating theories, a constant emerged: he remained inside my head. I heard his voice all the time, and I no longer wanted to. I had begun to feel as though he had found a way to inhabit me.

A single question continued to ring in my ears: Why? No single factor was emerging as the obvious catalyst for the dozens of scams, impersonations, and crimes for which he was responsible. As with us all, he was a tangle of genetics and environment. But of the tortured reasons he offered, there was one that seemed expansive enough to accommodate his own contradictions as well as the complexities of the scam. "They call Hollywood the city of broken dreams, right," he said one day, and his face had contorted into a rueful, awkward grimace. He had always wanted to write or direct or somehow be a part of the entertainment industry. Every aspect of the craft of making movies thrilled him. "It's what people do there that excites me," he said. "I wish I was a part of it." His dreams had never progressed further than the world of competitive speech. He seemed genuinely frustrated. "I was talented, man, I had *something*," he said. "I wasn't allowed! And that's the truth!"

Harvey grew up in a rarefied world surrounded by people with ties to the Indonesian film industry. Within the Sindhi community in Jakarta, it was assumed that kids would be industrious and successful no matter where they ended up. On one level, Harvey was a recognizable type: the immigrant pursuing the American dream. But when he got to the United States, he felt entitled to success in Hollywood, because that was always an attainable goal, even an expectation, in his own country. The reality was entirely different. And if he couldn't have his dream, no one else would, either. A shapeshifting entity whose purpose was to enable that destruction was born and found its way into the world from which Harvey had been exiled.

"I'm so confused," he said. "What did I do to my life?"

I, too, was confused. I hadn't expected contrition. "Oh my *God*, God," he said, "I'm so sorry. I'm so very sorry for everything. I hate what I did. Oh fuck. What did I do?" He had spent a lot of time trying to impress his family. He hated the role he played within his family then and hated it still. While other kids from his childhood were building families and receiving professional accolades, he had done nothing. At the age of forty-one, he was a failure. Friends had abandoned him. His family wanted nothing to do with him. "I know that a lot of people are now betting against me," he said. "Yeah, it was wrong. I'm willing to pay the price."

Was he?

Looking back on the videos I recorded of our conversations, I look haggard and exhausted. I was getting short with my family. Two days before Thanksgiving he called me three times. I contemplated telling him that his sister thought he was a psychopath, but the truth was, I didn't know if she was right. I wandered with Ali and the kids through our neighborhood looking at Christmas lights. It was the farthest thing from Indonesia that I could imagine, the farthest thing from the loneliness of his existence. I felt terrible for him sometimes, even though it was clear he was lying to me. Again and again he had hurt innocent people and tried to make them feel crazy. The blizzard of messaging—contradictory, pitiful, defiant—was disorienting. Amisha had written me another long email. I had told her by then that I was talking to Harvey, and she sent a worried message to a mutual acquaintance beseeching me to be careful. Going back through her correspondence, I was reminded that Amisha had once described her brother as an "evil entity." In any other context, *entity* was a neutral, almost bureaucratic term. But now it had taken on monstrous overtones, something mystical that influenced greatly the course of human events. "Most of his stories will be fabrications of his mind," she wrote. "As long as he is relevant and has a platform to unleash his tongue—it pleases him." This was troubling, as I had no wish to be the vehicle for his aggrandization.

The most generous interpretation I could muster was that the fragments of real remorse to be found in his occasional apologies were just that—temporary fragments he was using to further his own ends, which in this case was the construction, with my aid, of a different kind of artifice.

On November 25, 2020, Harvey and I spoke for ninety minutes. He consumed the first half with a manic rant that ranged from his persecution by his family to the ancestry of Nikki Haley, but eventually he settled down. He performed a couple of accents for me—an Irish brogue and a Scots bur—and explained the difference: it was all in the throat. I was reaching the end of my tether. Part of me longed for him to be arrested, just so I could have a break. Apart from my family and a couple of friends, I hadn't told anyone about my conversations with him. But as long as he was free and wanted to talk, I was to be his willing prisoner. After that hour-and-a-half call on the twenty-fifth, we finally hung up. He called back ten minutes later. He said he had forgotten to tell me something and began to laugh. He mentioned a prominent member of the Trump administration and asked me: Did I know that he had once had phone sex with this figure? I laughed, too. What more was there to say?

Then he had to go. He was off to volunteer at a soup kitchen. In the grand scheme of things, what he had done wasn't so bad, he said. Shouldn't I, as the journalist, weigh the good with the bad? He said he would call me the day after Thanksgiving. He wanted me to spend the day with my family.

The last thing he said to me was "Thank you for the story."

Harvey understood very well the contours of our relationship. I told him again and again that I was not his advocate, that I was more interested in the truth, whatever that was. He continued to speak to me. I never once called him; he always called me. But I did need him, and he, in a sense, needed me. He would say things like "You're going to write whatever you're going to write . . ." and then follow that up with pleas for understanding.

I told him I wanted to understand his side of the story. This was true, up to a point. But I had already determined that he was a cruel and sadistic manipulator who used people for his own ends, stole their money, and trashed their dreams. Mitigating circumstances were just that—mitigating. I was not offering absolution. Until I started writing this book, and then suddenly I wasn't so sure. And the more I spoke with him, the less sure I became. By the end, I had almost stopped caring what I thought. I just wanted it to end.

EVEN AS HE PLEADED HIS case with me, Harvey had continued his scams. I only discovered this later. On November 17, 2020, the same day he had pleaded for understanding from me, an actor in Los Angeles received an invoice. It had been sent by someone purporting to be Eka Rahmadia, an Indonesian instructor of *pencak silat* and other martial art variants popular in Indonesia. The instructor's facility was located in Jakarta, and a billing address was listed as a management firm located in Denmark. A description of the services rendered included: "Zoom Calls (18.65 hours at US$100 per hour) 100 * 18.65 = 1865; Customized Videos (32 videos at 45 mins long) Packaged = 550; Instructional PDF with a manual on lessons." Eighty percent of payment was due upon receipt of invoice; the remainder could be paid after the sessions were completed. Indonesian bank details followed. The actor who received this invoice had responded to an email from a producer who was interested in him for an upcoming role, that of Max Roberts/Admiral Max (age thirty-five to thirty-seven). Riddled with grammatical errors and comically far-fetched, the character and plot outline the actor received involved a Drug Enforcement Administration drug bust followed by a romantic interlude that culminated in the establishment of a secret, "ergonomically friendly" space colony, Colony X, run, of course, by

Admiral Max. It was sloppy and uninspired, but even in the era of Covid-19, or perhaps because of it, the pitch had worked. Though the actor never received any instruction, the total cost for the remote learning course of martial arts study came to $2,415 and most of it was paid that day, no doubt just a few hours before Harvey and I spoke, as rain once again accompanied dusk in Manchester and the hour best suited for *asmar*, "things of the evening," arrived.

Harvey had always been punctual. He had never missed our calls, had never been so much as a minute late for a scheduled telephonic rendezvous. Nor had he much compunction about calling unprompted, regardless of the hour. When the agreed-upon post-Thanksgiving Friday call never came, it was clear something was wrong. The minutes ticked by. An hour. Two hours. The silence that descended upon the house was immense, an aural and psychological void that filled up space like some noxious and unfamiliar fume—and unfamiliar quite suddenly, in the way a house can feel unfamiliar when one of its residents leaves, or returns after a long absence, and order and routine resume their proper, standoffish roles at the summit of domestic hierarchy. The visitor who had, in a sense, been living here, had left; gone—and gone with him were the stories.

After two more days, a source in the United Kingdom confirmed it. Harvey, going under the name Gobind Tahil, "a wanted fraudster," was in custody pending "extradition to the USA." His detention by the Greater Manchester Police had taken place under somewhat unique circumstances. Even though the authorities in the United Kingdom had conducted their own investigation into his alleged crimes and offenses, they had arrested him largely on the evidence and basis provided to them by the FBI. The grand jury indictment of a year earlier had been executed a few weeks earlier, which included one count of conspiracy to commit wire fraud, two counts of wire fraud, and five counts of aggravated identity theft—eight charges in all.

After an early-morning raid at the Light Boutique ApartHotel, at 20 Church Street, on Thanksgiving Day, he had been carted away in the back of a police wagon and classified as a "non-PACE" prisoner, which meant he hadn't yet been accused of any crimes within the borders of the United Kingdom, nor, in all likelihood, would he be. As a result, he would soon be sent to London, if he hadn't been already, to be processed for eventual extradition to the United States, assuming a judge found cause to comply with the request. He could, the source said, "get legal representation to delay that for say . . . Human Rights [*sic*] so could potentially be here a while." I broke the news of Harvey's arrest in the pages of the *Hollywood Reporter*, where the story had begun so many years before.

THESE DAYS, CALEB KOTNER LIVES in a small fishing town near Boston. One day in 2019, he sat down to watch the Golden Globes awards show. As the camera panned across the audience, it captured the director Quentin Tarantino leaning back in his chair to whisper something in the ear of a woman Caleb recognized. It was Amy Pascal. Caleb felt himself tensing up at the sight of her, even though the two had never even spoken. Years had elapsed since Caleb had returned from Indonesia but the uncomfortable sensation of intimacy between himself and the woman on the screen had lingered. Sitting with the feeling afterward, he realized that he felt that he had "done something wrong." He struggled to figure out a way to move past it. Looking back, Caleb was baffled by his own behavior. Some might call it a blind spot. But in reality, it was closer to a near-total suspension of disbelief and critical thinking—a lapse that led to the loss of roughly $65,000—his entire life savings.

Most nights of the week, Caleb wakes from bad dreams and he still suffers from intrusive thoughts that, while they don't always necessarily relate directly to the scam, nevertheless seem to have their roots there. A constant sense of unease and anxiety runs just below the surface of everyday life. He longs to "put the nail in the coffin" on the experience but isn't sure how to accomplish that; even now, so many years later, remnants of his experience with Amy Pascal in Indonesia find ways of surfacing. The standard Apple ringtone, for instance, haunted him. He was walking in a mall one day when he heard the ringtone and it immediately took him back to Jakarta. To me, his reaction sounded a lot like the post-traumatic stress disorder that veterans describe.

In 2019, Caleb's first child was born, a son, five weeks premature. The pregnancy and birth had been traumatic; Caleb's partner, Rachel, suffered massive internal bleeding. Adam was soon rushed to an intensive care unit, and as a result of the complications he was separated from his mother for the first week of his life. "A nightmare," Caleb said, which was soon followed by more distressing news. Adam, the couple learned, was completely deaf, struck down with auditory neuropathy spectrum disorder. "You want to be able to read to your kid and do all these things," Caleb said. "And you now realize that you have to learn a whole new language to be able to do that." Caleb found it difficult to contemplate Adam's troubles without getting angry all over again about the scam. If he still had his savings, might that have made Adam's earliest years easier? Better? Might it somehow have magically enabled them to avert Adam's condition altogether? The financial loss Caleb suffered was intimately tied up with his and his family's sense of well-being, and even with their material health. "It means I can't afford Adam's implant because someone took that from me," he said. "I want to have all those things that were taken from me that in turn happen to be valued in money. Nothing is more life changing than having a child, and the idea that you could have provided more but someone took it away is arguably the biggest impact I've had from all this."

Before Adam's birth, Caleb had understood his financial losses in largely theoretical terms; money was an abstraction, and so was its absence. But when Adam became its primary victim, that all changed.

I FOUND MYSELF LINGERING ON those elements of Harvey's stories that felt real, even if they weren't. He had told me about a time when he had traveled on ramshackle buses to a coastal town, skirting the Indian

Ocean. He arrived in a poor village and set up camp on a beach. It was Mala Satu Suro, the first night of the calendar year, and people, it was said, would cleanse their daggers by the light of the moon. The fading sky was red, the seas calm. He turned his phone off. He felt propelled by the sea, as if by a magnet. Then, a song from the deep, asking: What do you want from me? Was this the spirit of Nyai Loro Kidul, Queen of the Southern Seas, speaking to him?

Then there was the short fairy tale he spun for me one day. It went like this: An ambitious father wanted to be mayor of the town where he lived with his wife and two daughters. One night during Maghrib when the ghosts began to roam, the younger of the two daughters was visited by a small bird who perched on her window. "Tomorrow at your picnic," the bird whispered, "you will see me and follow me." Surprised to have encountered a talking bird, the little girl told her mother, who became upset and ordered the girl to return to her room and pray. But when the little girl saw the bird at the picnic the next day, she followed it. The bird led her to a portal that opened into another dimension.

The town rallied around the little girl's disappearance and vowed to find her. Meanwhile, the family secrets began to spill out. The mother, a modest and devout religious woman who always covered her head with the *jilbab*, was exposed as a whore, while the couple's other daughter was revealed as a closeted lesbian. The father found that he had a powerful and inexplicable attraction to his driver and bodyguard that culminated one day in a pregnant look, a moment of "love, of poetry, of surrender." It was at that moment that the wife intervened. She ordered the chief of police, with whom she had slept, to halt the search for the missing girl. "This is the perfect moment," she whispered to her husband. "People will empathize and pity you, as your daughter is *dead*." The search was called off and the husband was made mayor. "Your daughter," said his wife, "has given you the throne."

Was this tidy allegory how he wanted me to understand his life? Was *he* the little girl who had followed the bird and disappeared through the portal? Was it his mother who had abandoned him, literally, to another dimension? I couldn't help but be moved by the story, yet I wondered if he had actually written it, or made it up on the spot, or stolen it. Or if he even realized, as I thought I had, its significance. It was either a frighteningly intimate and sad window into his self-conception or a bitter and cynical twisting of the truth, a bid to place himself beyond the scope of censure by virtue of his own pain. Perhaps it was both. There was no way to know.

MY MOTHER HAD ASKED ME: How did it feel to be connected to a family in which evil had lurked? I had no answer for her at the time. Looking into the past, long-ago facts I once thought irrelevant no longer were. Under which conditions do all of us break? And under which do some, against all expectations, rise to the occasion? My wife asks me this: In an earthquake, would the Con Queen have helped others, or looked out for himself? I had no idea. Or perhaps I did, because another, more frightening question arose: What would the rest of us do?

OR PUT ANOTHER WAY: WHAT have the rest of us done? How often are we the purveyors of darkness, deliberately or not, in the course of ordinary life? I felt grateful, now, for having been led here, to this particular portal, where I was able to look through a window of my own. Here is a story I saw: myself, as a boy. That stepbrother, older by a few years, who found my mother's notebook and told me of its contents, hovering naked over me on a single bed. A baby blue blanket lay on the floor, exposing white sheets and the bastard form of us together, writhing like blind swamp worms. How did we wind up here? I have no idea, just as I don't recall what the true purpose was, or even who led whom down this particular rabbit hole. I have never really known how to understand what transpired between us then. It amounted to several clumsy episodes of childhood exploration over one humid and desultory summer. I have never fully understood them. It is difficult to extract them from the overstory of the abuse my mother endured, and which I learned about that same summer; it is equally hard to see those boys—us—as hapless marionettes whose actions are dictated by an act of history, as though we had no voice of our own.

We were two children grasping for the forbidden key contained within my mother's journals, which while it belonged to neither of us now united us. I can't know exactly why or how I wound up there, only that I must have been chasing an answer to a question I didn't even know I had, or perhaps I was trying to answer one for someone else; perhaps I, too, was lured into an unwelcome dimension. So the story that Gardner had begun—or had perhaps inherited himself, one can't be certain—took on new life; so shame finds a fresh host.

THE HALF-LIFE OF BAD ACTS, the impulse to harm, call it evil or dissociation or something else, can be long and twisting. When it came to Harvey, there seemed to be no one whose path he had crossed who hadn't come away altered. I thought about Caleb Kotner and his son, and the weeds that tethered them to Harvey. And about Harvey's sisters, Amisha and Yara, who according to Amisha had let the possibility of parenthood slip away because of Harvey. Or the scores of other people who even today harbored an intangible fear of him, who found it hard to trust other people, or themselves. I thought of the many people who spoke to me but then grew scared and quiet and slipped away again. The people who worried what might happen were he ever to find them again—and those who hoped to find him in order to hurt him. A former soldier had gone to Indonesia and then convinced a dozen or so of his friends, also soldiers, to do the same. Collectively they lost tens of thousands of dollars. The soldier confessed that he had hired someone in Indonesia and was trying to track down the culprit. I asked what he planned to do. He thought about going back to Indonesia, finding the driver, and "smashing his thumbs" until he got what he wanted. Others like him had expressed similarly gruesome fantasies: Torture. Murder. Disappearance. One soldier had proposed that he and a team of special forces operators track him down and take care of him. People, he guessed, would handle themselves in a thousand different ways. "Mine," he said, "is more violence."

I wanted nothing to do with that. Nor, for that matter, did Nicole, for whom the entire story had begun to wither and shrivel, splitting its seams, like a fruit exposed to too much sun. The behavior of the con artist who had once so bewitched her had come to seem more sinister, and more real. She turned away, retreating to her garden of Adriatic lilies, her roses and her tulips. Her flowers were the envy of the neighborhood. From their safety, she watched and she waited, more cautious now for the darkness Harvey had shown her, more prudent, perhaps wiser.

What I am left with, ultimately, is a fragment, a single, distilled moment in time: a home in Bungur with a window and a view of trees swaying in a gentle breeze, and inside of it a figure, silhouetted, waiting for someone to call his name.

Epilogue

There was one person I still hoped to find: Mr. Rusdi, the driver, who, perhaps more than anyone, had witnessed what transpired between Harvey and those of his victims who traveled to Indonesia. Rusdi remained an enigma to me and to many others as well. More than one traveler had confided in him, and in at least a few instances, Rusdi had reciprocated. He was integral to the duping but sympathetic to the duped, and he had spent more time with them than anyone else. If I could find him, I thought, perhaps he would illuminate for me how those disparate worlds connected. So, in July 2022, I boarded a plane in Seattle and flew to Jakarta.

Mr. Rusdi's last-known address was in a neighborhood known simply as "4," a warren of red-tiled roofs and jumbled electrical wires in West Jakarta. Men in Muslim skullcaps hawked tea and soda in green bottles from rust-colored rickshaws. I wandered down small lanes where barefoot kids played badminton in the street, to a narrow alley that culminated at the front porch of a modest dwelling. The house's owner, Anwar, emerged, accompanied by his friend Suparman.

About a year earlier, the men explained, the police had come looking for Mr. Rusdi. They were there at the behest of Malaysian authorities, who had received information about a fraud. When I showed them a picture of Rusdi, they shook their heads. The man they knew was younger, with fuller cheeks and eyes of a different shape and hue. He was a familiar figure in the neighborhood but had never lived in this particular house. "People keep looking for him here," Anwar said. They seemed as confused as I was. Then Suparman led me to his own house, just down the street. On his balcony, several colorful flycatcher birds sat in cages. Suparman provided me with an address in a neighborhood called Sepatan, along with two phone numbers for Ronny, one of Rusdi's sons.

Two hours later, in Sepatan, I arrived in what looked like a central town gathering area to find two women preparing for a festival. A small crowd of people, including dozens of children, greeted me warmly. A woman named Ani Cahynia pointed to a small, clean-looking house with white walls and curtained windows. For nine years, Cahynia said, Rusdi had lived next door to her. "He's known for taking foreigners around," she said. In 2021, no longer able to pay his bills, Rusdi had left Sepatan. She didn't know where he had gone, but Mr. Rusdi's best friend, Pa Gandhi, who lived just around the corner, did. Mr. Gandhi was busy with his evening prayers when I knocked on his door. His young daughter leaned against the wall of their porch and filmed me with her iPhone. Eventually Pa Gandhi emerged. Rusdi drove Americans around to tourist sites like Borobudur and Badang, he said. He was often gone for a week at a time and sometimes slept in his car. Rusdi lived about twenty minutes away by car, in yet another neighborhood. Pa Gandhi offered to take me to him. His daughter climbed on the moped, threw her arms around her father's chest, and the two set off, while I followed in a truck. The sun had set and darkness seemed to swallow the city. After an hour or so, we turned off the busy artery and the lights and noise began to fade, but as the truck wended its way into the neighborhood, the lanes grew so narrow that eventually the truck could no longer move forward. I abandoned it and continued on foot.

Pa Gandhi idled his scooter slowly up an alley barely wide enough to accommodate pedestrian traffic until he, too, stopped next to a small park. Up ahead, through a cloud of swirling dust and headlights, I could just make out the silhouette of a figure approaching from across the street. The two men embraced and talked for a few moments. Eventually Gandhi motioned for me to come forward and soon I found myself standing across from a diminutive man with a soft, open face and a wide smile.

"Mr. Rusdi?" I asked, extending my hand.

He nodded politely and gestured for me to follow him to his house, just a few steps away. A crowd of children and onlookers had gathered. We sat down on his front porch and the crowd settled in to watch this impromptu piece of street theater.

Mr. Rusdi had worked as a private driver for foreign visitors, he told me, but only for one year, in 2016. He explained that he had never met the people who sent him the clients, and only ever knew his employer as a disembodied voice, or series of voices, on the phone. At one point I showed him a picture of Harvey. He leaned over carefully, scrutinized the picture, and slowly shook his head. I tried several more pictures with the same result. He said he didn't know anything about a scam. He didn't know anyone named Harvey, or Hargobind, or Gavin.

Switching tacks, I showed him a picture of Will Strathmann, who had visited in 2017. Again, he shook his head. Then I pulled up a second picture, which Will had provided to me, of himself standing next to Rusdi.

"That's you, isn't it?" I asked.

Rusdi grinned. He remembered now, yes, an American photographer with whom he had traveled all over Indonesia. It was past 10 p.m. in Jakarta, but morning in America. I called Will and when his face materialized on FaceTime, I turned the phone around. On the other end of the line, I could hear Will struggling. The connection was poor and Will's face flickered in and out of view, but Mr. Rusdi kept shaking his head. I glanced back at the rapt crowd, and in their hope, I saw myself reflected.

Mr. Rusdi—Rusdi Samardi was his real name—would have been happy to host me on that balcony all night long, content to perform this charade. If I had been expecting a full-throated explanation, even a mea culpa, I now realized it was never going to happen. These long-ago events couldn't possibly be recollected with any certainty, much less understood, in the haze of forgetting that was now under way. Whatever fragments of actual human connection that did occur between Rusdi and his charges—the tender moment of bonding on a bridge that Jessie Evans had perceived came to mind—were perhaps best left in the past. And at the same time, the physical threats that I knew Rusdi himself had faced from angry travelers who blamed him for their predicament, and there were many, must have paled in the face of the economic imperative that drove him back to Harvey again and again.

In any case, it didn't seem likely that Mr. Rusdi had benefited much from his long years of service. After all, here we were at the end of a road, and the edge of a village, on the tilting precipice of a capital city that was swallowing him up. What possible reason would he have to align himself at this point with the man he surely now understood to be a crook, a cruel liar, and a thief. This is where Harvey had left Mr. Rusdi, and where I chose to leave him, too.

DHARMA GRAHA IS A TIDY, quiet campus of single-story offices interspersed among palm groves and a maze of carefully tended flowers and bushes. White-gowned nurses with their hair in tight buns walk in pairs across the sandy gravel grounds. On the day I visited, I sought out Dr. Yenny, a psychiatrist who had overseen Harvey's treatment. She declined to speak to me directly about her former patient, citing doctor-patient confidentiality. In general, however, she said that Dharma Graha's long-term residents suffered from both psychotic and nonpsychotic conditions, ranging from mild to severe, for which they received a variety of treatments, including in some cases therapy and pharmaceutical interventions. As a clinician, she had treated people with hallucinations, bipolar disorder, depression, borderline and narcissistic personality disorders, and, in a few rare instances, cases involving what she described as multiple personalities, even though this diagnosis has been largely abandoned by mental health professionals. Dr. Yenny wasn't eager to share more, and after a few minutes, she dismissed me. A short while later, a Mr. Suguy, Dharma Graha's operations manager, said, "The subject you're interested in is Gobind, and in that case we don't feel good about being associated." He explained that lawyers involved in "Gobind's" case had come to visit, but declined to say who they represented or what they hoped to achieve.

When I arrived at the gates of Doulos, on the other hand, Dr. Ruyandi Hutasoit, a tall, slender, and well-groomed man, greeted me with a big smile. He led me down a wide gravel entranceway and stopped beside an imposing two-story building. Behind him, in a large, grassy yard surrounded by palm trees and groves of dark foliage, a couple dozen lethargic patients were going through the motions of a vigorous calisthenics program. An instructor was shouting: Jump! Stretch! Jog in place! A couple of the patients seemed almost catatonic, fiddling absentmindedly with the grass or looking at the sky. Some laughed, danced, or groaned while others gazed dully ahead, attempting to complete the labors being demanded of them. One woman, having spotted me, broke into a huge smile and stood utterly still, arms draped heavily at her sides.

Hutasoit said Doulos was an explicitly Christian organization, and described the available course of "treatment," which included exorcisms, as "spiritual" in nature. He said patients suffered from gaming and sex addictions, kleptomania, and a wide variety of psychospiritual emotional problems. Arrivals to Doulos had to receive Jesus Christ as their savior, he explained. Then Doulos staff performed what Hutasoit described as an "exorcism check" to determine whether the incoming patient was possessed by any demons. "If they have anger and hatred in them, that's an open door for demons to come in," he said.

Hutasoit had no compunctions speaking about Harvey, who arrived here in 2002, and stayed for six months. Hutasoit and the other

Doulos staff members had conflicting memories. At one point in our conversation, Hutasoit told me that during the requisite exorcism check, Doulos's counselors determined that Harvey "did have a demon." When I repeated the question later, however, he told me Harvey had cleared the test, that no demons had been found. In time, the staff concluded that he was also a "paranoid schizophrenic." I asked Hutasoit whether the staff at Doulos ever conducted gay conversion therapy on homosexuals, like Harvey. "Yes," he said. "That is our duty."

On the far side of Doulos's main offices were the living quarters, a row of low-slung single-story buildings that looked as if they hadn't been updated since the 1970s, when Doulos first opened. The rooms were sparsely furnished, each with a small window, some cots, a sink, and a ceiling fan. Hutasoit showed me the room where Harvey slept, with two other patients, each on a cot. An image of Harvey gazing out at the world from atop his suite of luxury rooms in Manchester surged into view. The distance he had traveled from this place was so immense that it was difficult to believe anyone could pull it off. Yet somehow he had, stepping seamlessly from one into another, as if the laws of physics hardly existed at all. And yet it also seemed like sleight of hand, as though he had simply replaced one ward for another, one anesthetized existence for another. Then, not for the first time since my dealings with Harvey began, I was struck by a peculiar sensation. What if, I wondered, he had also transported me? What if my presence in Indonesia was somehow part of an escape plan whose outlines I couldn't discern?

WHILE IN INDONESIA, I MET many of the people with whom I had only ever been able to correspond via email or phone during the pandemic. The first time I spoke to Rudi Sutopo, Harvey's friend and inmate in Cipinang, he told me he had lost roughly $29,000 by investing in Harvey's Black Widow TV show project. Now he revised that story and said the actual figure was closer to $230,000. One afternoon, Sandra Djohan invited me to her home, a magnificent compound adorned with ancient teak beams and priceless family heirlooms. She cooked an elaborate and delicious meal of bakwan jagung, sambal, anchovies, and fried rice, along with fish, beef satay, and fried tofu in chile sauce. I also met Joko Anwar at his studios. He showed me a link for a movie that Harvey's father, Lal, had produced in 1980. It was called *You Were Made for Me*. The clip had generated over five hundred comments on YouTube. "The theme of the story isn't far from cheating, fighting over inheritance," wrote one person. "The main story is that everyone is very rich." Joko had just returned from Los Angeles, where he had met with his agents at WME and signed a deal for a show that would soon appear on Netflix. This, in the end, was the kind of world Harvey had wished to belong to, a world of creative movie producers and successful chefs. And in another version of his life, he could have.

I also found new sources of information, people who had known Harvey in other contexts. A former colleague of his from EMI told me how Harvey had racked up thousands of dollars in unauthorized expenses while organizing a record launch, a breach that ultimately led to his dismissal after angry vendors came looking for payment. A former colleague of his at the public relations firm Publicis divulged that Harvey had been fired after allegedly defrauding the company. As far back as 2003, I learned, Harvey had been posing as women and enticing men into phone sex while dangling offers of work. A former security guard at Cipinang told me how Harvey's fellow inmates referred to him as *wariya*, or half-man, half-woman. "They thought he was transgender," the guard said.

One day, I went to Bungur, Harvey's childhood home in central Jakarta. It was located in an unremarkable apartment bloc, just off a tree-lined avenue bustling with rickshaws. An office space next door advertised the services of a well-known lawyer specializing in bankruptcy law. Harris, a security guard who had worked at the apartment for more than twenty years and knew the family, often spotted Harvey standing on his balcony, gazing out over the city. Harris described the arguments that erupted from within the household each time Harvey's family discovered that he had once again run up an astronomical telephone bill. More than anything, Harris recalled the way Harvey walked, and he jumped out of his seat to mimic it for me: a confident, almost apelike saunter. In 2020, the police paid Harris a visit and said they had come to arrest Harvey. By that point, of course, Harris hadn't seen him in years.

On my last day in Indonesia, I sat down with Mushwida, an Indonesian lawyer who had represented Harvey for crimes he committed while still a prisoner in Cipinang. Mushwida's face was in constant motion, and she squinted and smiled in quick succession, alternating between an expression of puzzlement and worried skepticism. Mushwida said she loved Harvey—not in a romantic way, but simply for who he was. In her telling, Harvey was kind and generous, and deeply misunderstood. Her praise seemed bottomless and she teared up often when describing him. Theirs was also a pragmatic relationship, she explained. Harvey had never paid for her legal services; instead, he helped recruit new clients for her from inside Cipinang. When, toward the end of our conversation, I asked if there was anything else that she wished to say, she paused for a long moment. She claimed, without any evidence, that Harvey had been excised from the family inheritance. She went on: His sisters owed him a great deal of money. However, given that Harvey was currently imprisoned in the United Kingdom, he was in no position to collect it, much less look after it with any reasonable degree of care. Mushwida's face turned and twisted with increased vigor. Until Harvey could return to claim his inheritance, she concluded, Mushwida herself would volunteer to be the custodian for his fortune. As if on cue, she broke into tears again. A few moments later, she stopped abruptly and her face regained its composure.

A few months after returning from Indonesia, I traveled once more to the United Kingdom. Nearly two years had passed since Harvey's arrest. He had been languishing in London's Wandsworth, awaiting his extradition hearing. His case went to trial in September 2022, in trial room 1, on the first floor of the Westminster Magistrates' Court, in central London. Harvey appeared via video conference every day. Wearing a crisp blue dress shirt, he was clean-shaven and looked as if he had lost weight. But it soon became clear that he was, in all the ways that mattered, the same person. When asked if he had any religious affiliation, Harvey said he had converted to Judaism. He railed about the same things that were now so familiar to me and at several points broke down in tears.

I later learned that he was mostly keeping to himself in jail. He had taken to drawing. He often quarreled with his cellmates. Several expert witnesses for the defense had conducted psychiatric evaluations of him. His lawyers had compiled the highlights into a forty-one-page document that made for dizzying reading. One psychiatrist noted that Harvey was "accused criminally of an elaborate plot with many twists and turns—a type of behavior suggestive of a hypomanic disposition" that might fall somewhere on the bipolar mood disorder spectrum. Another psychiatrist disagreed, positing that Harvey's impulsive behavior was characterized by "psychopathic traits."

One day, before the proceedings began in earnest, Harvey appeared on-screen and called frantically for his lawyers. He needed to speak to them urgently, he said. "At least twenty minutes. No less." The imperiousness I had forgotten about came rushing back. He began ranting about me. His lawyers had apparently informed him of my presence in the courtroom and he was livid. "Scott Johnson . . ." he began, before his lawyers cut him off and quickly ushered me out of the room. One day a Danish actor appeared in the audience, accompanied by a journalist. Together they were producing a documentary about Harvey's Scandinavian victims, who were apparently legion. Until that moment, I hadn't heard a peep about them. There wasn't a corner of the world he had left untouched.

Harvey remains in custody in the United Kingdom, and is fighting extradition to the United States.

Acknowledgments

I would like to express my gratitude to everyone who helped in this book's creation. Michael Lerner and Alan Zarembo read early drafts, and their insights and moral support shaped the narrative. Liam Epstein, who knows this story as well as anyone, was a constant and energetic advocate. I'm grateful to Peter Kiefer for his probing questions, early feedback, and, most of all, his friendship. Amanda Griffin's keen editorial eye and sensitivity sharpened the story. As always, my father, Keith Johnson, offered support and advice, as well as the use of his cabin for writing. I am especially grateful to my mother for allowing me to share her story, and to Ben Riggs for his support. At Harper, the supremely talented Jennifer Barth was an early and avid supporter and helped me see the story clearly; Mary Gaule and Noah Eaker took up the baton with great enthusiasm and discernment, shepherding it through to completion. I'm grateful to Rachel Elinsky, Becca Putman, Edie Astley, and everyone on Harper's sales, marketing, and design teams. I'm particularly thankful for Jonathan Burnham's unwavering commitment. Chris Smith and the crew at Library Films offered encouragement and support with research, logistics, and travel. Ben Anderson provided help in key moments and much support along the way. If not for their whispers in my ear, I may never have gone on the plane trip that changed everything. Reid Meloy, an expert on psychopaths at the University of California, San Diego, helped me understand this story's murky psychological implications. Nigel Blackwood, of Kings College London, also provided key insights. Thanks to Salvatore Barba for his understanding of human nature. Maer Roshan made the introduction that launched this project. To Alex "Double" O'Donohugh for her *covert* assistance, and to Jon Mulligan, who helped crack the key to Harvey's world in Manchester—the eagle lands at dawn! Carol Chaski introduced me to the intricacies of linguistics. Josie Zanfordino helped me understand how voices shape our identities. At the *Hollywood Reporter*: thank you to Kim Masters and Matt Belloni; my editor David Katz deserves credit for the Con Queen moniker that has stuck and helped define this tale in virtually every incarnation that exists. Alex Ritman's reporting was very helpful. Thanks also to Costa Koralis. I'm grateful to David Kuhn and all the folks at Aevitas Creative Management. To my wonderful agent, the incredibly talented and patient Will Lippincott: you believed in me and in this project from the outset and helped bring it to life at every step along the way. The inimitable Allison Warren has championed the book in other areas, and it's thanks to her that the story will appear as a documentary and a scripted series. I wish to extend a special thanks to everyone in Indonesia, named and unnamed, who helped me and who looked out for my interests and my safety, in particular Sandra, Joko, Buce, and Evitarossi Budiawan, who provided invaluable support in Jakarta. To those people who remain anonymous or unnamed in the book, you know who you are, and how much I value your help. To my wife, Ali, and my children, Jesse and Willa, I owe you everything, and everything is for you. I love you with all my heart.

About the Author

SCOTT C. JOHNSON is the author of the highly acclaimed 2012 memoir *The Wolf and the Watchman*, which was long-listed for the National Book Award, and named a PEN Center USA finalist and a *Washington Post* Notable Book. A former *Newsweek* bureau chief in Baghdad, Mexico City, and Cape Town, Johnson has reported from more than fifty countries as a veteran foreign correspondent. His writing has appeared in the *New York Times*, the *Los Angeles Times*, *Foreign Policy*, *Granta*, and elsewhere. *The Con Queen of Hollywood* is his second book. He lives in France with his wife and two children.

DUE DATE	MCN	05/23	30.00

JCR

DISCARD

JUN - - 2023